RHETORIC IN AMERICAN COLLEGES,
1850–1900

SMU STUDIES IN COMPOSITION AND RHETORIC
General Editor: Gary Tate, Texas Christian University

Because this work has become such an important historical
document in the field of composition and rhetoric, it is being
published here without revision.

Rhetoric in American Colleges, 1850–1900

ALBERT R. KITZHABER

With an Introduction by John T. Gage

SOUTHERN METHODIST UNIVERSITY PRESS

DALLAS

First edition, 1990

Requests for permission to reproduce material from this
work should be sent to:
Permissions
Southern Methodist University Press
Box 415
Dallas, Texas 75275

Library of Congress Cataloging-in-Publication Data

Kitzhaber, Albert R. (Albert Raymond), 1915–
    Rhetoric in American colleges, 1850–1900 / Albert R. Kitzhaber.
        p.   cm. — (SMU Studies in Composition and Rhetoric)
    Includes bibliographical references.
    ISBN 0-87074-308-2. — ISBN 0-87074-309-0 (pbk.)
    1. English language—Rhetoric—Study and teaching—United States—
History—19th century.   I. Title.   II. Series.
PE1068.U5K48   1990
808'.042'071173—dc20   90-52657

Contents

INTRODUCTION   vii
PUBLISHED WORKS OF ALBERT R. KITZHABER   xxiii

I. Main Trends in Higher Education, 1850–1900   1
Changes in Psychology and Educational Theory   1
The Decline of Religious Influence on Higher
    Education   6
The Influence of Science and Technology on
    Education   9
The Influence of German Universities   12
Changes in the Curriculum Pattern   17
Two Poles: Yale and Michigan   20
    Yale: A Conservative College   20
    Michigan: A Progressive University   26

II. The Field of English   31
English at Harvard, 1850–1875   32
The Rise of Philology   36
Instruction in Literature   38
Organized Instruction in Speech   41
The Harvard Reports   43

III. Rhetorics and Rhetoricians   49
The British Rhetorics   49
Early American Rhetorics   55
The Big Four   59
    Adams Sherman Hill (1833–1910)   60

John Franklin Genung (1850–1919) 63
Barrett Wendell (1855–1921) 66
Fred Newton Scott (1860–1931) 69

IV. **Rhetoric, 1850–1900: Definitions,**
  Relations, Scope 75
  Definitions 76
  Relations 81
  Scope: The Rhetoric of Oral Discourse 83
  Scope: Belles Lettres and Literature 86

V. **Subject Matter and Logic** 95
  Invention 95
  Composition Topics 103
  Logic 109
  Unity, Coherence, Emphasis 113

VI. **The Forms of Discourse** 119

VII. **The Communicative Function of Rhetoric** 141

VIII. **The Paragraph** 153

IX. **Style** 169
  Style 170
  Figurative Language 175

X. **Diction, Usage, Grammar** 187
  Diction and Usage 188
  Grammar 191
  The Ideal of Correctness 199

XI. **The Shift from Theoretical to Practical**
  Rhetoric 205

XII. **Conclusion** 221

NOTES 229
BIBLIOGRAPHY 245
INDEX 265

Introduction

ALBERT R. KITZHABER'S 1953 dissertation, published here for the first time, has for thirty-seven years been legendary to students and scholars of composition. It has had an underground and grass-roots circulation, on microfilm and in multigeneration Xerox copies, and has been talked about as much as any secondary work in the field. It may be overstating the case to say that Albert Kitzhaber's is the most-quoted unpublished dissertation since T. S. Eliot's, but in terms of the effect it has had on an entire field of research, its impact has been arguably far greater. "Have you read Kitzhaber's dissertation?" is a frequent question heard by young American rhetoricians. "Where can I get a copy?" is their most frequent response. I have been on both sides of this exchange.

More than a necessary work for the student of contemporary composition to know if he or she wishes to understand the history of the discipline as it now exists, *Rhetoric in American Colleges, 1850–1900* is in fact one of the important markers of the beginning of that discipline. It is the first book-length historical study of this subject, by a scholar who helped to initiate the reevaluation of rhetoric in American education that made the so-called "paradigm shift" in composition during the 1960s possible.

Now that it is published and readily available to the burgeoning number of students and researchers who have made rhetoric and composition their chosen field in recent years, the importance of this study as a background for others' work will be abundantly clear. Its publication, even this late in the game, is an event to be celebrated by those who have already profited by reading copies of the dissertation typescript. Many have cited their indebtedness to it. James A. Berlin, for instance, in his *Writing Instruction in Nineteenth-Century American Colleges*, relies heavily on Kitzhaber's study, which he calls "groundbreaking" (Carbondale: Southern Illinois UP, 1984, 3). Donald Stewart, in his essay in *The Present State of Scholarship in Historical and Contemporary Rhetoric*, has written that "Kitzhaber provides the best overall picture of what happened in the nineteenth century" (Ed. Winifred Horner, Columbia: U of Missouri P, 1983, 155). Indeed, Stewart lists this study among the texts (beginning with Plato and Aristotle) that he believes should be required reading in the history of rhetoric for all English majors ("What Is an English Major, and What Should It Be?" *College Composition and Communication* 40, [May 1989]: 194). Robert Connors's debt to Kitzhaber's dissertation is fully acknowledged in his essay "The Rise and Fall of the Modes of Discourse" (*College Composition and Communication* 32, [December 1981]: 444–63), and other works. Stephen North lists in addition studies by John Michael Wozniak, Andrea Lunsford, Winifred Horner, and Patrick Scott to which Kitzhaber's influence may be traced (*The Making of Knowledge in Composition: Portrait of an Emerging Field*, Portsmouth, NH: Boynton/Cook, 1987, 68). North ends his list, as I must also, with "and so on."

Having already proven to be an influential work, as something of an underground classic, this book will open the door once again to fresh reconsiderations of composition's past. Kitzhaber has looked at nineteenth-century texts that others will now want to look at again, especially since this book's appearance will reveal how some of the more recent work done on this historical issue has relied on Kitzhaber's findings and interpretations without going back to the primary sources that Kitzhaber read so well.

In fact, there are reasons to think that the publication of

this study is especially fitting at this time. The field of rhetoric and composition, having grown and changed in the decades since this book was written, is presently passing through a "transitional" period that is not unlike the one Kitzhaber describes in the second half of the nineteenth century. Certainly those who have experienced the controversies that now inhabit our discourse about teaching composition will read Kitzhaber's opening sentences with some sense of familiarity:

> Until about 1870 few shifts in emphasis were apparent, the colleges continuing to operate much as they had since the eighteenth century. Dissatisfaction with aims, curriculum, and teaching methods was growing, however, through the middle years of the century, though the first attempts at reform had only limited success.

If the watershed year were changed from 1870 to 1970 and "eighteenth" changed to "nineteenth," few, I think, would quarrel with the accuracy of such a description applied to our own more recent history. The words raise the salient possibility that the discipline of composition, which seems to have changed so much in the past twenty years, has in fact changed relatively little, or has changed along familiar lines. It is perhaps comforting to know that the "revolution" in composition theory in our time seems less revolutionary when one understands that this is a discipline in which such revolutions have regularly come and gone. It is not comforting, of course, to those who naively assume—either through ignorance of history or preponderance of theory—that we have recently arrived at truths about composition and rhetoric that were unavailable to those who struggled in the past with the same issues we struggle with now. Whether comforting or not, it is important to see one's own time through the perspective of others'.

In what ways do current controversies in our field resemble those that characterize the transitional era Kitzhaber describes? I will mention only a few that rereading this study has suggested to me.

We too, like the nineteenth century, are struggling to discover the relevance of psychology to the composing process, although whereas it was a struggle against "faculty psychology" that conditioned a reinvestigation of rhetorical categories in the nineteenth century (with some attempts to apply the new science of experimental psychology), ours is an attempt to relocate rhetoric in a post-Freudian, post-Lacanian psyche or to reposition composing in light of principles from cognitive psychology.

As in the nineteenth century, recent developments in composition curricula have emerged in response to changes in the educational institutions and social structures, not without controversy or experimentation in either case. Such changes, in both eras, brought about the demand for teaching practical skills, which in turn led to the oversimplification of rhetorical concepts for the sake of prescriptive application.

Something like the same tension between composition and technical treatments of logic prevails now as it did in the late nineteenth century. As then, some methods of teaching writing assume knowledge of logic to be a precondition to argumentation, while others attempt to incorporate logical categories without the formalism of analytic logic, and others seek to escape logic altogether as a presumed hindrance to expression.

Similar tensions, then and now, characterize attitudes toward grammar: some lament student infelicities and seek remedy in formal instruction, while some attempt to incorporate grammatical principles into composing, and others blame emphasis on grammar as an obstacle to composing.

We also share with our nineteenth-century predecessors a choice between approaches that focus on the parts of a composition, to be applied later to whole compositions, and those that begin with whole compositions and consider various parts only in this context. Many of today's textbooks pay just as much attention to exercises in "the finer points" of diction, sentences, or paragraphs as do some of the textbooks that Kitzhaber discusses, while others treat the essay as a whole. The difference between a parts-to-whole and a whole-to-parts approach seems in fact to be much more characteristic of radical differences in methodology today, as in the nineteenth century, than the more commonly cited difference between "product or process."

The relationship between rhetoric and literary studies, fur-thermore, troubles our era as it did the mid-nineteenth century. The efforts of Fred Newton Scott, described by Kitzhaber, to find an appropriate way to study literature in the composition course were diminished by the usurpation by literary scholars of rhetoric's aims and methods, to the point where Kitzhaber could claim (in 1953) that "rhetoric has never fully recovered the ground lost then." Has it recovered that ground now, de-spite the interest among some composition specialists in the work of rhetorical critics such as Wayne Booth and Kenneth Burke?

The very question of whether "rhetoric" itself, as charac-terized by the classical tradition, has any relevance to composi-tion is another issue that we share with the nineteenth-century composition theorists, and on which we, like them, have not found agreement. While the form of this controversy in the nineteenth century has more to do with the relevance of specific rhetorical categories, such as invention, to the composing proc-ess (as we now call it), many today tend to view rhetoric as a whole system and to regard it as an alternative "approach" to composition pedagogy, whether for practical or for ideological reasons. At least the nineteenth-century pedagogs described by Kitzhaber saw distinctions among classical approaches, many of which are lost to those now who try to discredit the rhetorical tradition as entirely outmoded. But we, like our forebears, not only steal from the classical tradition what is most applicable, whatever our current allegiances may be or whatever new names we apply to old concepts, we reinterpret that tradition as needed. I am reminded of one of Richard Wilbur's epigrams:

> We milk the cow of the world, and as we do
> We whisper in her ear, "You are not true."

Just so have many recent pedagogs "milked" rhetorical con-cepts from the past, even while denying validity to that past as a place to look for answers.

Indeed, the reader who is familiar with the ideas of a number of contemporary theorists of composition but has not encountered those of the nineteenth century will be struck by a number of similarities between the ideas of Scott, Gertrude Buck, Joseph Denney, Alexander Bain, Henry N. Day, Arlo Bates, and others discussed in this book and the work of contemporaries who may or may not have acknowledged the parallels. In the work of the nineteenth-century rhetoricians we find a great many of composition's current interests prefigured, such as the need to engage the student's imagination or escape the influence of predigested forms, how to use writing as "problem-solving," how to teach "writing to learn," the need for heuristic procedures, how to adapt current concepts of logic and argument to composing, and even "writing across the curriculum" (although proposed by the curmudgeonly Samuel Thurber for reasons seldom advocated these days). I leave any specific comparisons undeveloped here for the sake of those who might want to use Kitzhaber as a guide and to follow through by reading the nineteenth-century rhetoricians in the original. While there are some ways in which contemporary theories might be seen as more sophisticated, it would not be unwarranted to conclude from such a comparative study that composition theory in the last half of the twentieth century is largely engaged in reinventing the late nineteenth century. The cost of such a conclusion might be to wear away some of the shiny newness of contemporary theory—and some of its aura of optimism that we have left the thinking of our forebears behind—to bring out instead its patina of age.

Yet the value of historical study of this discipline is not only to serve as a corrective to contemporary enthusiasms at having finally arrived at answers. Yes, some of the same questions remain, but new ones have emerged as well. But these also require historical consciousness to be understood. What are the reasons, for instance, that the nineteenth-century rhetoricians did not share our contemporary concern for the influence of gender on composition theory and practice, and that Kitzhaber (in 1953) did not make this a basis of critical assessment, as it often is today? Any critique of the history of rhetoric from a feminist point of view, then, would need an expansive cultural context to understand the omissions or assumptions made by the rhetoricians represented here. So, contemporary theory has much to add to our understanding of history, just as history is needed to inform contemporary theory.

Similarly, there are reasons that the intensity of current interest among rhetoricians in "epistemology" is not paralleled in the nineteenth century, even though philosophical treatments of language and knowing, e.g. those of Charles Sanders Peirce and William James, were presumably available for application. (We do find in this study an instance of James's psychology applied by one early twentieth-century rhetorician, Frank E. Bryant, but in a superficial way.) Present-day interest in Wittgenstein, Vygotsky, Ryle, Kuhn, Langer, Foucault, MacIntyre, etc., reveals a greater sense of the need to find connections between composition and philosophy than prevailed in the nineteenth century, and one wonders why. Not, certainly, because the rhetoricians were more poorly educated. The same may be said, perhaps, for connections between rhetoric and politics, or rhetoric and ethics.

The scope of rhetoric's interests today seems broader. I say "seems," however, because Kitzhaber looked primarily at textbooks, and one can well imagine a twenty-first-century Kitzhaber examining composition textbooks from 1960–1990 and noting with surprise the relative lack of such concerns in their pedagogy, compared to what the composition theorists and scholars were writing about in journal articles. Thus, another similarity emerges, considering Kitzhaber's assessment of the fate of "nearly all of the really vital ideas that appeared" in the middle years of the century: Given the demand for superficial correctness by the public and university officials, instruction

> had been cut off from all vital relations with other subjects in the curriculum and, in a sense, from life itself. . . . [R]hetoric had lost all status; teachers of a subject that, in its debilitated form, was regarded as valuable only insofar as it could eliminate errors from freshman writing would not be a receptive audience for ideas that were either radically new or that questioned long accepted beliefs.

Despite the degree of change and theoretical activity in our era, this situation seems not much improved. Kitzhaber's devastating critique of the "forms of discourse," taken up by others since, has not affected pedagogical practice as much as it should have. Richard Larson, for instance, testifies "to the persistence of the nineteenth-century 'modes' . . . in the thinking of scholars and teachers right up to the present day" largely because they offer a "system that ostensibly simplifies or even solves the problem of planning a text or organizing a course" ("Classifying Discourse: Limitations and Alternatives," *Essays on Classical Rhetoric and Modern Discourse*, ed. Robert J. Connors, Lisa S. Ede, and Andrea A. Lunsford, Southern Illinois UP, 1984, 204). These forms seem to have the same appeal to teachers now that they did for those of the late nineteenth century, and for the same reasons Kitzhaber cites. Furthermore, his assessment of the typical textbooks of Genung and Gilmore—that they "gave lip-service to a purposeful view of rhetoric as real communication, but their actual discussions of rhetorical categories revealed a static, formalistic conception of writing"—could be made just as accurately about many best-selling writing textbooks today. Perhaps the necessity of reducing abstract theory to get it into textbook form is a constant problem, one that we share equally with the nineteenth century, as is the "atrophy" that Kitzhaber attributes to textbook writers' practice of merely copying from other textbook writers.

Both our similarities to and our differences from the past—in this case a past that is not all that distant—help us to understand the present state of our discipline better. Even though Kitzhaber's study has already influenced historians of the subject who have come after him, it remains the most thorough (while at the same time the most comprehensive) treatment. These are among the many reasons the publication of this book is long overdue and ought to renew interest in the subject of its inquiry.

II

In recognizing the important contribution Kitzhaber has made to our understanding *of* the history of rhetoric in the last century, we should not neglect to credit Kitzhaber's place *in* the more recent history of rhetoric.

Although the Conference on College Composition and Communication had been founded in 1949, the "birth of modern Composition" as an academic field with new modes of inquiry is dated by Stephen North to 1963 (*The Making of Knowledge*, 15), the year in which Al Kitzhaber delivered a talk entitled "4C, Freshman English, and the Future" (published in CCC 14 [October 1963]: 129-38). It was the same meeting at which Wayne Booth gave his talk on "The Rhetorical Stance," Francis Christensen delivered "A Generative Rhetoric of the Sentence," and Edward P. J. Corbett spoke on "The Usefulness of Classical Rhetoric." Kitzhaber was then incoming president of the NCTE and had already served, in 1959, as chair of the CCCC. In his talk, Kitzhaber narrowed the focus of H. A. Gleason's call, a year earlier, for a "fundamental reorienting of the content" of English departments by applying a similar critique to composition, not only offering suggestions about how freshman English ought to be improved, but calling on the members of CCCC "to think through its assumptions, to agree on its aims and content, to take full advantage of knowledge available in such fields as language, logic, rhetoric, psychology" (133). At the same time he called on the CCCC to support and encourage "basic and applied research into the writing process and the teaching of writing" (138). While acknowledging the controversies that would emerge from such attempts, Kitzhaber asserted that without them no future reform in the way writing is taught would be possible.

Of course, this work had already begun. Kitzhaber's landmark study *Themes, Theories, and Therapy: The Teaching of Writing in College* also appeared in 1963, having been started in 1960 at Dartmouth College. It is still one of the most powerful statements about the vagaries of composition instruction, and its twenty-one concluding recommendations have not been surpassed even though they have yet to be fully implemented. Kitzhaber himself says that "a certain amount of the 'revival of rhetoric' started in 1960," when he debated University of Michigan's Warner Rice at the NCTE conference on the question of whether freshman English should be abolished. Kitzhaber's talk, entitled "Death—or Transfiguration?" warned against the same kind of atrophy he had observed in the nine-teenth century and called for composition to become a new kind of field. In his 1963 CCCC address, Kitzhaber also cited the studies and conferences that had taken place under Project English, a U.S. Department of Education effort involving a number of Curriculum Study Centers at locations throughout the country. Kitzhaber was one of fifteen experts invited to Washington by Kennedy's commissioner of education, Ster-ling McMurrin, to design Project English, which ultimately added to the study centers Summer Institutes (for high school teachers) and Research Planning Conferences (three of which were held).

Kitzhaber was chosen to direct one of the Curriculum Study Centers, and he decided on the University of Oregon as a prime location. Oregon's president at the time was Arthur Flemming, former education secretary under Eisenhower, and Flemming keenly supported the project, making the today unheard-of gesture of returning the university's overhead to the project. Oregon's English department also welcomed the project, even though at the beginning the project had to take what Kitzhaber describes as an "ambivalent" position on the role of literature in teaching writing. When McMurrin had appeared before Congress seeking some $400,000 from the NDEA to get Project English started, he was asked by one congressman whether any of the money would be spent "teaching novels and poems," an enterprise that the congress-man apparently viewed with some distrust. "Philosopher that he was," Kitzhaber recalls, "McMurrin assured the gentleman that the money would be directed to improving the teaching of writing, with the unstated reservation that, since kids had to write *about* something, literature could be bootlegged through the back door, as 'reading.' The people in the Office of Educa-tion, and the rest of us, winked at all this, but it is why the official title of our study center in Oregon was 'A Sequential Curriculum in Language, Reading, and Composition (Oral and Written), Grades 7 through 12.' As Project English developed over the next several years, this nonsense was quietly dropped and literature by that name was openly included in many of the centers."

A survey of Kitzhaber's career could easily take the form of a *curriculum vitae*, so perhaps this is enough to indicate that he was among those in the early 1960s who were not only calling for reform but also bringing it about. The composition program at Oregon became a model of his beliefs, under the leadership of Glen Love, another Washington PhD whom Kitzhaber had recruited from San Diego State. Together, they worked to make composition at Oregon a lively study in which the generation of and expression of ideas replaced exercises in forms for their own sake, as well as working simultaneously to improve writing instruction in elementary and secondary schools. Kitzhaber served the profession further during the 1960s, and determined its future directions, as leader of the CEEB's Commission on English Planning Institute for Composition, as consultant to the U.S. Office of Education, as member of the editorial board of *College English*, as a panelist at a White House Conference on Education, as leader of several MLA sponsored committees, and as the organizer of the Dartmouth College International Seminar on the Teaching of English. I'll forgo a recitation of the rest of his illustrious accomplishments. Suffice it to say that the author of this book ranks among the founders of the "revival of rhetoric" in the mid-twentieth century.

That career did not begin with this dissertation. Kitzhaber had already been a composition teacher for many years, and a director of composition, before he completed his PhD in 1953. It might interest readers to know a little bit about how this dissertation came to be written. It is a story that will sound familiar in some respects, but also marks a beginning. In preparing to tell this story (and much of the above), I enjoyed Kitzhaber's company and lively conversation, after not seeing him for a year or so, in his home in south Eugene, with its views of forested foothills, half clear-cut since my last visit. It was, for me, a panorama of change and its discontents.

After completing a BA degree in English at Coe College in 1939, Kitzhaber went to Washington State College (as it then was) as a teaching fellow in English and earned an MA there in 1941, going from there to Iowa State College as an instructor. He resigned that job to enter the twenty-six-week Intensive Russian course at the University of Iowa, which was followed by army service until the end of 1945, when he returned to Iowa State for three terms, and then went to Washington State again to teach English and Russian. (He claims with characteristic modesty not to have taught the latter subject very well.) His teaching of composition led him to the early conviction that this was the most important subject in the curriculum, but at the same time he realized it was not accorded the status it deserved. Iowa State's director of composition, Albert Walker, shared Kitzhaber's conviction and introduced him to Porter Perrin's *An Index to English*, a textbook that was reviewed in *Time* magazine and credited with closing "the breach between classroom English and spoken American" (August 7, 1939, 23). Walker's "liberal bias," as Kitzhaber calls it, was reflected in his choice of reading for composition students, namely *The Autobiography of Lincoln Steffens*, which every student had to read, discuss, and respond to in writing.

When Kitzhaber returned to Washington State, however, he found the environment less receptive to such innovations. There the director of freshman composition, an Anglo-Saxonist named Paul Kies, was more inclined to the traditional study and practice of sentence forms. A new director, Fred Dudley, took over in September 1947, and Kitzhaber was able to introduce Perrin's textbook into the curriculum—which, Kitzhaber remembers, "caused heartburn among the conservative literary types." It became evident to Kitzhaber that if he wanted to devote his career to teaching composition, he should work on his doctorate. Although Kitzhaber's motives for wanting to teach writing were what he calls "high-minded," he says he was also realist enough to know that such a career could be made respectably in an English department only if he were to be in charge of the writing program and not permanently "second-class." The pursuit of a PhD became especially attractive when he learned that Porter Perrin was at the University of Washington and taught courses in rhetoric at the graduate level.

Kitzhaber went to Washington, interviewed with Perrin, and entered the PhD program in 1948, sensing immediately that something different was happening there. Whereas in his previous experience, English departments either held rhetoric and composition in contempt or tolerated it as a source of "fodder" for graduate students in literature who themselves did not regard it as worthy of professional consideration, Kitzhaber found Perrin's program exactly suited to the ends he had chosen. Perrin taught courses in the history of rhetoric, current rhetorical theory, and style, while at the same time encouraging graduate students to explore the relevance of other disciplines to these subjects. Kitzhaber considers Perrin a "pioneer" in this regard, since he taught these subjects in relation to current psychological theories and social issues, such as freedom of the press, and was among the first to see the relevance of Kenneth Burke's ideas to composition. He was among the first, furthermore, to undertake such discussions within an English department, separate from the curriculum in speech. Perrin was not without opposition in the English department for initiating such a radical program of study, but he was the *de facto* leader of a sufficiently influential, and decidedly liberal, wing within that department, against the forces of the "Southern style of new criticism." Even so, Perrin wisely encouraged his graduate students to have literary arrows in their quiver, and Kitzhaber qualified in literary criticism, Shakespeare, American literature, and Spenser, while at the same time beginning his study of nineteenth-century rhetoric.

At the time it seemed merely to be the right kind of program for someone of Kitzhaber's interests, rather than a prototype for programs of the future. In fact, Kitzhaber completed one of the first doctoral degrees with an emphasis in rhetoric and composition awarded by an English department. There were few other English departments at that time in which such a thing could be done (the most notable exceptions being Michigan and the University of Chicago, where Perrin had himself taken a doctorate in rhetoric years before).

Even so, the dissertation did not come easily. Kitzhaber became interested in its subject because of his dissatisfaction with the routine way in which composition was most often taught, in comparison with the more progressive methods he had experienced at Iowa State, and he grew curious about where the entrenched methods came from. Kitzhaber began to see parallels between writing instruction in the 1930s and 1940s and that of the 1880s and to wonder why it was that educational doctrines could be successfully challenged in theory (as in H. B. Lathrop's 1918 article attacking the dogmatic triad of Unity-Coherence-Emphasis) "without making a ripple in practice" as Kitzhaber put it to me. He himself held no doctrinaire views about composition, but he knew that it could be more interesting than it generally was and that in fact it should be more interesting and vital since it touched every student and might be a genuinely liberating subject if taught well. But the search for appropriate methods took Kitzhaber more deeply into educational theory and psychology than he was expecting to go, and the dissertation changed shape in his mind several times.

Before completing it, Kitzhaber combined teaching and directing freshman composition at Utah State College in Logan, beginning in 1950, with further research on American rhetoric. Perrin, who had himself written a thesis on early American rhetoric instruction and theory, pushed Kitzhaber to read nineteenth-century American textbooks—Perrin mailed Kitzhaber apple boxes full of his own private collection of such texts. When it was time for Kitzhaber to defend the thesis orally, he returned to Seattle and completed the manuscript—reorganizing it entirely—in ten days while taking a room in a dorm that permitted typing until 10:00 P.M. He remembers well Perrin's first words on seeing the scotch-taped thesis manuscript on the table at his defense: "Is that the *corpus delicti?*"

Perhaps those words suggest some of the reasons Kitzhaber had misgivings about publishing the dissertation once he had finished it. Although before he finished the draft that he filed in 1953 he had already undertaken a new position, as director of freshman and sophomore composition and literature at the

University of Kansas, and was soon busy in the profession at a national level, it was not such distractions alone that led him to put the dissertation aside for an indefinite time. (In fact, he did publish the bibliography from the thesis in 1953.) Perrin had told him, and Kitzhaber had believed, that if he were to publish the dissertation he would have to spend at least one summer in the stacks at Harvard—a summer that never quite became available. His original intention had been to study the period 1850–1950, and he continued to think that the thesis should be brought up to date, even as the years added to the complexity of the task of arriving at the "present time." But he had worse reasons than these: Kitzhaber says he thought his method of "quote and paraphrase" was inadequate, and anyway, Perrin had told him, as dissertation directors sometimes do in their waggish moods, that "when you finish a dissertation, you won't be able to bear to look at it again for ten years." And perhaps it was ten years, by which time Kitzhaber was deeply involved in other administrative, leadership, and scholarly endeavors, before he saw Perrin's words as other than literal. "Since the study was somewhat ahead of its time," Kitzhaber says, "and no one else seemed to be interested in the grubby details of how freshman comp got that way, I sort of wrote the whole thing off as a learning experience to be noted and filed away."

It was not in the absence of offers to publish the dissertation that Kitzhaber demurred. Perhaps the "corpus delicti" seemed, to its vital and vigorous author, too much a thing of the past, or of the indefinite future. Often during his busy career he thought he might someday get around to rewriting the thesis, but one thing led to another, until he discovered that mice had gotten into his stored notes and shredded them for a nest. Why Kitzhaber did accept the latest offer to publish this book, without revision, nearly ten years after his retirement from teaching, I cannot say. But now that it is a thing of the present once again, we can be grateful that Kitzhaber's misgivings about publishing it have given way to mere reluctance, and not enough of that to deflect the urgings of Gary Tate on behalf of the SMU Press.

We need not know what Al Kitzhaber thought his dissertation ought to be before becoming a book in order to appreciate and use it now that it is one. A classic work in the field is now in print, and its history, however interesting, makes way for the future uses to which scholars and students of this protean, but timelessly relevant, discipline will put it.

John T. Gage
University of Oregon

Published Works of Albert R. Kitzhaber

BOOKS

————. *A Bibliography on Rhetoric in American Colleges, 1850–1900.* Special Bibliographies, No. 2, 1954. Bibliographical Center for Research. Denver: Colorado Public Library, 1954.

————, Robert M. Gorrell, and Paul Roberts. *Education for College: Improving the High School Curriculum.* The Report of the Portland High School Curriculum Study. New York: Ronald Press, 1961.

————. *Themes, Theories, and Therapy: The Teaching of Writing in College.* The report of the Dartmouth Study of Student Writing. New York: McGraw-Hill, 1963.

————, and Donald W. Lee. *Handbook for Basic Composition.* Englewood Cliffs, NJ: Prentice-Hall, 1961.

————, gen. ed. *The Oregon Curriculum: A Sequential Program in English,* grades 7–12. 24 vols. (12 student texts, 12 teacher manuals). New York: Holt, Rinehart & Winston, 1968–70. Second edition 1974, retitled *Concepts in Literature* and *Concepts in Communication.* 24 vols.

————, coordinating editor. *Spectrum of English,* grades 3–6. 4 vols. (student text). Encino, CA: Glencoe Publishing Co., 1978. Second edition 1984, retitled *Glencoe English.* 4 vols.

ARTICLES

"Götterdämmerung in Topeka: The Downfall of Senator Pomeroy." *The Kansas Historical Quarterly* 18 (1950): 243–78.

"Mark Twain's Use of the Pomeroy Case in *The Gilded Age.*" *Modern Language Quarterly* 6 (1954): 42–56.

"The University of Kansas Course in the College Teaching of English." *College Composition and Communication* 6 (1955): 194–200.

"Teachers and Teaching." *Proceedings of the Northwest Association of Secondary and Higher Schools* Nov.–Dec. 1959: 53–59. Also in *Oregon Higher Education* 3 (1960): 23–30.

"Death—or Transfiguration?" *College English* 21 (1960): 367–73.

"But What Are We Articulating With?" *English Journal* 51 (1962): 167–79. (Attributed to the NCTE committee on High School-college Articulation but written entirely by ARK and later incorporated into *Themes, Theories, and Therapy*.)

"New Perspectives on Teaching Composition." *College English* 23 (1962): 440–44.

"The Coming Revolution in English Teaching." *Proceedings of the Northwest Association of Secondary and Higher Schools* Dec. 1962: 54–60. Also in *Iowa English Yearbook* Fall 1964: 3–8.

"Rethinking: A Prerequisite to Reform." *English Journal* 52 (1963): 230–33.

"4C, Freshman English, and the Future." *College Composition and Communication* 14 (1963): 129–38.

"The Two-Year College and the Teaching of English." Published as a pamphlet by NCTE, Nov. 1963.

"Current Developments in the Teaching of English." *College English* 25 (1964): 450–58.

"Foreword" to Syrell Rogovin, *Modern English Sentence Structure*. New York: Random House-Singer, 1964.

"English Instruction in Two-Year Colleges: Problems and Possibilities." *Research and the Development of English Programs in the Junior College*. Cooperative Research Project No. x-004. NCTE 1965: 1–6.

"Reform in English." *College English* 26 (1965): 337–44. Also in *English Journal* 2 (1965): 73–80, under title "NCTE Presidential Address."

"English Composition: The Hardest Subject." *University of Kansas Bulletin of Education* 19 (1965): 112–23. Also in *Kentucky English Bulletin* 14 (Winter 1964–65): 3–16.

"A Time of Change." *College English* 28 (1966): 51–54. Also in *English Journal* 55 (1966): 911–14.

"General English Curriculum Development Programs: University of Oregon." *Summary Progress Report of English Curriculum and Demonstration Centers*. NCTE Commission on the English Curriculum (Nov. 1966): 25–26.

"What Is English?" *Holt's Dialog* Winter 1967: 1–17. Published by Holt, Rinehart & Winston. One of the two opening papers read at the Dartmouth International Seminar on the Teaching of English, Aug. 1966.

"A Search for Better Ways to Teach Writing." *California Teachers Association Journal* 63 (1967): 13–15.

"The Government and English Teaching: A Retrospective View." *College Composition and Communication* 18 (1967): 135–41.

"Project English" (Interview). *Education* 20 (1971): 4–12. School Publication Branch, Department of Education, Wellington, New Zealand.

"A Rage for Disorder." *English Journal* 61 (1972): 1199–1219. Reprinted, slightly condensed, in *The Use of English* (Sheffield, England) 25 (1973): 103–16.

"A Review of Hirsch's *The Philosophy of Composition.*" *The Rhetoric Society Quarterly* 8 (1978): 149–54.

Main Trends in Higher Education
1850–1900

CHAPTER ONE

T HE SECOND HALF of the nineteenth century was a period of transition in American higher education, a time in which the philosophy and methods of education underwent important changes. Until about 1870 few shifts in emphasis were apparent, the colleges continuing to operate much as they had since the eighteenth century. Dissatisfaction with aims, curriculum, and teaching methods was growing, however, through the middle years of the century, though the first attempts at reform had only limited success. By 1870 the pressure for change had become so acute that major revisions began to appear, at first only in a few institutions with enterprising presidents, but finally, as the century drew to a close, in even the most traditional colleges. Throughout the period, developments in rhetorical theory and practice were tied quite closely to the changes taking place in educational philosophy. It is for this reason that a brief survey of the chief trends in American higher education during these fifty years is needed as a background against which to study the single discipline of rhetoric.

CHANGES IN PSYCHOLOGY AND
EDUCATIONAL THEORY

The most prominent educational theory in American colleges up to 1870 was based on the ideal of mental discipline. The human mind was widely regarded as consisting of certain faculties or powers: the will, the feelings, the judgment, the imagination, etc. It was believed that these faculties could be exercised and strengthened in much the same way as muscles. Educators, therefore, saw their function as twofold: to discipline and strengthen these separate faculties through drill and exercises; and secondarily to supply the student with a store of general principles in the light of which his trained faculties would, in later professional life, make needed particular applications. The best sort of education was that which offered the best opportunities for rigorous drill, and that which stressed generalizations thought to be universally useful. The curriculum that best suited this approach was the traditional one centered chiefly around mathematics and the classical languages. Most of the curriculum was required, and deviations from it were discouraged since it not only provided essential mental discipline but it also furnished the sort of generalized culture thought to be most valuable. Instruction was by recitation, a method calculated to strengthen the faculty of memory: the student often memorized the pages of his textbook and repeated them to his teacher verbatim. Questions from the student usually were not encouraged, since the teacher did not consider it a part of his responsibility to add anything of his own to the lesson.

This theory of education was long buttressed by the popular study of mental and moral philosophy (or mental and moral science, as it was often called).[1] The evangelical churches (whose clergy were in charge of most American colleges in these years) had not, since the time of Jonathan Edwards and his "New Light" theology, had a systematic philosophical basis for their faith. The rationalism and skepticism of the eighteenth century; the philosophy and psychology of men like Berkeley, Hartley, Kant; the increasingly urgent claims of science for a rational and experimental rather than supernatural approach to nature—all these had put the advocates of revealed religion on the defensive before the nineteenth century opened. The popularity in America from about 1820 of the books of the Scottish "Common-Sense" philosophers (chiefly Thomas Reid and James Beattie) marked the beginning of the mental and moral philosophy movement. The "Common-Sense" school, using what was basically a faculty psychology, divided the powers of the human mind into mental and moral. Mental science provided the psychological justification for moral science. The essential feature of this psychology was the combating of skepticism by elevating plain common-sense to the rank of a distinct mental faculty which tells us plainly through the senses and through consciousness itself that we exist, have minds, can think and know. Having thus cleared the air of skepticism and associationism, the "Common-Sense" school then outlined a system of moral philosophy distinguished by orthodox theology. Thus, if one accepted the psychology he had a philosophical basis for religious orthodoxy.

Reid's *Intellectual Powers of Man* (1785) and *Active Powers of Man* (1788) were gratefully received by the clergymen who made up the faculties of most American colleges, and by the 1830s American texts on mental and moral science, based on Reid, were appearing in quantity. The new studies were intended to offset the materialism encouraged by the increase in scientific investigation and discovery as well as the threat that Transcendentalism was posing to orthodox theology. Courses in mental and moral science were given in nearly every college in the country for at least two generations, and usually were required. The movement is significant here because it is evidence of the hostility to new developments in various branches of inquiry that kept the American college relatively static for so long. It is of even more direct interest in that a number of the earlier American authors of textbooks on rhetoric were also authors of texts on mental and moral science, and based their rhetorical theory on the faculty psychology of mental science. After the middle of the century some of the psychological theories of Sir William Hamilton were added to the discussions of mental science, and ultimately carried over into rhetorical textbooks. The items of theory selected from Hamilton, however, were not his most significant contributions to psychology but rather a classification and arrangement of mental powers neater and more precise than the ones that had appeared earlier.

Shortly after 1850 faculty psychology slowly began to give way before attacks made on it from several directions. Hamilton was himself primarily an associationist and tried to correct the oversimplified view of the mind that had been advanced by earlier associationists as well as by Reid and his followers. He still spoke, however, of mental powers, and his theory was mechanical. Alexander Bain, professor of logic, mental philosophy, and English literature at the University of Aberdeen from 1860 to 1880, was also an associationist, but he differed from Hamilton and in fact from all preceding psychologists in realizing the need for a thorough knowledge of physiology in order to understand properly the workings of the mind. His two chief books on psychology (*The Senses and the Intellect,* 1855, and *The Emotions and the Will,* 1859) contain the most comprehensive attempt made up to that time to encompass the whole range of human experience in one systematic psychology. As an associationist he attacked the view of separate mental faculties (the titles of his books are somewhat misleading); in addition, his knowledge of physiology gave him an advantage over earlier associationists by keeping before him the realization that mental activities are extremely complex, involving the whole body. Bain's textbooks on psychology were among the standard ones in England and America till near the end of the century and did much to combat the neat but unrealistic division of the mind popularized by the faculty psychologists.

Other influences also helped to undermine the older view of the mind, and with it the whole philosophy of education based on mental discipline and a required curriculum. Darwinism, for example, with its emphasis on individual differences, was in conflict with a system of education that sought to force all students into the same mold. More important, however, was the rise in Germany of modern experimental psychology under Wundt, whose *Principles of Physiological Psychology* was published in 1873–74. Wundt and his steadily increasing number of disciples went much farther than Bain in studying mental phenomena in terms of physiological stimuli and reactions. Wundt established in 1879 his famous psychological laboratory, to which students from Europe and America soon began flocking.

4

The first American to study under Wundt was G. Stanley Hall, who on his return went in 1883 to the Johns Hopkins University, where he set up a laboratory modeled on Wundt's. Among the first students to work in Hall's laboratory was John Dewey, who published his *Psychology* in 1886 and did much to supply a rationale for the new developments in education that crested in the 1890s. William James began publishing articles on psychology in the late 1870s and issued his great *Principles of Psychology* in 1890. About 1885 the influence of Herbart finally began to make itself felt in the United States. Herbart's theory of apperception meant, pedagogically, that the student must be guided carefully from familiar material to material unfamiliar but related to what he already knows. Since the required curriculum did not do this, the effect of Herbartian ideas was to give greater impetus to the movement for curriculum reform, as well as to help overthrow the faculty psychology which underlay the older philosophy of education. In the 1880s, chiefly under the leadership of G. Stanley Hall, child psychology assumed great importance in America and soon began to influence teacher-training, pedagogical methods, and the curriculum. Closely tied with this movement, as well as with Herbartianism, was the rapid growth of chairs and departments of education. The first permanent chair of pedagogy was established at the University of Michigan in 1877.[2] Growth was slow until the 1890s, when it suddenly accelerated. There were 11 chairs or departments of education in the country in 1891; two years later there were 83; by 1894 the number had more than doubled, reaching 174; and by 1899 there were 244.[3]

By 1890, then, faculty psychology had been pretty thoroughly discredited. The mental discipline ideal of education, with its required curriculum, still had a good many supporters, and they were very vocal; but the ground had been cut from under them, so that their arguments sounded much less convincing in the 1890s than they had thirty years earlier when mental science gave them the appearance at least of being based on laws of the human mind. The death blow was finally given to the mental discipline approach by E. L. Thorndike and R. S. Woodworth in 1901 in an article called "The Influence of Improvement in One Mental Function upon the Efficiency of Other Functions."[4] The authors, after considerable experimentation, concluded that skill in one function does not transfer to other functions unless there is a close similarity between the functions, and even then the amount of transfer depends directly on the degree of similarity.

THE DECLINE OF RELIGIOUS INFLUENCE
ON HIGHER EDUCATION

Until well after the Civil War, the colleges of America were still largely in the hands of the Protestant clergy. One of the main functions of the American college from the founding of Harvard had been the training of clergymen, though throughout the eighteenth century other professions—notably law—claimed the interest of an increasing proportion of college students. The great religious revival of the early nineteenth century, however, caused for a time an increase in the number of young men who, stirred with the religious fervor of the period, determined on the ministry as a career. At the same time, individual denominations which were expanding their missionary activities in the more settled parts of the western frontier found the available supply of clergymen too small. Partly as a result of this need for more ministers in the West, partly perhaps from a sort of denominational imperialism, and partly from the desire to establish small centers of Christian culture and enlightenment in the rough towns of the frontier, Protestant sects began to found denominational colleges. Between 1800 and 1830 only 17 such institutions had been established; but between the latter year and 1861, 133 colleges, nearly all of them sectarian, were founded.[5]

Clerical influence dominated not only these new colleges, but most of the older ones as well; the tradition of the clergy as the chief guardians of learning and teachers of youth was slow to die out. It is reasonable to assume that the resistance to change that marked American higher education during so much of the nineteenth century was due in considerable measure to normal human inertia. At the same time it seems likely that clerical domination of most colleges intensified this resistance. The introduction of untried and possibly

6

dangerous subjects into the curriculum, the growth of inductive and hence anti-authoritarian methods of studying traditional subjects like history and language, the appearance from Germany of the "Higher Criticism" of the Scriptures—all these influences were vigorously opposed by most colleges until after the Civil War, and by some to the very end of the century. The denominational colleges clung to the traditional ideal of establishing and maintaining a Christian community through education. As Julius H. Seelye, president of Amherst from 1876 to 1890, said, "Unless we make Christian culture the informing idea of all our educational edifice, unless we make the Bible its corner stone and top stone, the edifice itself will crumble."[6]

In the 1870s clerical influence on higher education began to lessen perceptibly, in part because of a widespread feeling that this influence had narrowed education and was keeping it out of touch with the times. Andrew D. White, first president of Cornell University, voiced this dissatisfaction in an address before the National Education Association in 1874. White pointed out that though the United States then had some 360 institutions calling themselves universities or colleges, none of them was worthy of being ranked with the average European university. Faculties were incomplete, libraries inadequate, laboratories and equipment nonexistent. For these conditions White blamed partly the apathy of the public, but chiefly the domination of higher education by church groups. He cited numerous instances in which membership in a given sect had been a prerequisite to holding a professorship and declared that from the time when Cotton Mather forced the resignation of Henry Dunster as president of Harvard College because of religious nonconformity, "the sectarian spirit has been the worst foe of advanced education."[7] The system of sectarian colleges had resulted, he said, not only in a scattering of effort that made the creation of a few strong schools impossible, but it also had cramped intellectual inquiry. Since these institutions depended for their maintenance on particular denominations whose ideal was not so much the growth of the student as of the denomination, all the studies in the curriculum were made to conform to a sectarian pattern. The effect of this, White charged, had been to warp the student's mind, not educate it (p. 60).

After 1870 the denominational colleges were on the defensive. They found themselves in opposition to nearly all the new trends that were beginning to appear; coeducation, courses in laboratory science, higher standards of scholarship, all ran counter to their traditional ideals and mode of operation. John W. Burgess, returning to Amherst in 1873 from Germany, tried to introduce German methods of study and teaching but found the opposition so strong that he resigned and went to Columbia, where he was able to found a political science faculty.[8] Thomas LeDuc, writing of Amherst but stating really the case for many denominational colleges, has summed up the situation:

> Amherst was founded squarely on the belief that the role of the college was to transfer to each new generation a body of accepted truth. The validity of these doctrines was not to be questioned. The German ideal [of research] played havoc with this tradition. It suggested, in the first place, that truth was, perhaps, not yet entire. In the second place, it cut even more sharply into the old faith, for it declared anew the validity of human reason, of man's power to discern for himself, without divine revelation or intuitive perception, the nature and content of truth.[9]

The sectarian college was faced with the choice of accepting the new ideas and revising its methods and curriculum accordingly, or of losing students. The religious enthusiasm of the earlier half of the century that had nourished these colleges was now on the wane. The young men who had come to them earlier with the purpose of training themselves for the ministry were now fewer. The new times were overwhelmingly secular in spirit. Some idea of this can be gained by citing a few enrollment figures in schools of theology as compared with schools of science and commercial and business colleges. Figures for the years 1871 and 1880 are the most significant, because between these two dates the new trend began. In the former year there were, according to the Commissioner of Education's

Report for 1880, some 94 theological schools in the country, enrolling 3,204 students. In the same year, 60 business and commercial colleges had an enrollment of 6,460, and 41 science schools had 3,303 students. In 1880, however, although the number of theological schools had grown to 142, total enroll-ment was still only 5,242. In contrast with this, 1880 showed 162 commercial colleges with an enrollment of 27,146, and 83 science schools with 11,584 students.[10] According to these fig-ures, schools of theology continued to increase in number, but their enrollment did not rise correspondingly. Institutions that offered more "practical" training, however, flourished as never before. These included especially the new land-grant colleges and universities, which were offering a type of education that a large part of the population wanted. Between 1885 and 1895 enrollment at 8 state universities, all but one in the middle west, showed a 300 per cent increase; during the same years, 8 well-known denominational colleges in the same area had only a 15 per cent increase.[11]

By the end of the century the near-monopoly of control over higher education that the clergy had exercised earlier in the century had vanished. Many small sectarian colleges still flourished, of course, but the characteristic institutions of the new century were the large state universities and colleges estab-lished under the Morrill Act, and the universities like Cornell, Chicago, and the Johns Hopkins founded and heavily endowed by private philanthropy. Both types were nonsectarian.

THE INFLUENCE OF SCIENCE AND TECHNOLOGY ON EDUCATION

The most disturbing idea offered by science in this period was of course the theory of evolution. America showed much interest in evolutionary thought from the beginning. The first American edition of the *Origin of Species* in 1859 was completely sold out in two weeks,[12] and the works of Spencer, Mill, Comte, Huxley all found a wide audience in this country. Tyndall lectured in the United States in 1872-73, Huxley in 1876, Spencer himself in 1882.[13] In 1876 the New York *Tribune* devoted an extra issue to a reprint of all the addresses Huxley had delivered in America.[14] In

9

addition, the Americans John Fiske and E. L. Youmans worked assiduously to popularize Darwin's ideas. Shortly after Charles W. Eliot was inaugurated as president of Harvard in 1869, he engaged Fiske to lecture on Positivism. Clergymen at once protested what they called "Harvard's raid on religion." Eliot was not daunted but had Fiske repeat the lectures the next year and also give a series on evolution.[15]

Though Darwinism did not have any immediate effect on education, it served in the long run to undermine traditional views of many fields of study and thus contributed indirectly toward a weakening of faith in the existing curriculum. By substituting the idea of dynamic growth for static notions, by stressing the functions of an organism, evolution caused profound changes in such diverse fields as economics, sociology, anthropology, literature, history, psychology, and in the case of one or two advanced theorists at the end of the century, in rhetoric as well. Evolution challenged the *status quo*. Its acceptance necessitated a thorough reassessment of many academic subjects; its rejection placed one on the defensive, which, tactically, is a weak position.

The fact that technological advances after 1850 were beginning to affect, in one way or another, the entire population of the United States hardly needs to be elaborated. The ordinary aspects of existence were taking on a new appearance as rapid communication destroyed continental distances; as the products of factories were priced within the reach of an ever greater proportion of the nation; as improvements in medicine, agriculture, engineering, and countless other fields made their contributions to the national life. The prestige of science and technology rose steadily as it became apparent what miracles they could accomplish in the subjugation of nature to man's use.

It is not surprising, therefore, that after the middle of the century a good deal of pressure was exerted on the colleges to give more adequate recognition to scientific studies. Book instruction in some of the sciences had of course been the custom for many years, but what was wanted now was laboratory courses in experimental science. Perhaps the most influential of the many spokesmen for the admission of science to academic respectability was Herbert Spencer. His series of four essays published under the title *Education: Intellectual, Moral, and Physical*[16] found a wide audience both in England and in America. The first and most important of the four, entitled "What Knowledge Is of Most Worth," was an ingenious and uncompromisingly practical attack on the traditional classical education. Spencer began by saying that a rational curriculum was urgently needed, and the way to determine such a curriculum was to find out which subjects minister most directly to the activities of existence. He arranged these activities in a hierarchy, beginning with the most important (those which contribute directly to self-preservation) and ending with the least important (those "ornamental" activities which help to occupy one's leisure time). Since no system of education could hope to train the individual equally well in all possible activities, Spencer reasoned that the most significant ones should receive most attention. He found, however, when he looked about him and surveyed the education of his time, that the ornaments were usurping the place of important studies. Values, he thought, had perversely been turned upside down: the arts, mere ornaments of life, were the core of present education, and the indispensable facts of science were being ignored. He disclaimed any animosity toward the arts, but insisted they "should be wholly subordinate to that knowledge and discipline in which civilization rests [that is, science]. *As they occupy the leisure part of life, so should they occupy the leisure part of education*" (pp. 74-75). Spencer argued further that science would be quite as effective as the classical languages in promoting mental discipline, and insisted that it could equally well inculcate moral discipline and even "religious culture."

The argument is undoubtedly strained, the logic faulty; but it was good ammunition with which to attack the classical curriculum, since it made a show of justifying science not only on the obvious premise of its practical utility but even on the very grounds of mental discipline and culture that defenders of the classics used themselves to support their own position.

The insistent pressure for laboratory science courses in American colleges finally began to yield a few results. Harvard made a start in 1846 with a laboratory course in chemistry,[17] but such innovations were still not regarded favorably by most colleges, since they meant a break with the long-established way of doing things. Special technical or scientific schools began to appear about the middle of the century, in part as a protest against the lack of adequate instruction in science and technology in the regular colleges. In 1847 both the Sheffield Scientific School at Yale and the Lawrence Scientific School at Harvard were established. The Massachusetts Institute of Technology was founded in 1865. The most powerful impetus to scientific and technical education came, however, in 1862, with the passage of the Morrill Land-Grant Act for the founding of colleges of agriculture and mechanic arts. Within five years after the act became law, twenty-three states had availed themselves of its provisions.[18] These new state institutions, founded squarely on the notion that it was the responsibility of American colleges to offer a wider selection of courses than had been commonly available before, were very influential in breaking up the older pattern and in supplying a new one for the next century.

THE INFLUENCE OF GERMAN UNIVERSITIES

American students had begun going to Germany for advanced study before 1820, though at first there were few of them. Accurate figures on American enrollment in German universities are hard to come by, but it has been estimated that before 1850 fewer than 200 Americans studied in Germany. Then a sharp increase began. Between 1850 and 1860 there seem to have been some 300 American students enrolled; in the next 10 years the number jumped to about a thousand; the figure held at near 1,000 from 1870 to 1880 but crested in the decade ending in 1890, when over 2,000 Americans were enrolled.[19] From 1890 the enrollment declined sharply, and a survey made of American attendance for the winter semester 1901-02 shows only 411 American students in 30 German universities.[20]

The obvious reason for the heavy attendance of Americans at schools like Göttingen, Berlin, Giessen, Leipzig, Fulda, is simply that these institutions offered a type of training that the

American colleges of the period did not. The opportunity for graduate study, which was the chief reason why young Americans flocked to German universities, was almost nonexistent in America before 1870. The university plan of organization with its distinct graduate college, first established in Prussia, had not yet gained acceptance among the governing authorities of American educational institutions. Moreover, neither faculties nor library and laboratory facilities at American colleges were yet able to sustain research on the graduate level. As a result, while German universities were approaching their peak in prestige and enrollment, there were in 1868-69 only eight graduate students in residence at Yale, five at Harvard, and none at all at Brown, Columbia, Princeton, or the University of Pennsylvania.[21]

There were other reasons too why Americans were attracted to German universities. The secular control of German higher education had fostered a different sort of system with a broader educational philosophy underlying it. In contrast to the often narrow sectarian control of inquiry and instruction in American colleges, the German institutions adhered to the ideals of *Lernfreiheit* and *Lehrfreiheit*. They insisted on the right and duty of the scholar to pursue truth disinterestedly; they assembled first-rate faculties who were there to teach, not to hear recitations and maintain order in the classroom. Such conditions came as a revelation to students accustomed to American colleges. And when these students returned to America, with or without a German *Doktorat*, they were often impatient with what they considered the backwardness of higher education in this country. James Morgan Hart, for example, later a president of the Modern Language Association, received a Ph.D. in Germany; when he returned to the United States he wrote a book on German universities which consisted of almost unqualified praise of the German system. The idler of Germany, he declared,

> has forgotten twice as much as the idler of America, the industrious student knows twice as much as the industrious under-graduate, and the future scholar of Germany is a man of whom we in America have no conception. He

13

is a man who could not exist under our system, he would be choked by recitations and grades. What he studies, he studies with the devotion of a poet and the trained skill of a scientist.[22]

Another critic was F. H. Hedge, who after graduating from Harvard had gone to Germany for further study. Though Harvard in the 1860s was still, in popular estimation, the most distinguished American university, Hedge delivered in 1866 an address to Harvard alumni in which he insisted that Harvard was not a university at all, compared with German institutions, but "simply a more advanced school for boys, not differing essentially in principle and theory from the public schools in all our towns." In both Harvard and the schools, he said, boys were required to recite lessons and write compulsory exercises, and they were graded on their proficiency in these activities. Coercion was the ruling principle—"Hold your subject fast with one hand, and pour knowledge into him with the other." Hedge found it deplorable that half of the most distinguished German universities were younger than Harvard.[23]

It is obvious that men like Hedge and Hart idealized the German system considerably beyond its actual merits. German higher education, after all, was an instrument of German nationalism, and political interference with academic freedom was by no means uncommon. The German scholar's view of research, his disdain for style, his passion for fact-grubbing and influence-tracing were themselves to prove finally as much a curse as a blessing to American higher education. But to most German-trained men of these years the shortcomings either were not apparent or were insignificant alongside the positive benefits that German universities were offering.

With advocates like Hart and Hedge pressing the superior claims of German training, it became the fashion to round off one's schooling with a period of study in Germany. Some students, like the young Lincoln Steffens, returned without the doctorate, and sometimes with more knowledge of Berlin music halls and Munich beer than of Teutonic scholarship. But, as Thomas LeDuc has written, "Whatever its real merit, the experience of studying in Germany endowed the individual with a prestige that carried a cash value in America. It was fashionable to adorn the college faculty with these German doctors."[24] By 1883 at Amherst a third of the faculty had had German training, and the proportion increased later.[25]

These returning scholars exerted a great influence on the American college and university through their efforts to pattern the curriculum, teaching methods, and the very aims of higher education itself after the German model. Harvard had had its course disturbed momentarily in the 1820s by George Ticknor and George Bancroft, who after returning from a period of German study had tried to introduce such innovations as the elective system and instruction by lectures. In the 1850s a second attempt was made by a group including George Martin Lane, Francis J. Child, Josiah Parsons Cooke, and William Watson Goodwin. All these men had studied in Germany and upon their return had accepted chairs at Harvard.[26] Like the 1820 reformers, however, they accomplished little at the time. The recitation system was still firmly entrenched and was now backed up by a peculiarly rigid system of grading known as the "Scale of Merit." But the size of classes at Harvard had become too large—as many as a hundred students—for the recitation plan to function well, and as a result the new men finally did succeed in getting written examinations substituted for oral, both for the Overseers' annual examination of each class in each subject and also for some of the examinations during a course.[27] The latter was the first definite break with the recitation system at Harvard, and after it the system rapidly collapsed.

At other institutions also the German plan was making considerable headway. Henry P. Tappan, president of the University of Michigan from 1852 to 1863, had visited Germany; when he came to Ann Arbor he tried consistently and with some success to introduce German ideals and methods. Opposition to his reforms, however, caused his dismissal by the regents in 1863. Cornell University, under the leadership of its first president, Andrew D. White, aimed from the beginning to make itself a true university on the German plan. A dramatic sign of German influence was the founding of the Johns

Hopkins University in 1876 expressly as a graduate university ministering to the needs of mature students who wanted thorough and scholarly training. A distinguished faculty, nearly all German-trained, was assembled, and provision was made for each man to do research as well as teaching. A program of graduate fellowships was also established which, like other features of the new university, quickly became the model for similar developments in other schools.

When enrollment of Americans in the universities of Germany finally began to decline after 1890, it was simply because facilities for acceptable graduate training had become available in the United States. The influence of the Johns Hopkins University in stimulating the formation of graduate faculties was great, but other institutions were already moving in this direction even before 1876. Yale established a graduate school in 1871, and had in fact conferred the first American doctorate of philosophy in 1861.[28] Harvard announced in 1872 that it would award the degrees of Ph.D. and Sc.D., and the University of Michigan followed suit. Harvard's first Ph.D. was granted in 1873, Michigan's in 1876.[29] An indication of how American universities rapidly began to meet the needs of graduate students who formerly had gone to Germany is seen in the rapid expansion of graduate enrollment at Harvard. Though in 1868-69 only 5 graduate students were in residence, the number had grown to 28 by 1872. Four years later there were 61, and by 1889-90 the number had risen to 111. Between 1873, the date of the first doctorate, and 1898 Harvard conferred 212 doctor's degrees.[30] In 1898-99 there were more than 3,600 graduate students enrolled in 24 American institutions, 1,000 of these students being women. In 1898 alone, 246 doctorates of philosophy were awarded in America.[31]

In the remaining years of the century other American colleges gradually fell into line, adopting—often, as at Yale, over strong opposition—many features of the German university system. It is difficult for us today to realize how profoundly indebted the modern American university is to the German university of the nineteenth century. The elective system, the graduate school, the Ph.D. degree, the graduate seminar, the lecture system, the concept of academic freedom, the ideal and even the methodology of research—all these and more we owe chiefly to the German university.

CHANGES IN THE CURRICULUM PATTERN

As a result of the influence of the German university, of the impact of science, of the Morrill Act, of a weakening faith in the credibility of the old faculty psychology, the 1870s saw the beginnings of extensive revisions in the traditional curriculum. The changes were heralded by the inaugurations of six great educational leaders as presidents of important universities: Andrew D. White, Cornell (1867); James McCosh, Princeton (1868); Charles W. Eliot, Harvard (1869); Noah Porter, Yale (1871); James B. Angell, Michigan (1871); and Daniel Coit Gilman, Johns Hopkins (1875). All these men had strong personal followings and wielded great influence. The significant thing, however, is that only two of them were defenders of traditional education—McCosh and Porter. The other four were all keenly alive to the educational pressures and trends of the time and pledged themselves to remodel their institutions, fitting them more efficiently to present and future needs.

There can be little doubt that of these six men the one who was most influential, especially in curriculum revision, was Eliot of Harvard. A forceful speaker and prolific writer, Eliot made himself the leader of the forces that wanted to admit new studies. (The opposition was spearheaded by McCosh and Porter.) Eliot was the model of the university executive, and through a combination of tact and stubbornness was able to win the consent of the Harvard Overseers and Corporation to nearly all the changes he recommended. The battle was essentially, of course, between rival theories of education—between the advocates of literary as opposed to scientific subjects as the staple of college work. Eliot's tact can be seen to advantage in his inaugural address in 1869, when he declared there was no point to the controversy over whether literary or scientific education was the better. "This University recognizes no real antagonism between literature and science, and consents to no such narrow alternatives as mathematics or classics, science or metaphysics. We would have them all, and at their best."[32] He was proposing, in other words, to modify the curriculum not by excision but by addition. In point of fact, however, the result was about the same. Eliot's introduction of modern languages and literatures, and of the experimental sciences (he was himself a chemist), had the effect of deemphasizing the classics and ultimately of nearly wiping them out—whether this was what he intended or not.

Consistently with this desire to add to the curriculum, Eliot made in the same address a plea for specialization, one of the most prominent features of higher education in Germany, where he had studied. Specialization, however, meant the end of the prescribed curriculum that had been intended to develop and train equally all the separate faculties of which the student's mind was presumed to consist. Consequently, Eliot championed the introduction of the elective system into American higher education. It is a little difficult today to realize how much heat this matter generated in the last thirty years of the nineteenth century. It was undoubtedly one of the most spirited disputes in the history of college education in America.

Agitation for the elective system had been begun by George Ticknor at Harvard in the 1820s after his return from studying in Germany. He was not able to accomplish much, nor were other German-trained young men able to do much more at Harvard in the 1850s. Nevertheless, there was a good deal more freedom of choice for the student at Harvard before Eliot's inauguration than at any other American college, though this freedom was under severe constraints.

Eliot, again in his inaugural address, made his own position with regard to electives unmistakably clear. The entering student, he said, "ought to know what he likes best and is most fit for. If his previous training has been sufficiently wide, he will know by that time whether he is most apt for language or philosophy or natural science or mathematics. If he feels no loves, he will at least have his hates" (p. 14). The old plan of required courses declined more rapidly at Harvard than elsewhere, but Harvard's example facilitated the gradual spread of the elective system throughout the country.[33] In the academic year 1874–75 the required work at Harvard, except for a few courses in history, rhetoric, philosophy, and political economy, was entirely in the freshman year. By 1883-84 electives had been extended into the freshman year too, and the only required courses left were freshman English, freshman German or French, themes and forensics in the sophomore and junior years, and two short lecture courses in chemistry and physics.[34]

The elective system was, for a variety of reasons, an almost inevitable development in this period. Perhaps the most obvious reason was the rapid increase in knowledge, chiefly scientific and technical, and the great complexity of this knowledge. The traditional curriculum had been formulated at a time when it was thought that the content of this curriculum provided an educated man with just about all he needed to know. But by 1870—in fact, well before this—the volume of knowledge available on individual subjects had become so vast that it would have been nearly the work of a lifetime to master completely any one subject. This, coupled with the growing complexity of society itself and the premium that society placed on specialization, contributed heavily to spell the doom of the required curriculum. There were other causes for its decline too. The psychology which underlay the disciplinary ideal of education was under attack, as we have seen. In the lower schools more attention was being paid to the individuality of the pupil, his preferences and capacities, and it seems probable that some of this interest militated against the uniform curriculum in higher education. Finally, a knowledge of Latin and Greek did not seem, in this period of industrial expansion and quick fortunes, to have the practical value that a knowledge of civil engineering or mining technology did.

The entrenched position of Latin and Greek began to crumble perceptibly in the 1880s as the elective movement gained force. At Harvard the two languages had been dropped as required subjects for the freshman year; and when finally in 1887 the entrance requirement in Greek was done away with, the classical languages were left on the same footing there as any other subject, and in some respects on a shakier one than English. By 1900 the elective system had won out practically everywhere in the United States, though it was seldom extended to as

many subjects as it was at Harvard. Students in 1900 did, however, have a good deal of choice, and more and more of them
used the privilege to reject Latin and Greek and concentrate
their efforts on what they felt were more practical subjects.

TWO POLES: YALE AND MICHIGAN

One of the best ways to make clear the conflict of the old
with the new in this period is to contrast two institutions,
Yale College and the University of Michigan. There are reasons for choosing these particular schools. In the first place,
Yale, dominated by clerical influence, remained one of the
most conservative of major American colleges till near the end
of the century; its three presidents between 1846 and 1899
were attached to the older system and steadfastly resisted innovations. Michigan, on the other hand, was hailed in the sixties
and early seventies as the only true university in America.
Under President Tappan, and later under President Angell, it
was one of the most successful examples of the new system of
higher education. Both schools were influential. Particularly
under President Porter, Yale was regarded as a stronghold of
the traditional view of education, and the fact that many of its
graduates found their way into administrative or teaching
posts in other colleges widened Yale's influence. Michigan, by
its early adoption of many aspects of the German university,
was a rallying point for advocates of change.

Yale: A Conservative College

The condition of Yale toward 1850 was not much different from
that of most other American colleges. The curriculum was of
course nearly all prescribed. The second Timothy Dwight, writing his reminiscences of the college as it existed in the late 1840s,
said there were some elective courses in languages and mathematics in the third term of the junior year and the second of the
senior year, but he added that they "were merely supplemental
to the required studies." Two class-hours a week were the maximum time allotted to them.[35] The philosophy underlying Yale's
approach to education was stated succinctly in a quotation that
Dwight drew from a catalog of the time:

The object of the system of instruction to the undergraduates is not to give a partial education, consisting of a few
branches only; nor on the other hand to give a superficial
education, containing a little of almost everything; nor to
finish the details of either a professional or a practical
education; but to commence a thorough course, and to
carry it as far as the time of the student's residence will
allow. It is intended to maintain such a proportion between the different branches of literature and science, as
to form a proper symmetry and balance of character. In
laying the foundation of a thorough education, it is necessary that all the important faculties be brought into
exercise. When certain mental endowments receive a
much higher culture than others, there is a distortion in
the intellectual character. The powers of the mind are
not developed in their fairest proportions by studying
languages alone, or mathematics alone, or natural or political science alone. The object, in the proper collegiate
department, is not to teach that which is peculiar to any
one of the professions; but to lay the foundation which is
common to them all (p. 91).

Here is, one might say, the classical expression of the older
theory of education. All the features are present: a prescribed
curriculum in which mathematics and the ancient languages
have the central place, the ideal of training and strengthening
the mental faculties, the emphasis on generalized knowledge,
and the consequent disavowal of specialization.

Instruction at Yale in 1850, when Andrew D. White was a
student there, was conducted for the lower classes by tutors,
who supported themselves in this way while going through the
divinity school. "Naturally," White added, "most of the work
done under these was perfunctory. There was too much reciting by rote and too little real intercourse between teacher and
taught. The instructor sat in a box, heard students' translations
without indicating anything better, and their answers to questions with very few suggestions or remarks."[36] It was, in short,
the same system that was used in the lower schools of the time.

In his *Autobiography* White recurred often to the evils of the recitation system at Yale in his day. For it was not only the tutors who used it, but the most gifted of Yale's senior professors as well—Professor James Hadley, for instance.[37]

The Library at Yale in the 1850s was inadequate to the needs of good scholarship. The combined library resources of all New Haven amounted to only 70,000 volumes, including the library of Yale itself; and Yale's library was smaller than the collections of two of the college literary societies. The student had to pay a fee if he wanted to borrow a book, and even then he could visit the library only during the five-hour period on which the college library was open on weekdays. The main hall of the library was not even heated in the winter.[38]

The situation with regard to English studies at Yale in mid-century was not particularly good. White declared that during his whole course at Yale there was not a single lecture "upon any period, subject, or person in literature, ancient or modern. . . ."[39] C. F. Thwing quotes an unnamed graduate of 1854 as saying that "If the name of a single English author was ever mentioned in the classroom by an instructor during my whole college course, then I have forgotten the fact. We had instruction—a little—in composition, but for English Literature we were left to our private reading."[40]

This work in composition was given by Professor William A. Larned, whose predecessor had been Chauncey Allen Goodrich, professor of rhetoric at Yale from 1817 to 1839, best known now for his anthology, *Select British Eloquence.* In 1839 Goodrich was given the professorship of the Pastoral Charge in the divinity school and devoted the rest of his career chiefly to sacred rhetoric. Larned took over Goodrich's former duties, and although the title of the chair was changed from "Rhetoric and Oratory" to "Rhetoric and English Literature," there seems to have been little practical change in the nature of instruction. Students did not meet Larned until their senior year, since tutors handled all instruction before then.[41] Furthermore, Goodrich continued to deliver his lectures on the British orators to the senior class, and Larned therefore was able to do little.

Given Yale's philosophy of education in this period, it at first seems strange that Yale should have had a "Professorship of the Sanskrit and its relations to kindred languages, and Sanskrit literature," and that the occupant of this chair should have been William Dwight Whitney, the foremost American philologist and linguistics scholar of the nineteenth century. The explanation is quite simple. The chair was named for and endowed by Edward Elbridge Salisbury, the wealthy Sanskrit enthusiast who on his own initiative had given courses in Arabic and Sanskrit at Yale before the coming of Whitney, and under whom Whitney had studied. Neither Whitney's presence at Yale nor his position there was due to the enterprise of the Yale faculty or administration.

From the middle of the century until 1888 the fortunes of Yale were controlled by two presidents, Theodore D. Woolsey and Noah Porter. Woolsey came to the presidency in 1846, having been professor of Greek at Yale for fifteen years before that time. Few changes occurred at Yale during Woolsey's presidency—both he and Porter, said Dwight, "were believers in the older system of required studies, and were strongly attached to it."[42] About the only innovations that appeared during Woolsey's term of office were the announcement in the 1860-61 catalog that Ph.D. degrees would henceforth be conferred,[43] and the gradual substitution of written for oral examinations— tried at first hesitantly, but later adopted officially when the size of classes made oral examinations impossible.[44]

Noah Porter, one of President Eliot's most vigorous and outspoken opponents in the 1870s and 1880s, succeeded Woolsey in the presidency in 1871. He had studied theology at Yale, had held two pastorates in New England, and had studied for two years in Berlin. During this time he had become interested in the study of mental and moral philosophy, and his two texts on the subject, *The Elements of Intellectual Science* (1871) and *The Elements of Moral Science* (1885), are perhaps the best-written of the dozens that the movement produced. He had occupied the chair of philosophy at Yale for nearly a quarter of a century before becoming president of the College. Throughout his term as president he continued to teach courses in mental and moral philosophy. He was, as Dwight said, a conservative; more than that, he was a strong executive and usually managed to get his way. There seem, for example, to be only two important instances recorded when he had to give ground on curriculum revision. One came in 1876, when the faculty forced through a plan to make almost half of the junior and senior courses elective; the other was in 1884, near the end of his presidency, when all senior courses except mental science were made elective[45]—over "the emotional protests of President Porter," as Wilbur L. Cross recalls.[46]

Porter's educational theories were expressed in great detail in a book published in 1878, *The American Colleges, and the American Public.*[47] His position in this book was uncompromisingly in favor of the older system. "We contend," he said, "not only that the colleges have judged rightly in giving to the study of language the prominence which it receives, and that the Greek and Latin deserve the special preëminence which has been assigned them, but that there are peculiar reasons why they should be even more thoroughly and earnestly cultivated than they have been" (p. 40). Here is a measure of Porter's effectiveness in debate: though his position was under attack from many sources at this time, he seized the offensive himself and asked for even more emphasis on the classics. His argument rested on the conviction that no study was so effective as the classics in providing "mental discipline."[48] The training of the ear, eye, and hand which Eliot prized as of superior value, and which he maintained that the experimental sciences could best supply, was dismissed by Porter with the statement that such a "discipline of the senses" does not require "either the *culture* or the *discipline* of the intellect" that the classics provide (p. 40). In an equally summary way, Porter disposed of the claims then being advanced for modern languages and the historical study of English as substitutes for the classics in furnishing mental discipline.

The ideal of mental discipline was at the very center of Porter's theory of education—quite possibly as a consequence of his belief in the faculty psychology of mental science. He said plainly that "certain studies may be of the greatest value for discipline which possess no other obvious and direct utility" (p. 69). It was on these grounds that he challenged the criticism that training in the ancient languages did not prepare a man for the conduct of practical affairs. On the contrary, Porter insisted, this was actually the best sort of education for future business men since it trained the intellect to "habits of method, of analysis, and of comprehension"—all of them qualities essential to the successful business man (pp. 71-72).

Porter was unwilling to admit a single flaw in his philosophy of education. He even defended the recitation method of teaching as "Socratic," and insisted that in the traditional curriculum "There is not a single study that is superfluous. Not one should be displaced, because not one can be spared" (p. 95). It was Porter's totally uncompromising attitude that kept Yale's curriculum and methods relatively unchanged during the years that many other American colleges were rapidly adapting themselves to new conditions.

Porter was succeeded as president in 1886 by the second Timothy Dwight, who served until 1899. During Dwight's administration, a steady pressure from students, faculty, and alumni gradually extended to Yale more of the features of the German university, but none of the changes could be regarded as spectacular. Dwight himself, though a little more open to compromise than Porter, was still regarded at the end of his life as "a conservative in educational matters, even a non-progressive."[49] And it should be added that during a part of Dwight's presidency both Woolsey and Porter were still alive and in close touch with the college; Porter, in fact, continued to teach there. It is reasonable to suppose that these men exerted some influence over college policy, and that this influence was generally opposed to innovation.

The influence of Yale on higher education was strong throughout the nineteenth century. At the bicentennial celebration of Yale in 1901, Cyrus Northrup, president of the University of Minnesota, stated that the first president of 19 colleges had been Yale men, and that 105 Yale graduates had at one time or another served as presidents of some 85 colleges and universities. Many of these institutions were among the most important of their time: Princeton, Columbia, Dartmouth, Amherst, Rutgers, Trinity, Hamilton, and the Universities of California, Chicago, Pennsylvania, Illinois, Minnesota, Wisconsin, Iowa, to name only a few.[50] Johns Hopkins and Cornell drew their first presidents from Yale, though these men, Gilman and White, were not typical representatives of the Yale pattern. Better instances were the founders of Beloit College, who in the words of Northrup were motivated by "the same old conservative Yale ideas which have so generally characterized Yale educators, whether at home or abroad" (pp. 591–592). Most Yale-trained educators, said Northrup, "have had on them all their lives the stamp of Yale College, and have cherished the Yale ideas and have followed the Yale methods. No other single word describes what these are so well as 'conservatism.' They have held fast to what was good and been slow to enter new and untried paths. The education that in the past had succeeded in giving men power has seemed good enough for the future, and they have been slow to accept knowledge without discipline or culture without power" (pp. 589–590).

Michigan: A Progressive University

Until the installation of its first permanent president, Henry P. Tappan, in 1852, the University of Michigan did not differ greatly from other colleges of the time. A single classical curriculum was prescribed, and instruction was by recitation. But there were certain conditions that favored the growth of a university of the new type. The founders of the educational system of Michigan, John Davis Pierce and Isaac Edwin Crary, had been so impressed with Cousin's report on Prussian education[51] that they had made provision in the state constitution for a Prussian-type educational structure in the state, with the common schools at the base and the university at the apex. They were sympathetic too with the German ideals of higher education, and Pierce urged successfully that faculty appointments be made on the basis of professional qualifications, not denominational membership.

Tappan had been a professor of intellectual and moral philosophy at New York University, but he was a broader man than most such philosophers. He was a Presbyterian, though a very tolerant one. He once said in a sermon:

> If any one ask me, why I am a Presbyterian? I cannot answer, that it is on account of doctrine; for other denominations hold the same system of doctrine. Nor can I say it is on account of Polity; for other denominations have polities which appear to accomplish the same ends. I dare not say I am a Presbyterian because I believe my Church to be the only true church, or even better than others; for I find the most perfect forms of Christian character developed elsewhere. I am a Presbyterian from taste, association, habit and education; and, because, being this, I can see no sufficient reason for changing to anything else. I suppose most of us of the different denominations, to be candid, would say about the same thing.[52]

A statement like this is significant coming from a university president in the middle of the nineteenth century. It is unusual in its freedom from dogmatism and sectarian bias; and it suggests a willingness to tolerate diversity of opinion, which was not a particularly common trait of most college presidents of the period. At the end of his career at Michigan, Tappan was able to say that during his presidency not a single man had been hired with regard to his denominational connection; instead, men were engaged on the basis of their ability in their own fields.[53]

Shortly before the middle of the century Tappan had made an extended visit to Germany, where he formed an admiration for the German university system. His book *University Education*, published in 1851, was chiefly an exposition of the German plan. When, therefore, in the next year he was called to the presidency of the University of Michigan (on the recommendation of George Bancroft), he at once set about overhauling the institution. In his inaugural address he announced that since the University at present was really no more than a college or *gymnasium*, the first task would be to perfect this college. To accomplish this he proposed the establishment of a scientific course to run parallel with the existing classical course. "There will be comprised in it, besides other branches, Civil Engineering, Astronomy with the use of an Observatory, and the application of Chemistry and other sciences to agriculture and the industrial arts generally." The student in the scientific course would, at the end of the usual four years, receive a bachelor of science degree.[54] He also proposed the adoption of the elective system.[55] Once the undergraduate college had been regenerated, Tappan intended to establish facilities for postgraduate work, thus making the institution into a true university on the German model.

Tappan's course was not entirely smooth, but he did lay a sound foundation for the true university that had begun to take shape before he left. His proposed course in civil engineering was established, a chemistry laboratory was set up in 1857, and what appears to have been the second distinct chair of history in an American college was filled in 1857 by the brilliant young Andrew D. White.[56] In the year 1855-56 elective courses were offered for the first time, though they were limited to the senior year.[57] The lecture system at Michigan apparently had its beginnings under Tappan but did not become well established until later.[58] Tappan was dismissed in 1863, partly because of opposition from the small sectarian colleges in the state and partly because of what seems to have been demagoguery in the legislature. His constant urging of European innovations caused the charge of un-Americanism to be brought against him, and he was forced out.[59]

But the University of Michigan had charted its course. The next president, E. O. Haven (author of a rhetoric to be discussed below), was chosen apparently for little more than his ability at conciliation; even so, during the six years until his resignation the University continued in the path recommended by Tappan and in fact added pharmacy to its curriculum.[60] Henry S. Frieze, who served as acting president from 1869 to 1871, was a man who had come to agree wholeheartedly with Tappan. During a tour of Europe in the 1850s he had studied the European university system. Returning to Ann Arbor with an entirely new conception of higher education, he became one of Tappan's warmest supporters.[61] His two years in the presidency saw two far-reaching changes: the authorizing of coeducation in 1870, and the so-called "diploma" connection with high schools of the state. The first of these was accomplished at the instance of the Regents, who were under considerable popular pressure to admit women to higher instruction. Frieze and the faculty generally seem to have been somewhat distrustful of the measure.[62] The second, however, which concerned the qualifications of entering students, was directly due to Frieze himself. At Harvard in the 1870s the problem of determining the fitness of candidates for admission was met by the imposition of entrance examinations. At Michigan, where the University was considered an integral part of the entire state educational system, Frieze urged the adoption of what has now become known as high school accreditation. The plan was outlined in the catalog for 1869-70, this being the first appearance of the system in the United States. It was widely copied by other universities later in the century.

In 1871, on Frieze's recommendation, James Burrill Angell, former newspaper editor, professor, and then president of the University of Vermont, was appointed to the presidency. He too had been in Europe and moreover had studied at Brown University under President Francis Wayland, one of the most progressive educators of the first half of the nineteenth century. Angell was thus a fortunate choice, for he was already in agreement with the Michigan philosophy. In his inaugural address he urged the establishment of a sound graduate school,[63] he recommended that entrance requirements be raised so as to leave the University free to do work of real university grade (pp. 17-21), and he suggested that a special course of study for persons intending a career in journalism be set up (pp. 25-26). Not all these aims were accomplished at once, but innovations continued to appear. In 1871-72, for instance, Professor Charles Kendall Adams introduced the German seminar method of teaching in his courses in history, and shortly afterwards Professor Moses Coit Tyler of the English Department followed his example.[64] In 1877, because of pressure from Angell, the first chair of pedagogy in the country was established.[65] In the same year nearly half the studies leading to the bachelor's degree were made elective; the change was so popular that, according to B. A. Hinsdale, there was a 20 per cent increase in enrollment in the Literary (that is, Collegiate) Department the following year.[66] A new course of study was established in 1877 leading to a bachelor of letters degree, work in the course consisting chiefly of history, and of English, French, and German languages and literatures.[67] Under Angell the first permanent set of entrance requirements for medical schools was established (1874), and the first college instruction in forestry was offered (1882). Angell continued throughout his administration to press for a distinct graduate school; but, though Michigan granted many graduate degrees during that time, the graduate school was not separately organized till 1910, a year after his retirement.[68]

Though the University was not always well supported in the later years of the century, it somehow managed to keep outstanding men on its faculty. It is possible that Angell's attitude helped to create a congenial atmosphere that outweighed other considerations. Until the late 1870s Michigan was almost unchallenged as the only real university in the United States. From then on, it shared its advanced position with an increasing number of other schools—Harvard, Johns Hopkins, Columbia, Chicago, and other state universities—but it remained among the most distinguished institutions in the country throughout the century.

The Field of English

CHAPTER TWO

INSTRUCTION in rhetoric had been given in American colleges throughout the seventeenth and eighteenth centuries and, especially in the last quarter of the eighteenth century, there was usually some work offered in composition, belles lettres, and criticism. Though occasionally men like John Witherspoon, president of the College of New Jersey, delivered rather elaborate series of lectures on rhetoric to undergraduates, the teaching ordinarily was done by tutors and seems more often than not to have been perfunctory. During and after the Revolution a keen interest in political problems led to greater emphasis on instruction in oratory and debate, but the simultaneous rise of elocution tended increasingly to narrow this training and restrict it to one aspect of the rhetorical process—delivery. During the first half of the nineteenth century oral rhetoric came to be identified even more closely with elocution, which usually had its own texts and professors. The study listed in college catalogs of the time as rhetoric usually meant the rhetoric of written composition, and toward 1850 some study of literature as well, though chiefly at second hand through historical manuals of literature. Chairs and departments of English had not yet made their appearance; near the middle of the century, however, a number of chairs whose earlier titles were rhetoric and oratory came to be called chairs of rhetoric and English literature.[1] There does not seem to have been much actual writing done by the students, and what little existed was ordinarily corrected by tutors rather than by the professor of rhetoric. In keeping with the prevailing theory of education, most attention was given to reciting the numerous rhetorical principles in the textbook. Rhetoric was studied, that is to say, as a body of knowledge worth knowing for its own sake, somewhat apart from its practical application to speaking or writing. It was the "formal rhetoric" so much to be condemned a few decades later.

There seems to have been more opportunity for practice in writing and speaking, and for literary culture as well, afforded by the college literary societies than by the courses in rhetoric. These societies had originated in the eighteenth century, partly as a student protest against the narrowness of a prescribed curriculum. At first they provided greater opportunities than the classroom offered for speaking and debating in English instead of Latin. As student demand for knowledge of English literature grew in the first half of the nineteenth century, and as the shift from oral to written rhetoric became more pronounced, the members of the societies read and discussed literary works and often read and criticized papers written by members. The societies accumulated libraries sometimes larger than those of the colleges themselves. The Linonian Society of Yale, for example, had a collection of over 10,000 volumes by 1846.[2] The literary society began to decline shortly after 1850, however, giving way to the secret Greek-letter fraternity. The chief reason for its decline seems not to have been competition from a rival sort of organization, but instead the fact that after 1850 the colleges slowly began to make more adequate provision for instruction in literature and in written composition.

ENGLISH AT HARVARD, 1850–1875

The fortunes of English studies at Harvard in the third quarter of the nineteenth century are fairly typical of what happened at other schools then or a little later. But it is important to look at Harvard for another reason as well. Under Eliot, Harvard became one of the foremost leaders (and certainly the one best publicized) in educational reform. In the admission of English and other modern languages and literatures, as well as the sciences, Harvard helped to establish the pattern that nearly all other colleges would be following by the end of the century. From 1875 to 1900, the most influential English program in America was Harvard's.

In his inaugural address in 1869 Eliot had condemned "the prevailing neglect of the systematic study of the English language,"[3] and he never ceased to regard English as central in the scheme of American education. In 1884, after he had already accomplished much to raise the status of English studies, he still felt dissatisfied with what had been done. In that year at Harvard, he said, "less than half as much instruction, of proper university grade is offered in English as in Greek or in Latin. The experience of all other colleges and universities resembles in this respect that of Harvard."[4] In the same paper he declared that "The first subject which, as I conceive, is entitled to recognition as of equal academic value or rank with any subject now most honored is the English language and literature" (p. 97). ". . . English should be studied from the beginning of school life to the end of college life . . ." (p. 121).

Consistent with these beliefs he had made several changes at Harvard that had given more importance to English. One of his first moves seems to have been the relieving of Francis James Child of the Boylston Professorship of Rhetoric (probably at Child's request),[5] and the promotion of Adams Sherman Hill to the Boylston chair. (Eliot had brought Hill to Harvard in 1872 as assistant professor of rhetoric.) This action freed Child for research and teaching in Anglo-Saxon, history of the language, and literature; and it gave to Harvard a man who was to make his career in rhetoric instruction and ultimately to have great influence on the study of rhetoric in American colleges. Evidence of the early improvement in English instruction that Eliot brought about can be seen by comparing the course offerings of 1858–59 with those of 1874–75. In the former year, C. H. Grandgent writes, in *The Development of Harvard University*, "the Freshmen had Lessons in Orthoepy and Lessons in Expression; the Sophomores, Lessons in

Expression, Lessons in Action, Themes; the Juniors, Themes, Declamation, Rhetoric; the Seniors, Forensics: nothing more." Grandgent adds, however, that James Russell Lowell was offering a senior elective in modern literature that year.[6] By 1874–75, English offerings included prescribed rhetoric throughout the freshman year, a prescribed half-course in rhetoric in the sophomore year, a similar prescribed course in the junior year but with different texts, and prescribed themes and forensics in sophomore, junior, and senior years. Child was offering three electives—two in Anglo-Saxon and history of the language, and one that consisted of a study of Chaucer, Shakespeare, Bacon, Milton, and Dryden.[7] In 1873 elocution had finally been dropped as a required subject, so that freshmen and sophomores henceforth studied rhetoric instead of orthoepy, action, and expression.[8] English as a separately designated field of study had appeared in 1868–69, just before Eliot's inauguration.[9]

Perhaps the most far-reaching development in English to come out of Harvard in this period was the requiring of entrance examinations in English—far-reaching because the action set the precedent for similar moves later by many other colleges and also because these examinations had certain consequences that finally came to a boil in the 1890s. The first hint of any sort of entrance requirement in English at Harvard appeared in the catalog for 1865–66: "Candidates will also be examined in reading English aloud." In the catalog for 1869–70 English was given a separate heading for the first time in the list of entrance requirements; the examination, however, like the earlier one, consisted of reading aloud, though this time Shakespeare's *Julius Caesar* and Milton's *Comus* were specified as the works the candidates were to prepare. In 1872–73 the following sentence appeared: "Correct spelling, punctuation, and expression, as well as legible handwriting, are expected of all applicants for admission; and failure in any of these particulars will be taken into account at the examination." A formal requirement in English composition was first imposed the next year:

English Composition. Each candidate will be required to write a short English Composition, correct in spelling, punctuation, grammar, and expression, the subject to be taken from such works of standard authors as shall be announced from time to time. The subject for 1874 will be taken from one of the following works: Shakespeare's Tempest, Julius Caesar, and Merchant of Venice; Goldsmith's Vicar of Wakefield; Scott's Ivanhoe, and Lay of the Last Minstrel.

Four years later, correctness of paragraph division was added. Beginning in 1882 every candidate was also "required to correct specimens of bad English given him at the time of the examination." And with this final addition the entrance requirement in English at Harvard remained substantially unchanged almost to the end of the century.[10]

Adams Sherman Hill, who as Boylston Professor had charge of composition work at Harvard from 1876 to his retirement in 1904, wrote in 1879:

It was hoped that this requirement would effect several desirable objects,—that the student, by becoming familiar with a few works holding a high place in English literature, would acquire a taste for good reading, and would insensibly adopt better methods of thought and better forms of expression; that teachers would be led to seek subjects for composition in the books named, subjects far preferable to the vague generalities too often selected, and that they would pay closer attention to errors in elementary matters; that, in short, this recognition by the College of the importance of English would lead both teachers and pupils to give more time to the mother tongue, and to employ the time thus given to better advantage.[11]

Not all these objects were achieved at once, Hill admitted. For several years, he said, the preparatory and high schools did not take the requirement seriously; some "deemed it a high crime and misdemeanor to take an hour for English from Latin, Greek, or mathematics." Besides, the Harvard faculty, "posted on the heights of the classics and mathematics, descended with difficulty to petty questions of spelling, punctuation, and grammar." The belief was common, said Hill, "that a good writer had no advantage over a poor one in the studies of the Freshman year, and but a slight advantage in the subsequent years of the course. . . ."[12] By 1879, however, Hill believed (though somewhat too confidently, as will later appear) that there was better cooperation all around. "More work is done in the schools; greater proficiency is demanded from the candidate for admission; the Faculty frankly accept the requirement in English as standing upon a par with the other requirements; and many of the college instructors take account of a student's ability or inability to express his ideas with precision and clearness."[13]

THE RISE OF PHILOLOGY

The first half of the nineteenth century had seen the rise of philology and linguistics in Germany, with men like Jakob and Wilhelm Grimm, Franz Bopp, Eduard Mätzner, and Moriz Heyne doing historical research in European languages. The new methods of language study employed by these men came as a revelation to scholars in both Europe and America. For the first time languages could be examined scientifically. Their origins could be determined with some accuracy, their historical developments traced and explained. The modern form of a language was seen in an entirely new light against the historical background of its earlier forms. In America the study of philology began to take hold in the 1850s. The works of several of the German philologists, such as Mätzner and Heyne, who had written on Anglo-Saxon and English philology, were known and admired in this country. But the great vogue that English philology was soon to enjoy in America resulted from a number of other reasons. One was undoubtedly the high estate of science and scientific method in the period; philology provided the opportunity to make the study of language into a science and thus place it in the forefront of new developments. Another was that, in the last half of the century particularly, as evolutionary thought penetrated America, the idea of growth and development was carried over into the study of many fields outside the physical sciences. In English it took the form of the historical approach, both to language and to literature. A third reason was that philology, in the hands of those advocating increased study of English, became a weapon with which to attack the monopoly held by Greek and Latin. Defenders of the classics belittled the study of modern English as a substitute for Greek and Latin since the lack of inflections made it unsuitable to provide adequate mental discipline. Anglo-Saxon, however, was highly inflected, and it was urged that the purposes of mental discipline would be well served by the close grammatical study of the language of *Beowulf* and Alfred.[14]

The first American college course in Anglo-Saxon appeared in 1825 at the University of Virginia, where Thomas Jefferson, impressed by Horne Tooke's argument (in *The Diversions of Purley*) favoring Anglo-Saxon, had insisted that it be taught from the opening of the school. It was given at Amherst from 1838 to 1843 by William C. Fowler, a son-in-law of Noah Webster, and Francis J. Child introduced it at Harvard in 1851.[15] John S. Hart, principal of the Central High School in Philadelphia, taught Anglo-Saxon to his pupils for several years, but in 1854 it was discontinued. A writer in Henry Barnard's *American Journal of Education* for 1858 says that Hart was forced to abandon it because a "popular clamor" against the subject had been aroused.[16] Francis A. March, who had studied at Amherst when Fowler was there, held a professorship of English Language and Comparative Philology at Lafayette College for about half a century, beginning in 1858. March himself claimed that this was "the first authoritative recognition [in America] of the English and Anglo-Saxon as a separate department of philological study coordinate with Greek and Latin, and the central object of comparative study."[17] March exerted a good deal of influence through his several textbooks on Anglo-Saxon and philology, among the first American texts to appear.[18] William Dwight Whitney, coming to the chair of Sanskrit at Yale in 1855, was not mainly concerned with Anglo-Saxon, but his influence in general philology and linguistics was great until his death in 1893. In 1868 Hiram Corson began teaching Anglo-Saxon at St. John's College, and when in 1871 he went to the newly opened Cornell University he continued to give the course.[19]

The rapid growth in popularity of the new subject can be judged from a Bureau of Education survey that March summarized in 1877. Twenty-three of the colleges polled were offering work in Anglo-Saxon; eight more said they were studying it incidentally along with work in English literature. Nearly all these schools had begun the study within the last four years. Of the colleges that did not give work in the subject, nine either expressed regret for the fact or said they were planning to offer it soon. Only sixteen of the colleges reported merely that they did not teach Anglo-Saxon and apparently did not plan to.[20]

By the end of the century philology and Anglo-Saxon had a firm grip on the American college. The Commissioner of Education's *Report for 1888–89* contained a listing of the courses of study at 101 colleges and universities. Forty-four had courses in Anglo-Saxon, and the same number (though not always the same schools) had courses called variously "English philology," "philology," "comparative philology," "linguistics," "history of the English Language," etc.[21] Often enough it was not just one course in philology and another in Anglo-Saxon. Lake Forest University, for example, offered courses in Anglo-Saxon, transitional English, accidence, comparative philology, and phonetics.[22] The College of New Jersey (soon to be Princeton University) gave Lounsbury's *History of the English Language* to freshmen, March's *Origin and History of the English Language* to sophomores, March's or Sweet's Anglo-Saxon readers and Harrison's *Beowulf* to juniors.[23] Columbia offered courses in historical English grammar, history of the English language, Anglo-Saxon grammar, readings in Anglo-Saxon, historical grammar of the Anglo-Saxon and English languages, and the language and poetry of Chaucer.[24]

INSTRUCTION IN LITERATURE

Along with the historical study of the English language came the historical study of English literature. In the 1850s and 1860s manuals of literary history were the colleges' answer to demands for work in English literature. The most popular were probably Thomas B. Shaw's *Outlines of English Literature*[25] and the posthumous revision of it called *A Complete Manual of English Literature.*[26] These manuals consisted of separate little articles on English authors, arranged chronologically, with a few words on the chief works of each. They were inaccurate and unscholarly, and never brought the student into contact with the actual works of literature. They were designed to be assimilated page by page and recited to the teacher.

One of the earliest courses in English literature where the students actually read the works for themselves was Child's at Harvard, already mentioned. According to Wilbur L. Cross,[27] however, Child was anticipated by Thomas R. Lounsbury at the Sheffield Scientific School, who had begun such a course in 1870. Lounsbury had accepted his appointment at Sheffield on condition he be allowed to give a course in English literature, though his title was that of Instructor in English Composition. He devised a combined program of composition and literature for sophomores, the literature being in the form of a historical survey course beginning with Chaucer. The students read the works for themselves. To freshmen he gave a course in the history of the English language, for which a little later he wrote his well-known book in that field.[28] He succeeded so well that a year after the course had begun he was promoted to full professor. Cross says, "Without the slightest doubt Lounsbury rescued the study of English literature at second hand from untrustworthy historical manuals. . ." (p. 114). On the evidence of Lounsbury's wife, Cross states that for twenty years after 1870 English professors from all over the country visited Lounsbury to learn about his methods and theories of teaching literature (p. 112).

It is significant that this sort of instruction should have appeared first in a school dedicated to training scientists, rather than in an institution devoted to liberal education. It is a measure of how wary of new approaches most regular colleges were. The staff of the Sheffield School, said Cross, "were in agreement that specialized work in science should be preceded by or carried along with a wide range of studies in the modern languages and literatures, in history, economics, and government. They held to three years of Latin as a requirement for entrance but discarded Greek as too remote for education in a new age. English grammar and composition they regarded as an essential study for every boy either in school or college" (pp. 111-112). For contrast, one should set this attitude alongside that of the faculty of Yale, to which college Sheffield was attached. For many years Yale was unquestionably the most conservative major college in the United States, resisting new tendencies and holding as long as possible to the traditional scheme of education. The establishment of Sheffield, in fact, entrenched the conservatism of Yale for several decades because the technical school siphoned off those students who found Yale's curriculum obsolete and confining. The College thus was free to continue on its customary path.

From about the mid-1870s English studies, and especially literature, took up an ever larger place in the curriculum of all colleges. Separate departments of English became fairly common before the end of the 1880s, and by the middle of the next decade they were the rule. By this time the compulsory classical-mathematical curriculum was pretty much a thing of the past. Elective studies had become prominent, courses in Latin and Greek were diminishing, and courses in English, science, modern European languages, history, economics, and so on, were rapidly multiplying. Work in English at most colleges was divided into three main areas: language, literature, and composition and rhetoric. Almost invariably the courses in literature outnumbered those in the other two fields. At the University of Michigan, for example, in 1894-95 there were five courses in linguistics, six in rhetoric and composition, and ten in literature.[29] In the same year the University of Indiana had four courses in rhetoric and composition, six in language, and eight in literature.[30] Harvard, in 1896-97, offered nine courses in composition and rhetoric, seven in language, and nineteen in literature; this did not include one course each in elocution, oral debate, and versification.[31]

The Harvard entrance requirement in English, which specified a knowledge of certain major works of literature as a requisite for admission, probably contributed to this development. The attention of the preparatory schools, first, was focused on literature since they had to fit their students for college entrance. Later, as Harvard's entrance requirement was copied by other colleges, the colleges themselves began to take more notice of literature. More important, however, was the general trend of the period away from the old curriculum toward more modern studies. As the study of Greek and Latin literature declined, courses in English and sometimes American literature took its place. The appearance of the elective system accounted at least in part for the great increase in the number of literature courses: if students were to choose for themselves a considerable part of their courses, they must be supplied with adequate range of choice.

ORGANIZED INSTRUCTION IN SPEECH

The beginnings of organized instruction in speech, as opposed to elocution, lie between the late 1870s and the early 1890s. Historians of the teaching of speech have curiously done very little with the rise of speech departments and of credit-bearing courses in speech[32] (elocution was usually given without credit). Thomas C. Trueblood, who was one of the pioneers in the movement, has told some of the story.[33] In 1879 he and a colleague named Fulton opened a private school for speech instruction in Kansas City. In a short time they began to get requests from surrounding colleges in Kansas and Missouri to offer short courses on the campus. The courses bore no credit, and the instructors had neither academic rank nor any financial connection with the colleges. They collected tuition fees directly from the students who enrolled. Trueblood and Fulton gradually expanded their activities and soon were giving courses in the Universities of Kansas, Missouri, Kentucky, Ohio Wesleyan University, and Washburn, Park, and William Jewel Colleges. Both men were dissatisfied with itinerant instruction, and both wanted to see speech courses put on a regular academic footing in the colleges. Trueblood, therefore, called on President Angell at the University of Michigan to see what interest there might be in establishing systematic instruction in speech at that institution. Angell welcomed the suggestion that Trueblood give a trial course, and at its conclusion offered him an instructorship. Trueblood declined because of the low salary, but he returned to Michigan for several years to give his courses (pp. 5-7). Finally in 1887 the University agreed to give credit for the work in speech and, moreover, yielded to pressure from the students of the Law and Literary Colleges to grant free tuition. Trueblood accepted a permanent appointment at the University and was paid on the same basis as the rest of the faculty. In 1892 he was promoted to a full professorship and was given a separate department of public speaking. This seems to have been the first permanent department of speech in the country. Meanwhile Fulton was appointed to a professorship at Ohio Wesleyan and was made dean of a "School of Oratory" there. He taught credit courses both at that school and at Ohio State (pp. 7-8).

The rise of credit instruction in speech was no doubt connected in large measure with the decline of the old literary and speaking societies on college campuses. The decline had become marked by 1850 as the Greek-letter social fraternities rapidly supplanted the older organizations. A course in "Oral Discussion," first offered at Harvard in 1878, was really a course in debate designed to fill the need for oral argument that the speaking societies had once satisfied. A course offered at Amherst by H. A. Frink in the early 1890s was of much the same sort; Frink defended the existence of such a course in the curriculum on the grounds that "the literary society as a rule no longer flourishes, even if it exists, in the American college. Nor, as many hope, can it be restored to a place of general influence and usefulness. Wherever its successor, the Greek letter fraternity, thrives the public society has little, if any, vitality."[34] The courses in elocution, which were still being given at the end of the century, did not supply the student with much more than a knowledge of vocal intonations and various gestures; what was needed was training of a fuller sort. Since the popular rhetoric textbooks of the 1880s paid little attention to the claims of oral rhetoric, they also contributed to the rise of separate instruction in speech.

THE HARVARD REPORTS

One of the reasons behind the Harvard entrance requirement in English had been the desire to relegate to the lower schools the responsibility for the more mechanical details of writing so that the university could devote itself to higher instruction on the pattern of European institutions. Harvard was able, through this requirement, to exert a good deal of pressure on the preparatory schools to give more attention to work in English, both literature and composition. What the schools really did, however, was concentrate on fitting their students to pass the Harvard examination rather than try to give a rounded course of training in English. The result was that great gaps existed in the students' preparation; freshmen were usually able to write a passing paper on one of the works which they had crammed, but when it came to writing on other subjects, as they had to do once they were admitted to classes, they often were almost helpless. The prestige of Harvard as a leader in educational reform helped to popularize the Harvard plan of entrance examination, and so perhaps did the fact that college teachers were quite willing to let teachers in the lower schools have the responsibility for teaching the elementary principles of correct writing. As the 1880s advanced, the Harvard plan spread across the nation, bringing with it the same problem that Harvard was encountering: the lower schools were obediently reorienting their English courses to meet college entrance requirements, but were doing little more.

In the 1890s the whole situation came to a boil. A great many students were still failing the various entrance examinations in English or passing them with low grades, and the colleges of the country were having to devote more and more labor to freshman composition instruction. The matter was aggravated by sharp increases in college attendance, especially in the 1890s, that were making classes unusually large. Enrollment of men in coeducational institutions as well as in colleges and universities solely for men increased 62.4 per cent between

1889-90 and 1899-1900; enrollment of women in coeducational institutions increased 153.3 per cent in the same period.[35] What this meant in actual class size may be inferred from the fact that at the University of Michigan in 1894-95, 1,198 class enrollments were handled by a staff of 4 full-time teachers and 2 part-time graduate assistants.[36] Since this proportion was not uncommon, the desire to lighten the teaching load became acute—especially in composition work, where great numbers of themes had to be read. Though Harvard was peculiarly fortunate in having a staff of 20 to take care of a little under 2,000 class enrollments,[37] there was much dissatisfaction there over English A, the required course in freshman composition, which it was thought took a disproportionate amount of staff time and labor.

In 1891 the Board of Overseers of Harvard College appointed a committee of three laymen—Charles Francis Adams, E. L. Godkin, and Josiah Quincy—to study the composition and rhetoric problem as it existed at Harvard and submit a report on it. Their findings, published in 1892 as the "Report of the Committee on Composition and Rhetoric,"[38] consisted mainly of complaints that have been heard periodically ever since, both from college administrators and from many college teachers of English. Beginning with a description of English A and the quantity and kind of writing required in it, the committee turned at once to an attack on the necessity for making college teachers engage in such "stupefying" work as correction of English A themes. "It is obviously absurd," said the Report, "that the College—the institution of higher education—should be called upon to turn aside from its proper functions, and devote its means and the time of its instructors to the task of imparting elementary instruction which should be given even in ordinary grammar schools, much more in those higher academic institutions intended to prepare select youth for a university course" (p. 119). As a part of the investigation of composition, the committee had asked English A instructors to secure from each student in the course a short theme describing his English training in preparatory school. The papers were read by the committee, and there was a good deal of sarcasm in the Report over the quality of the writing. Specimen themes were reprinted in the Report, and some were even reproduced in facsimile to call attention to poor hand-writing and lack of neatness. The committee also examined the compositions written as part of the entrance examination in June 1892 and found the same faults there. Forty-seven per cent of these themes either were conditioned or "passed unsat-isfactorily." Two per cent passed "with credit," 20 per cent failed completely (p. 151).

The conclusion of the committee was that the preparatory schools were to blame. The schools trained their students to pass a certain examination, and no more. The solution recom-mended was that preparatory schools devote more time to Eng-lish, and specifically to English composition. The committee believed that it was "little less than absurd to suggest that any human being who can be taught to talk cannot likewise be taught to compose. Writing is merely the habit of talking with the pen instead of with the tongue" (p. 155). More practice in writing in the lower schools, then, was the answer. The com-mittee urged that theme-writing be classed once and for all as a part of elementary education and not a concern of the univer-sity or college. When and if this was done, the higher institu-tions could turn their efforts to instruction more in keeping with their true purpose—advanced education. It was urged that admission requirements in English be raised immediately to a point where the lower schools would be forced to take the matter in hand or see most of their graduates barred from admission to Harvard College.

The committee issued two further reports in 1895 and 1897.[39] The former was a scathing criticism of the quality of translation English tolerated in the lower schools by teachers of Latin and Greek. The latter covered the same ground as the 1892 report, though it was based on different papers—1,300 of them, which were duly bound and placed in the Harvard library as a testimony to what had come to be known as "the growing illiteracy of American boys." The same recommendations were made in this report as in the earlier one: since the fault lay with the lower schools, let Harvard raise its entrance requirements and make the schools mend their ways. Meanwhile the Reports had been well publicized. Magazines and even newspapers took up the cry and joined in deploring the bad English used by American college students; the blame for this state of affairs was regularly fastened on the lower schools. In 1894 the *Dial* ran a long series of articles on the state of English teaching in the colleges, the articles being written by ranking professors in the English departments of a selected list of representative colleges. In 1895 the articles were published in book form.[40] In the next year the Harvard University Press reprinted in book form a series of essays on English work at Harvard written by members of the Harvard staff over a period of twenty years;[41] a good deal of space in the book was given to an explanation and defense of the Harvard entrance requirement.

As a result of this unprecedented outcry that had made correctness in English a national concern, certain steps were taken. In July of 1892 the National Council of Education appointed a committee on secondary education (known as the "Committee of Ten") which arranged nine conferences to study and discuss nine different subjects in the secondary school curriculum; none received more publicity than the Conference on English. Other efforts were directed toward standardizing college entrance examinations in English, since one of the chief difficulties the secondary schools were laboring under was the great variety of reading lists specified by different colleges and universities. In the secondary schools themselves there were earnest attempts to eliminate the conditions that were causing all the criticism. More writing was demanded of pupils, and some schools went so far as to adopt college-level textbooks in rhetoric, hoping thus to forearm the pupils going on to college. This in turn, however, was denounced as ill-advised and presumptuous.[42]

The comparative docility of the secondary schools under this criticism was quite remarkable. Only a few voices objected that the problem was not as simple as the Harvard Committee believed. When the Committee proposed in 1896 to print the entrance examination papers of all candidates for admission to Harvard together with the name of the particular school from

46

which each candidate had come, the principals of the preparatory schools most likely to be affected protested to the Board of
Overseers that the schools should not "be held solely responsible for evils which are chiefly due to the absence of literary
interest and of literary standards in the community."[43] A writer
in the *Nation* in the same year pointed out that under good
conditions the composition teacher in secondary schools had
forty-five minutes a day for three school years "in which, besides teaching something of the history of literature, he is to
counteract influences that have fifteen years the start of him,
and fifteen times as great present opportunity. The only remarkable thing is that, under such circumstances, he accomplishes anything at all."[44]

The Harvard Reports had, in the long run, both desirable
and undesirable effects on English instruction. On the credit
side, they centered attention on the inadequate provisions for
English training in the lower schools and no doubt did a good
deal to help establish English there in a prominent position.
On the other hand, their approach was both oversimplified
and tactically wrong. The Reports tried to raise standards in
English by coercion and intimidation—as Fred Newton Scott
said, "by the hair of the head."[45] They used the secondary and
preparatory schools as whipping-boys, asserting that the colleges had no responsibility in the matter at all. They assumed
that the solution of the problem was simple and obvious,
and that only the lassitude and ineptness of the lower schools
were responsible for the problem's continued existence. Finally, and most serious of all, the Reports emphasized only one
aspect of composition—mechanical correctness. This was perhaps natural since the authors of the reports were not English
teachers themselves but only interested laymen; they had no
real firsthand knowledge of what was involved. This emphasis
on superficial correctness, however, contributed in no small
measure to the ideal of superficial correctness that was to dominate composition instruction for many years thereafter.

Rhetorics and Rhetoricians

CHAPTER THREE

T HESE BRIEF surveys of the general conditions in American higher education in the last half of the nineteenth century and the developments that took place in English studies during the same period provide a setting in which to view in more just perspective a single academic discipline. For rhetorical theory and practice in the colleges reflected, in the main, the emphases that marked English studies and higher education generally through these fifty years. It was in this period that American colleges made the transition from British rhetoric texts to books written in this country; and because at first the break with earlier British rhetorical doctrine was far from complete, it will be necessary, before turning finally to a detailed consideration of the American books themselves, to give some attention to the most influential of the British texts. A number of works on rhetoric had, of course, been produced in the United States before 1850, and though none of them had any noticeable influence on doctrine after the middle of the century, a few words should also be said of them to give some notion of earlier American theory.

THE BRITISH RHETORICS

Although some works on rhetoric were written in America in the first half of the nineteenth century, by far the most widely used texts were of British origin. Heading the list was Hugh

Blair's *Lectures on Rhetoric and Belles Lettres,* first published in England in 1783, brought to America in the same year, and reprinted in Philadelphia the following year.[1] A measure of Blair's popularity in this country is suggested by the fact that the Harvard library now has on its shelves no fewer than twenty-six separate printings of the *Lectures* issued between 1789 and 1832.[2] And this is by no means a total list of the reprintings; they continued to appear throughout the century, though less frequently after the Civil War. Warren Guthrie has cited evidence that before 1850 Blair's book was used in twenty of forty-three American colleges whose catalogs he has examined, it being by far the most popular rhetoric text. It remained in use at Yale and Williams till 1850,[3] and the University of Notre Dame was employing it as late as the 1880s.[4]

The *Lectures on Rhetoric and Belles Lettres*[5] did not comprise a systematic treatment of rhetoric in the classical sense, but were instead a loosely organized body of opinions and injunctions concerned more with literary composition and criticism than with the oral rhetoric of the ancients. The lectures were divided roughly into five groups: taste, its nature and pleasures; language; style; eloquence; and the kinds of verse and prose composition. Scattered throughout were "critical examinations" of various authors.

One of the most distinctive aspects of the *Lectures* was the numerous abstractions used to refer to qualities of style. Sublimity of style, for instance, depended on simplicity, conciseness, and strength. Style itself had to have perspicuity in words and sentences. Perspicuity in words required purity, propriety, precision; and in sentences, clearness and precision, unity, strength, harmony. The ancients, Blair said, had divided kinds of style into plain, median, and high, but he found this an oversimplification. Hence he offered the diffuse and the concise styles, the nervous and the feeble, the simple, the affected, the elegant, the vehement, the dry, plain, neat, etc. No part of Blair's book was so widely adopted as this tendency to categorize and abstract. Many later rhetoricians used his identical categories and terms.

Blair gave some place, as one would expect, to figurative language and to individual figures of speech. His discussion was traditional, being notable chiefly for its restraint, since only ten figures were mentioned. He divided prose composition into classes that were to persist, in main outlines, well into the nineteenth century: historical writing, philosophical writing (including dialog), epistolary writing, and "fictitious history" (novels and romances). Poetry was similarly classified into pastoral, lyric, didactic, descriptive, epic, and dramatic. Included in the lectures on poetry were a discussion of the nature, origin, and development of poetry, and a few pages on prosody. All these features were found often in later American rhetorics.

In his discussion of eloquence (oratory) Blair made a distinction between convincing and persuading that was to be copied by a host of American rhetoricians in the next century. The difference was stated in terms of faculty psychology: "Conviction," he said, "affects the understanding only; persuasion, the will and the practice." That is, a man may be convinced of something, yet not feel impelled to do anything about it. Persuasion, on the other hand, causes him to *act*, since "the passions" and not just the understanding have been addressed (pp. 315–316).

Blair accepted the classical division of the parts of a discourse—introduction, division, narration, etc.—but he departed sharply from classical doctrine in excluding invention, or the finding of subject matter, from the province of rhetoric. Proper arrangement and expression are fit concerns of the rhetorician, he said, and invention is no doubt of great importance. "But, with respect to this, I am afraid it is beyond the power of art to give any real assistance. Art cannot go so far, as to supply a speaker with arguments on every cause, and every subject. . . . For it is one thing to discover the reasons that are most proper to convince men, and another, to manage these reasons with the most advantage. The latter is all that rhetoric can pretend to" (p. 427). This question of whether invention is or is not a legitimate function of rhetoric was debated all through the nineteenth century, and with such equal force on both sides that no clear decision was ever gained. Blair's exclusion of invention was characteristic of his belletristic bias, which caused him to pay more attention to style than to any other aspect of rhetoric.

George Campbell's *Philosophy of Rhetoric*[6] was first printed in 1776 in Edinburgh, and though copies found their way to America in the 1780s it seems not to have been reprinted here until 1818.[7] Beginning about 1820, however, its popularity rose so rapidly that it soon became a strong competitor of Blair. Guthrie lists seventeen colleges that used the text before 1860.[8] Campbell's book was much more a rhetoric of oral discourse than Blair's. There is occasionally some ambiguity in his use of the term "discourse," and he took up some matters that are more properly esthetic than rhetorical; but the book was aimed specifically at the spoken word. This did not, however, prevent much of what he said from applying equally well to written composition. It was indeed as a composition textbook that the *Philosophy* was mainly used.

Rhetoric for Campbell was not, as it was for Aristotle, an "offshoot" of logic, but instead he regarded logic as merely, like grammar, an essential tool of rhetoric. "Now it is by the sense," he said, "that rhetoric holds of logic, and by the expression that she holds of grammar" (p. 54). Believing this, Campbell did not hesitate to regard invention as a proper part of rhetoric, and he devoted two chapters to it. Grammar (interpreted broadly) came in for a very extended treatment, and it is this part of the *Philosophy* that was most influential on later rhetorical theory. Campbell set up usage as the criterion that governs grammatical matters. "It is not the business of grammar," he declared, "as some critics seem preposterously to imagine, to give law to the fashions which regulate our speech. On the contrary, from its conformity to these, and from that alone, it derives all its authority and value" (p. 162). Good use must meet three requirements, he continued: it must be "reputable" (used by "authors of reputation"); it must be "national" (opposed to foreign and provincial); and it must be "present" (opposed to archaism) (pp. 162–174). After this came a series of "canons of verbal criticism" governing doubtful or divided usage. Then, under the heading of "grammatical purity," Campbell discussed at considerable length such offenses against purity as "barbarisms," "solecisms," and "improprieties" in both words and phrases. This doctrine of reputable, national, and present use enjoyed great currency through the entire nineteenth century, and it is not uncommon to find it in composition texts written well into the twentieth century. For many years, it was an exceptional rhetorician who omitted Campbell's theory.

Like Blair, Campbell spent a good deal of time on abstract qualities of style. Purity he classified as a grammatical quality, but among rhetorical qualities he listed perspicuity (appealing to the understanding), vivacity and elegance (appealing to the imagination), animation (directed to the passions), and music (for the ear). The most essential of these was perspicuity, under which head Campbell discussed obscurity, ambiguity, and "the unintelligible." Vivacity was given three additional chapters in the concluding section of the book, where it was treated in a threefold way: as depending on the *choice* of words, on the *number* of words, and on the *arrangement* of words. Rhetorical tropes were mentioned under choice; tautology, pleonasm, and verbosity under number; and under arrangement he discussed simple, complex, loose, and periodic sentences. The material of this section, like that of the one on usage, was for a time almost universally adopted by rhetoricians in America.

The *Elements of Rhetoric*,[9] published in 1828 by Richard Whately, Archbishop of Dublin, almost at once rivaled the popularity of Blair and Campbell in America. It did not usually supplant the other two works but instead was used with them. Guthrie has found it in use at nineteen colleges before 1850,[10] and it was still in the course of study at several in the late 1880s.[11] The *Elements of Rhetoric* differed from the works of Campbell and Blair chiefly by restoring to rhetoric the Aristotelian emphasis on logic. Whately, the author of a successful text on logic,[12] agreed with Aristotle that rhetoric is "an off-shoot from logic."[13] Of the four divisions of his book, therefore, he devoted the first and longest to invention. "The *finding* of suitable ARGUMENTS to prove a given point," he said, "and the skilful *arrangement* of them, may be considered as the immediate and proper province of Rhetoric, and of that alone" (p. 40).

His treatment of the process of rhetorical invention was rigorously logical, beginning with a form of the classical doctrine
of "status"—testing the propositions first by asking "What,"
"Why," and "What Consequence" (p. 39)—then proceeding to
an exhaustive classification of kinds of arguments, and a discussion of their uses and best order for specific purposes. This
emphasis on logic was, in the main, a healthful influence on
rhetorical theory in America, keeping it from a too exclusive
preoccupation with style and underlining the importance of
substance in composition. Whately saw clearly (what many
of the American rhetoricians of the nineteenth century did not)
that students must be given composition subjects that are interesting to themselves and within their range of ability. He objected to assigning topics of which the student had little or no
knowledge and suggested it would at best lead only to the pol-
ished utterance of commonplaces (pp. 28-30).

Whately was really more concerned with written composition than with oral, though he recognized the claims of
both and tried to adapt his book to make it useful for both
speaker and writer. He mentioned some of the causes why
writing had assumed greater importance than speaking in the
modern world and admitted that rhetoric "in the widest ac-
ceptation that would be reckoned admissible, comprehends
all 'Composition in Prose.'" But between this and the nar-
rowest interpretation—merely persuasive speaking—he took
a middle road. It was his intention, he said, "to treat of 'Argumentative Composition,' *generally*, and *exclusively*" (p. 17).
This position was in line with his bias in favor of logic and
made the book somewhat narrower in scope than those of
Blair and Campbell.

As a result of this intention, for instance, his two main
divisions of composition were simply argumentation and persuasion. Not only was his treatment of invention and arrangement restricted to these two sorts of composition, but the
section on style was devoted to those matters that "have
an especial reference to Argumentative and Persuasive works"
(p. 181). Perspicuity was naturally considered of paramount
importance in style, and energy (Campbell's vivacity) was the

next most valuable since it aided persuasion.[14] He listed elegance as a third stylistic quality but, since he had little interest in the belletristic side of writing, he gave it scant treatment.

EARLY AMERICAN RHETORICS

Apparently the first rhetorical work of importance produced in America was John Witherspoon's *Lectures on Moral Philosophy and Eloquence*,[15] delivered between 1768 and 1794 at the College of New Jersey, later Princeton, of which Witherspoon was president. These lectures, rather similar in substance to Blair's though written in a firmer and more incisive style, were not published in America until 1810, sixteen years after Witherspoon's death. They had no perceptible influence on later American rhetorical theory. The same may be said of John Quincy Adams' *Lectures on Rhetoric and Oratory* (1810),[16] which offered a rather full though conventional restatement of the classical doctrine. Adams was the first Boylston Professor of Rhetoric and Oratory at Harvard, occupying the chair between 1806 and 1809, during which years he delivered these lectures to Harvard seniors.

The first American rhetoric specifically designed as a textbook, and the first one to have any currency outside the institution where it was produced, was Samuel P. Newman's *A Practical System of Rhetoric*, first published in 1827.[17] The book, which was exclusively a rhetoric of written composition, was centered mainly around style and criticism. It showed some few evidences of classical influence, as in the traditional linking of logic with rhetoric,[18] the relative importance given to invention, and the discussion of the Ciceronian division of a speech (though here a written composition) into five parts. The influence of Campbell revealed itself in the section on language, where the earlier writer's doctrine of usage was adopted almost verbatim. The emphasis of the book as a whole may be judged from Newman's list of the advantages of rhetorical study: an acquaintance with the philosophy of rhetoric, the cultivation of taste and the exercise of the imagination, skill in the use of language, skill in literary criticism, and the forming of a good style.

There was a good deal in the book on taste, with an extended treatment of literary taste in particular, though nearly all of the latter section was devoted to a treatment of figures of speech. The material in general had nothing especially original about it; it appears to have been drawn from the eighteenth century English estheticians and rhetoricians. Style was discussed in terms of abstractions—correctness, perspicuity, vivacity, euphony, and naturalness—and the usual antithetical pairs of style types—concise and diffuse, barren and luxuriant, neat and elegant, and so on. Here and there Newman showed some awareness of the communicative function of language. Style will vary, for example, according to the individual personality of the author, according to the subject and the occasion, and according to the different classes of writing. Some adaptation of style to meet these circumstances will therefore be necessary. In the discussion of introductions, Newman mentioned the need for enlisting the interest of the reader, and he said that skillful use of language means "that the writer selects his words and composes his sentences, in a manner, which accurately and clearly conveys to those able to read this language, the thoughts existing in his own mind" (p. 117). There was also a classification of the kinds of composition according to purpose that has some interest because it approached so nearly to the "four forms of discourse" of the 1890s. Newman listed didactic, persuasive, argumentative, descriptive, and narrative (pp. 28–29). The didactic would correspond roughly to what was later called exposition.

Joseph McKeon, second holder of the Boylston Chair at Harvard (1809–1818), seems to have left no rhetorical writings. His successor, Edward Tyrell Channing, lectured on rhetoric and criticism for thirty-two years (1819–1851) and, after his death, his lectures were published with an introduction by R. H. Dana, Jr.,[19] one of his most distinguished students. There is no evidence to suggest that Channing's published lectures influenced the course of rhetorical theory in America, though Channing himself as a teacher had the most profound influence on American literature. Nearly all the writers of the New England renaissance were trained under him at Harvard—Dana,

Thoreau, Emerson, Holmes, Motley, Parkman, to mention only the chief. Van Wyck Brooks has remarked that, judging from results, "one might almost say that Channing sowed more of the seeds that make a man of letters—when the seeds fall on a fortunate soil—than all the other teachers of composition and all the writers of textbooks that have ever taught a much-taught country."[20]

The period 1830-1850 seems to have witnessed the appearance of a number of minor rhetoricians in the United States whose theories never gained wide currency. The influence of these men appears usually to have been local, confined to the schools where they taught. It is difficult to be sure how many there were, since it is likely that their lectures were not always published. An example is Ebenezer Porter's *Lectures on Eloquence and Style* (1836).[21] Porter held the Bartlett Professorship of Sacred Rhetoric at Andover Academy from 1813 to 1831 and during those years delivered the lectures that were published after his death. He was the author of a highly successful textbook on elocution, but the *Lectures on Eloquence and Style* do not seem to have made a mark outside Andover. Porter's view of rhetoric was a narrow one. Eight of his ten lectures on eloquence concerned elocution, and the remaining seven lectures were on style. The latter were undistinguished as theory; they showed the influence of Campbell's doctrine of usage and listed traditional eighteenth-century qualities of style—Perspicuity, Strength (dependent on Unity, Brevity, and Good Arrangement), Beauty (dependent on Harmony and Elegance), and Sublimity. The only original note was a defense of Americanisms in diction, which appeared in the lecture on "What Constitutes Good Use."

John A. Getty's *Elements of Rhetoric* (1831),[22] though occasionally showing the influence of Blair, was mainly a mosaic of quotations from the standard classical rhetoricians of Greece and Rome. It was written in the old catechetical style that shows it was designed for the recitation method of study. The nature of the questions and answers, which made up the body of the text, may be judged from the definition given of rhetoric: "What is Rhetoric? 'Rhetoric is the art of Speaking

in such a manner as to obtain the end for which we speak.'"
A footnote credited the quotation to Blair. "What is its principal end? 'To instruct, to please, and to move.'"[23] This was attributed to Quintilian. These footnotes, however, quoted other definitions from Bacon, Vossius, Aristotle, and Cicero. The footnotes, in fact, probably took up more of the book than the text itself. The latter, consisting mainly of quotations, was in three languages—Latin, Greek, and English, depending on the nationality of the rhetorician quoted. The rhetorical doctrine was basically that of the Roman school, full of elaborate divisions of rhetorical terms and functions.

Just as derivative was James R. Boyd's *Elements of Rhetoric and Literary Criticism*,[24] a larger book than Getty's and apparently a more popular one. It appeared first in 1844, but in four years it had gone into a sixth edition, an eighth coming out in 1867. The reason for this popularity seems to be that the book presented standard rhetorical doctrine in a simple form intended to make it intelligible to common-school and academy pupils. There was nothing original in the book—Boyd called himself the "compiler" rather than the author, and urged as the main value of his book the fact that it had been derived "from the best and most recent sources" (p. xii). The doctrine itself was strictly that of written composition. Boyd covered nearly everything, from spelling and punctuation to figures of speech, kinds of composition, history of the English language, and finally included short anthologies and histories of British and American literature.

Similar to Boyd's book in general outline was Richard Green Parker's *Aids to English Composition* (1844).[25] This text was designed for "students of all grades" and seems to have been used even more widely than Boyd's; by 1858 it was already in its twentieth edition. It too was a large book and covered a great variety of subjects, all related to written composition. It contained no section devoted specifically to literary extracts, though frequent examples appeared throughout. Like Boyd, Parker derived nearly all the material of his book from other writers, a list of whom appeared at the end of the volume (p. 419). One aspect of the book deserves special mention—a list of 863 topics for compositions. Examples of a few of them chosen at random will give some idea of the nature of composition assignments about 1850: "Curiosity"; "Nature"; "The Religious Institutions of Egypt, Greece, and Rome"; "History, Biography, and Fiction"; "Byron and Ezekiel"; "On the Comparative Prevalence and Strength of the Principles of Loyalty and Independence in Man."

THE BIG FOUR

Beginning about 1850 rhetorical textbooks began to appear in quantity in the United States. Not a great many were published for the first ten or a dozen years, but they gradually increased until in the 1890s there was a flood of them. The earlier books showed an understandable dependence on Blair, Campbell, and Whately, whose texts were still the most popular. In the 1870s, however, American textbooks began to take on a more distinctive character. This tendency increased in the next decade, and by the last years of the century the break with the older British rhetoricians had, in most respects, been accomplished.

The period 1850–1900 can hardly be called a particularly distinguished time in the history of rhetoric. Very few of the rhetoricians were original thinkers, and very few exerted any lasting influence on rhetorical theory. Most of the books during these fifty years are of interest here more for the evidence they supply of general trends—and sometimes fads—than for any great significance they have individually. An exception must be made, however, for the books of four men, and for these men themselves. Adams Sherman Hill, John Franklin Genung, Barrett Wendell, and Fred Newton Scott are figures of importance in this period, though perhaps only Scott could be called an original theorist. The texts of these men were not only very popular, but they were widely imitated by minor writers. In time, they extend from 1878 to the end of the century, and in many respects they epitomize the main emphases of rhetorical theory in these years. As far as personalities can be determined at this distance, it seems quite plain that the rhetoric texts of all four men reflect, to a considerable extent, certain predilections and traits in their characters. For this reason it is worth while to sketch something of the men themselves. Their books, forming as they do a part of the evidence for the detailed discussion of rhetorical doctrine to follow, will be mentioned here only to point out their general qualities.

Adams Sherman Hill (1833–1910)

It is difficult to find out much about Hill. He is not mentioned in the *Dictionary of American Biography*, and *Who Was Who* lists only a few bare facts. Except for occasional passing references, none of the men directly associated with him seems to have written about him; and though his imprint on rhetorical instruction in the last quarter of the century was pronounced, he seems not to have been the sort of teacher who has a large personal following among his students.

Hill graduated from Harvard with an A.B. degree in 1853, in the same class with Charles W. Eliot. Two years later he took a degree in law, then went to New York, where he worked on the New York *Tribune* under Horace Greeley. Eliot became president of Harvard in 1869 with the avowed intention of giving more prominence to English studies, and particularly training in composition. In 1872 he summoned Hill to Harvard as assistant professor of rhetoric. Francis J. Child, occupant of the Boylston chair since 1851, was anxious to be relieved of the chore of correcting compositions so as to be free to pursue literary research. After a probationary period of four years, Hill was elevated to the Boylston Professorship in 1876. Hill shared Eliot's belief in the necessity for work in English composition. In 1879 he published an article in which he urged that English be put on a par with Latin and Greek, and that students be given more frequent opportunities for practice in speaking and writing English. It would not be enough, he said, for just the colleges to give this instruction. "From the beginning to the end of the pre-collegiate course, the one thing that should never be lost sight of is the mother-tongue. . . ." Until a boy "knows how to write a simple English sentence, he should not be allowed to open a Latin grammar."[26]

Early in his career Hill apparently met some opposition from his colleagues in other departments as he struggled to get increased recognition for English. Besides this, he does not seem to have got along well with most students. His technique in theme correction was, according to LeBaron R. Briggs, "common sense ruthlessly applied; surgery; wounds which left scars, and at first, it may be, bitterness toward the operator. . . . No man could take the conceit out of a pupil more rapidly, or with more memorable phrasing." Briggs admired, however, Hill's shrewdness as a critic of student writing and says that the first resentment of a student who had suffered under Hill's lash often changed later to "gratitude and affection" as the justice of the criticism became apparent.[27] That this transformation did not always take place is suggested by Rollo Walter Brown's recollection that Hill's students "sometimes hummed pleasant academic melodies while he read a man's themes in the classroom."[28] But in spite of these difficulties, as well as the frail health that plagued him all his life, Hill persevered and gradually built up his English program. By 1883 he had a full-time staff of three, including Barrett Wendell and LeBaron Briggs.

Until 1885, Hill's required course in rhetoric was taught in the sophomore year. There were other courses in writing—electives—introduced in the late seventies, but Sophomore Rhetoric was the big course at Harvard. It was, as Hill pointed out in 1879, the only course required for every student after the freshman year; all others had been made elective. In that year Hill had recommended that sophomore rhetoric be put in the freshman year: "Could the study be taken up at the threshold of college life, the schools would be made to feel that their labors in this direction [increased attention to English] were going to tell upon a pupil's standing in college as well as upon his admission."[29] However, none of the departments then occupying the freshman year would yield him any of their time. In 1885 Hill was finally successful: freshman English (called "English A") was inaugurated—the parent of all later courses in freshman composition. Its demise at Harvard was not observed until 1951. For the remaining years of the nineteenth century it was regarded as a model course in rhetoric and widely imitated throughout the United States.

In the 1880s, as Hill's health became even more precarious, he delegated many duties to Briggs and Wendell. Though he continued to teach until his retirement in 1904, the number of courses he offered became steadily fewer. He died in 1910.

Hill wrote a number of textbooks on rhetoric, but the best known and most influential—the one known to two generations of students simply as "Hill's Rhetoric"—was his *The Principles of Rhetoric, and Their Application*, first published in 1878, then revised and enlarged in 1895. This book was the standard text at Harvard from the time it first appeared until some years after Hill's death. It was widely adopted in other colleges and universities, in part no doubt because of the considerable prestige enjoyed by the Harvard English department. But there were other things as well that recommended the book. For one thing, its doctrine was largely traditional, drawing heavily on Blair, Campbell, and Whately but usually giving a fresher cast to the material through rephrasing and some simplification. Thus it combined the advantages of familiarity with those of apparent novelty. Besides this, Hill had a fondness for writing *ex cathedra*, for delivering pronouncements on matters of usage and rhetorical effect in such a way as to suggest that there was only one rational answer, and here it was. A dogmatic tone, most of us would like to think, should count against any textbook. Yet for inexperienced teachers, or those who are heavily burdened with paper correction, or those who have no particular interest in teaching composition, who look at it as something to be got through as quickly and painlessly as possible—for all these a dogmatic text is often valuable. It discourages questions from students, it simplifies the teacher's job of exposition, it saves time. During the years when Hill's book was popular, these types of teachers were very commonly engaged in composition work—as perhaps they still are today. College enrollments, in their rapid expansion, outran the available supply of trained instructors, so that large numbers of inexperienced young men, or sometimes men trained in other fields such as moral philosophy or Latin, were drawn into composition work to meet the urgent need. When Hill's book finally lost favor, it was not so much because of its dogmatic tone as because the doctrine by then had too obviously become antiquated. Even so, there is a report that in the early 1930s a professor of English at an eastern institution tried to prevail upon the publishers to reissue the book so he could use it once more in his classes.

John Franklin Genung (1850–1919)

Genung was a graduate of Union College, having received his A.B. there in 1870. He attended the Rochester Theological Seminary after this, graduating in 1875 and being ordained a Baptist minister. He then joined the hundreds of young Americans going to Germany for graduate study. From the University of Leipzig he received an A.M. degree, and in 1881 a doctorate of philosophy, his dissertation being a study of Tennyson's *In Memoriam*. When he returned to America he went to Amherst at the invitation of President Julius H. Seelye. The various titles Genung bore at Amherst are a graphic record of how the emphasis changed in English studies. When he began his career there in 1882, there was a good deal of importance attached to philology, since the philological approach to the vernacular was thought to be the one that would provide enough gristle for the purposes of mental discipline. His first title, therefore, was Instructor in the English Language. In 1884 he became Associate Professor of Rhetoric, Oratory, and English Literature; the last of these fields was beginning to assert itself. When in 1889 he was promoted to Professor of Rhetoric and English Literature, oratory had become the concern of a professor of public speaking—H. A. Frink. Finally, in 1906 Genung was made Professor of Literature and Bible Interpretation. Early in the twentieth century the study of rhetoric under that name had almost ceased to exist. Part of its former province had gone to literature, now a thriving field in its own right; the rest had become known as "English composition."

No formal biography of Genung has been written, though there are numerous records of him made by former students. All of them agree that one of the most prominent traits of his character was thoroughness—heightened, perhaps, by his German training. John Erskine, once Genung's student, writes: "No scholar in his generation had a finer training in the ancient literatures and languages, as well as in English, and none was more thorough than he, yet he had no mind for specialization; with him it was the whole subject from the ground up, with all its implications."[30] It is this quality that so distinguishes his *Practical Elements of Rhetoric* —a compendious book in which all aspects of rhetorical theory, as they appear to the author, are systematized and presented in clear if sometimes dogmatic prose. Another Amherst alumnus remarks on his industry: "He was a prodigious worker, doing a day's task before most of us had left our beds, and still having time for a walk before breakfast." Genung always prepared each lecture and recitation with meticulous care, and read painstakingly the themes handed in to him.[31]

As a teacher of literature he acted on the theory that the literature itself would provide all the stimulation the class needed; as a result, some students took advantage of him and indulged in various classroom antics, which he serenely ignored. Yet he seems to have exerted a deep and beneficent influence on many students, who often did not realize the extent of it till many years after graduation. Genung was fond of literature—as fond of it as of rhetoric. One of his former students has listed the composition subjects given out for two-thousand-word essays, several of which were required in the third term of the rhetoric course: "The Use of the Supernatural in 'Macbeth'"; "A Comparison of Malory's 'Morte d'Arthur' and Tennyson's 'Idylls of the King'"; "Sir Thomas More's 'Utopia.'"[32] In the evenings Genung sometimes gave public readings of poetry; Browning and Tennyson were favorites of his, and he read them well. These evenings became cultural events to be looked forward to in the life of the town. He also liked music and played the viola in a chamber group. John Erskine recalls that once a distinguished gathering of theologians invited Genung to address them on hymnology. "Of course," he told Erskine, "it's of no use to talk about hymns without giving examples, so I've arranged to have four or five hymns sung. Do you know," he added with a smile, "I'm writing them myself, words and music."[33]

One of his students remembers that Genung was deeply conscious of artistic form, whether in literature, music, or painting. Another speaks of his "devotion to method and order." His handwriting, whether in a manuscript or in a notice to his classes, was as precise as the engrossing on a document. A manufacturer of types once asked permission to cast a font of some of his letters. When writing a manuscript he habitually illuminated the first letter in each chapter. Erskine, when he once called on Genung, found him working devotedly over such an illuminated letter with red and black ink and a quill pen. "But having found something to criticize in the page, he had rewritten it, with another illuminated capital—and this he had done four times, still finding something to improve."[34]

Knowing these aspects of Genung's character and habits, it is not hard to understand the precise and orderly arrangement of material in his *Practical Elements*, the emphasis on form in composition and literature, the finely drawn and numerous distinctions on points of rhetorical doctrine. Genung's book is perhaps one of the most systematically ordered textbooks on rhetoric ever written, whatever may be thought of his theories on the subject. It was no doubt in part this well-planned organization of the book that led to its great popularity. One gets the reassuring impression from a book so neatly organized that all the problems of which it treats have been satisfactorily solved and duly pigeon-holed. One man, referring to the popularity of this book, wrote at the time of Genung's death in 1919 that "For the generation now coming into middle age the first sentence of this admirable textbook, 'Rhetoric is the art of adapting discourse, in harmony with its subject and occasion, to the requirements of a reader or hearer,' is probably as familiar as 'Omnia Gallia est divisa.'"[35] One of Genung's favorite stories, illustrating the vogue of his book, concerned an alumni dinner at which he was speaking. A cub reporter dropped in to pick up the names of the speakers and asked, "Who's the one in spectacles and a gray beard?" "Genung," someone told him. "Genung's 'Rhetoric'?" "Yes." "Well, *damn him!*"[36]

Genung was a gentle and kindly man. When students became unusually obstreperous in one of his classes, he would never scold them; tradition has it that he would go to his office and get out a little black book in which he kept a list of students who annoyed him, arranged in order of degree. He would move the names of the two or three offenders down a notch, light his pipe, and at once be as genial as ever. He once said to a friend, "When I die, I hope someone will say: 'Is John Genung dead? It's too bad.'" The Amherst alumnus who tells this story adds, "His hope was fulfilled a thousand fold."[37]

Barrett Wendell (1855-1921)

There is no greater contrast between the tone of Genung's *Practical Elements of Rhetoric* and Barrett Wendell's *English Composition* than there was between the personalities of the two men themselves. Genung, the patient scholar and self-effacing teacher, too kindly to rebuke an unruly student; Wendell, the brilliant dilettante and dramatizer of himself, capable of telling a girl student who wrote in a theme, sincerely if unwisely, that she had come "to sit at his feet and gather inspiration from his lips"—telling this girl she had written "disgusting slop" and that he had never seen a woman make such a fool of herself in one page. Wendell was, at the least, colorful; C. H. Grandgent tactfully characterizes him as "a highly original type."[38]

Wendell, a native Bostonian and representative of one of the old families, graduated with an A.B. from Harvard in 1877. After a year in the Law School, he accepted in 1880 an appointment as Instructor in English at Harvard. In 1888 he was made Assistant Professor, and was Professor from 1898 till his resignation because of ill health in 1917. In 1902-03 he lectured at Trinity College, Cambridge, and at the Sorbonne in 1904-05. The impression he made on the French was sufficiently favorable that a room at the Sorbonne was named for him. In 1913 he received a Litt. D. from Columbia, and in the next year was an exchange professor from Harvard to the University of Berlin. He was an authority on the Elizabethan period, wrote books on early American literature (*Cotton Mather*) and the seventeenth century in England (*The Temper of the Seventeenth Century in English Literature*), and produced several novels and plays.

Rollo Walter Brown, who says that Wendell as he crossed Harvard Yard gave the impression that he was "a caddish gentleman out of the age of Queen Elizabeth," has described his appearance and mannerisms:

> He cultivated a very "un-American" beard. He parted his hair precisely in the middle. He talked in a roaming, high-pitched voice that seemed to be artificially modulated to produce the effect of British speech. He carried his walking-stick on his little finger. He paced back and forth on the platform of his lecture-room and twirled his watch chain—and sometimes his watch—while he talked about the Puritans of 1642, "who feared that they might be damned for thinking," and the followers of Charles II in 1660, "who weren't certain that they were not going to be damned, but who were certain that they weren't going to be damned fools"! He participated in academic pomp with an air of such grave solemnity that when he once stepped upon the bottom of his gown as he mounted the platform to speak in a foreign university the onlookers were more amused than sympathetic. Usually when a whole-hearted country boy first encountered this very professorial professor, he came away with a numb feeling that there never had been much in the world worth doing, and that most of this had already been done—no small part of it by Wendell himself.

"No man ever lived," says Brown, "who could build around himself a more formidable outwork of somebody else."[39]

One of Wendell's best friends, LeBaron Russell Briggs, wrote that Wendell was widely misunderstood. Most thought him "a jaunty, rather trivial, amusingly picturesque person, highly sophisticated, inclined to snobbery, thick with 'Britannia plate.'" Behind this mask, according to Briggs, Wendell was "deeply serious, simple-hearted and true, frank and merciless in judging himself, genuinely humble, imitating none."[40] Wendell as a teacher used the shock technique. His classes were never dull. He was fond of saying that whatever success he had had as a teacher was the result of his indiscretion. "His pupils knew that he kept nothing back, that he was never warily on his guard, that they had whatever was in Barrett Wendell's mind, and that the mind was fertile, original, and bold."[41] He had a facility for synthesis and generalization. Whatever he read to his classes he immediately characterized in a phrase or two which, while not always meeting with acceptance, would not easily be forgotten. Briggs says, "It is doubtful whether any teacher or writer in America has equaled him in the quick and clear perception of literary relations, in the power of generalizing."[42]

In the 1880s, after Briggs had been teaching freshman composition for several years and Wendell had been working with a class in advanced composition, the two men decided to trade courses for a while. Wendell, as a result, had to prepare a new set of lectures. In November and December of 1890 he gave the lectures at the Lowell Institute in Boston as well. In 1891 they were published in book form under the title *English Composition.*

Except for one or two items, there is not much essentially new doctrine in the book, but the approach and tone are strikingly new. The most prominent feature of the book is its comparative simplicity and informality. Nearly all the ideas in it are drawn from older rhetorical doctrine, but Wendell's power of synthesis reduces complicated theory to a few broad and simple generalizations expressed in an easy conversational tone that makes them seem much less formidable than, say, Genung's or Hill's statements of the same principles. This was something new in books on rhetoric. It was perhaps the first text in the history of the subject that, while avowing the aim of simplifying rhetorical theory, actually had some success in doing so. The book is full of mannerisms—as Wendell himself was. The pronouncements are often cocksure, the tone is slightly condescending, and many of the illustrations seem designed as much to show off the author's wide general culture as to elucidate the text. Yet all these mannerisms keep the book lively; it is interesting to read. It is unusual and refreshing to find in a textbook on something as academic as rhetoric statements like "To clever people, no matter how philanthropic their general scheme of life, there are few more unlovely facts than the average man"; or "To fastidious people there will always be a charm about what other people do not know enough to appreciate. . . ."

Wendell's book was immediately popular and for years had a wide influence. The publishers say it was reprinted some twenty times, though in rather small editions, between 1891 and 1925. In his later years Wendell abandoned work in composition as an impossible task. Students still wrote badly, and he lamented the years he had spent teaching the unteachable. He insisted that composition courses ought to be thrown out of the college curriculum. Yet he did a service for the cause of composition training. His book marked the transition from the massive, heavily formal texts of the earlier period to the simpler and more direct books that were to follow. Not the least important thing he did was to turn the attention of rhetoricians away from mere correctness in details to effectiveness of the larger units (paragraphs and whole compositions) as determined by what impression the writer is trying to make on the reader.

Fred Newton Scott (1860–1931)

Of these four men, Scott alone could be called an original thinker. Hill and Genung offered traditional theory, arranged more systematically than the earlier British rhetorics and sometimes given a different emphasis, but still making no distinct break with the past. Wendell, though he gave the impression of originality, really did no more than simplify existing doctrine and give it a fresher and more persuasive expression. Scott, however, made a genuine effort to formulate a comprehensive system of rhetorical theory drawing on new developments in such related disciplines as experimental psychology, linguistics, and sociology. More than this, he tried earnestly to vitalize rhetorical instruction both in the secondary schools and in the colleges; but, though he met with some success for a time in the 1890s, most of his ideas were too new, his recommendations for change too fundamental to be generally accepted. Rhetorical instruction fell in behind the Harvard group instead, with the result that the brief flare of activity in the nineties that for a time looked so promising was quickly extinguished, and both theory and practice were once more narrowed and cut off from those relations that supply rhetoric with a realistic function.

Scott's entire career, both as student and teacher, was spent at the University of Michigan. Entering the University as an undergraduate in 1880, he had taken bachelor's, master's, and doctor's degrees there by 1889. As soon as he had received his doctorate, he was appointed Instructor in English, and a year later was promoted to Assistant Professor of Rhetoric. In 1896 he became Junior Professor, and finally reached the rank of Professor of Rhetoric in 1901. Though the term "rhetoric" was out of favor in the new century, Scott insisted on retaining the word in his title throughout his career; in 1903, in fact, apparently at his request, the University established a Department of Rhetoric separate from that of English. Scott retired from teaching in 1927, dying four years later.

During the 1890s Scott seems to have had assigned to him most of the advanced courses in criticism and rhetoric. By 1902 he was teaching two essay-writing courses, one in description and narrative, the other in exposition and argument; a course in the "Principles of Style" (which by then he had been teaching for a dozen years); a course in "Theory of Prose Narrative"; one in the teaching of composition and rhetoric; one in advanced composition; and two seminars in the history and theory of rhetoric.[43] When the new Department of Rhetoric was set up under Scott's direction the following year, Scott took with him these courses, as well as the freshman courses in "Paragraph Writing," and added four new ones: "Interpretations of Literature and Art," "Newspaper Writing," "Reviews," and one that was unique, "Prose Rhythms."[44] The course in newspaper writing seems to have been Scott's earlier course in "Rapid Writing," first offered in 1890-91, though now under a new name. According to Clarence D. Thorpe, the course in "Rapid Writing" was probably the first college course in journalism in America.[45] A. S. Hill had come to rhetoric-teaching from journalism, though there is no evidence in any of his books or in his rhetoric program at Harvard that he was aware of possible relations between rhetoric and journalistic writing. Scott, however, had recognized at the beginning of his career the growing importance of journalism and showed a steadily increasing interest in it during the rest of his life. The only further change that took place in his title, in fact, was his designation as Professor of Rhetoric and Journalism in 1921.

As a scholar, Scott chose not to break with tradition, but rather to find out what the tradition was, where it was going, and what his place in it was. "He had little patience with noisy reformers who would break with the past," a friend wrote of him.[46] Yet he was far from being a traditionalist in the sense that Hill, Genung, and Wendell were; he wanted to retain what was still valid in traditional doctrine, but to use this as a foundation on which to build new theory. His ideas often seemed strikingly unconventional to many people. Students coming to him who had been trained to look at language as primarily a matter of mechanical correctness found that Scott had a more functional view. Correctness was necessary but far from being the chief purpose of composition work. Scott "looked on words as a cabinet maker looks on his tools—things that just must be right and unabused throughout or the work will be bad. The tools were not what he was *making*; it was the *product* that basically interested him." The former student of Scott's who makes this statement adds that "we came to look on the misuse of a word much as an artistic woodworker would look on the employment of a chisel for screwdriver purposes; it was childishly destructive of a necessary tool."[47]

Scott's textbooks on rhetoric, all written in collaboration with Joseph V. Denney, did much to guide the reform movement of the nineties. Valuable also were his efforts to furnish a wider variety of materials for use in rhetoric instruction. He edited and published Spencer's *Philosophy of Style* and George Henry Lewes' *The Principles of Success in Literature*; he collaborated with C. M. Gayley on *An Introduction to the Methods and Materials of Literary Criticism*, believing that rhetoric and criticism were closely allied and each should contribute to

71

the other; for over twenty years he edited a series of research publications entitled *Contributions to Rhetorical Theory*, which provided an outlet for the theory being developed by graduate students in rhetoric working under his direction. Besides all this, he wrote a great many papers on composition problems and was an active participant in meetings of secondary school and college English teachers. His work with the secondary schools was especially useful. At Harvard, where secondary school English was looked on with something not far from contempt, teachers of English in the schools were blamed for all the linguistic shortcomings of entering freshmen. Scott took a different approach. He tried to reduce the gap between the high school teacher and the college teacher, to show that both had essentially the same problems. For years he labored to bring about willing cooperation and understanding for the benefit of both groups. He was in thorough agreement with the plan that had established a pyramidal educational structure in Michigan, with the elementary schools at the base and the university at the apex, each level having responsibilities toward the others. He called it the "organic" plan, as opposed to the "feudal" plan followed by Harvard.

One of Scott's most important contributions, though it is impossible to evaluate it exactly, was his graduate program in rhetoric. Even before a separate department of rhetoric was established in 1903, Scott had been giving graduate courses in the field; a number of master's degrees and one doctorate in rhetoric were conferred before 1900. From 1904 to 1930, when the Department of Rhetoric was absorbed by the English Department, 140 master's degrees in rhetoric were awarded, and 23 doctorates. The popularity of Scott's program may be judged by the fact that in the same period only 25 doctorates were granted by the English Department.[48] Part of the attraction that this program held for graduate students seems to have been due to Scott's effectiveness as a teacher. In the classroom he seldom expressed his own opinions; students looking back found they rarely could say Scott had told them this or that. Instead he used the Socratic method almost entirely, leading students to make their own discoveries and form their own conclusions. "He made us possess ourselves of *more* than *judgments,*" writes one of his former students; "he made us acquire criteria. . . ."[49] Students also found his attitude toward his subject stimulating. His keen awareness of the relations of rhetoric to other disciplines, his alertness in keeping abreast of new developments in these disciplines, his view of language as a social phenomenon serving definite human needs, his liberal and informed attitude toward linguistic usage—these, together with his impelling curiosity about literary effects and his conviction that these effects are capable of being studied and described, made graduate work in rhetoric a challenging and rewarding experience. How far his influence extended through the impression that his ideas made on his students it would be difficult to say. Certain of his students, however, such as Sterling A. Leonard and Ruth M. Weeks, both of whom took master's degrees in rhetoric under Scott, were leaders in the movement that tried to promote a more liberal and scientific view toward language matters in composition courses and textbooks.

No man was more influential than Scott in the reform movement of the nineties, and no man offered more sensible leadership. His recommendations were always thoughtful, always conscious of the larger implications of rhetorical problems. He never advocated change merely for the sake of change, but, as a friend wrote of him after his death, "he kept an anchor in the past."[50] He tried, though unsuccessfully, to secure the adoption of a fuller conception of rhetoric, one that would restore to it the great social importance that it has sometimes had in its long history. Unfortunately, English teachers were not ready then to adopt such a view. Instead, the narrower philosophy of the Harvard group won out, with the result that rhetorical instruction in America until well into the 1930s became, for all practical purposes, little more than instruction in grammar and the mechanics of writing, motivated almost solely by the ideal of superficial correctness.

Rhetoric, 1850–1900:
Definitions, Relations, Scope

CHAPTER FOUR

THE FIRST TWO or three decades after 1850 were a period of transition between the theory inherited from the British rhetorics and a native theory reflecting contemporary American conditions and needs. It was a period of some confusion as to exactly what rhetoric is and what its chief purposes are. The classical rhetorical tradition had largely evaporated by this time, except for a few vestiges that survived in British doctrine. The British rhetorics, still in 1850 the most popular texts in American colleges, had in effect established by this time a tradition of their own. Their abstract and "philosophical" approach to the subject had fitted them well to the main emphases of American education until mid-century. After 1850, however, as major changes began to penetrate our educational system, the doctrine of Blair, Campbell, and Whately became increasingly unsatisfactory. It seemed poorly fitted to the needs of the new generation of students who were clamoring for "practical" education; and, being tied closely with faculty psychology and the mental discipline theory of education, it began to seem less credible as experimental psychology undercut the older view of the mind and as a new educational philosophy appeared. Thus American rhetorical theory from 1850 to the 1870s showed a good deal of uncertainty. On the whole, the theory in these years was traditional, as was American higher education itself;

but there were stirrings of change. The uncertainty was due largely to the writers' inability to see clearly what the changes were and where they were tending.

Since the disciplinary ideal of education still flourished, however, nearly all the books before 1880 did have in common a formal and abstract tone suggesting that the rhetorical laws and principles contained in them were designed to be assimilated and thus to help in the formation of a disciplined intellect. Most writers in these first twenty or thirty years of the period were careful to establish whether rhetoric is a science or an art, what other subjects are related to it, and what may be included within it. On none of these points, however, was there any clear agreement.

In the late 1870s, as the older curriculum began to break up and yield to the elective system, and as faith in the mental discipline theory and the psychology on which it was based began to weaken, rhetorical theory became less elaborate. Fewer books advanced rhetorical "systems"; instead, doctrine became simpler, and a more concrete approach appeared in the textbooks. Consequently, after 1880 there was a rapidly diminishing interest in defining rhetoric in the philosophical fashion of earlier years. With a new, more flexible, and more diversified curriculum, it no longer seemed either necessary or practicable to establish the exact position of rhetoric with relation to other subjects. Explicit statements of the scope of rhetoric became fewer, but the scope itself became increasingly narrow, confined finally at the end of the century to practical rules to guide written composition—and, more often than not, only the more mechanical aspects of this. All these tendencies may be illustrated by an examination of the rhetorics during these fifty years.[1]

DEFINITIONS

There was in these first years a tendency to view rhetoric as a science, as a coherent body of laws or principles that were worth learning for their own sake, more or less apart from their practical application to writing. A. D. Hepburn, for example, in his *Manual of Rhetoric* (1875),[2] defined rhetoric as "the

Science of the Laws and Forms of Prose. It investigates the method and general principles to which every discourse must conform that is designed to instruct, convince, or persuade" (p. 13). By discourse, Hepburn meant to include all sorts of literary composition, whether spoken or written, omitting only poetry. In the same way, David J. Hill, in *The Science of Rhetoric* (1877),[3] maintained that "Rhetoric is . . . the science of the laws of effective discourse" (p. 37). Hill's book has some interest as being perhaps the most elaborate attempt to make rhetoric into a "mental science." Like other sciences, Hill declared, rhetoric cannot make laws; "but it can *discover* them, and explain why poetry pleases and eloquence wins, by referring their effects to the laws of mind and language" (p. 8).

Neither of these men, however, was entirely consistent in regarding rhetoric as a science. Hepburn, though he defined the subject as a "science," actually discussed it more as though it were an art; and Hill, in spite of the imposing scientific pretensions of his book, wrote another one the next year (*The Elements of Rhetoric and Composition*[4]) which said little or nothing of science but instead professed to be a practical guide to actual writing. Equally confused were those writers who insisted that rhetoric is not a science but an art. Henry N. Day, in *The Art of Discourse* (1850, 1867),[5] defined rhetoric simply as "the Art of Discourse"; he stressed the word "art" because, he said, a science aims only at knowledge but an art aims at practical skill. Consistent with this was his view of the function of rhetoric, which is purposeful communication. All rational discourse "must ever be communication, not mere objectless utterance." It "implies a communication from one mind to another. It involves ever the three essential elements, of a subject, object, and a relation between them; in other words, of a mind addressing, a mind addressed, and the act itself of addressing" (p. 6). The actual discussion of rhetoric in the book itself, however, was in sharp contrast; it was abstract, extremely complex, and heavily formal (in the strict sense of the term). Day seems to have lost sight entirely of the communicative function. The same may be said of M. B. Hope's *The Princeton Text-Book in Rhetoric* (1859)[6] and John Bascom's *Philosophy of*

Rhetoric (1872),[7] both of which professed to regard rhetoric as a practical art but actually treated it more as a self-sufficient science.

Perhaps the best single example of this confusion over the nature and function of rhetoric was James DeMille's *The Elements of Rhetoric* (1878),[8] where three separate definitions were given. The preface said that "The study of rhetoric may be regarded as an analytical examination of literature" (pp. v–vi). In the opening chapter there were two other definitions, one referring to subject matter, the other to mode of presentation. In the former, rhetoric governs choice and arrangement of subject matter, where the author's purpose is to instruct, convince, or persuade; "Here it may be defined as the art of persuasion." In the latter "it relates to the manner of expression, where the writer treats his subject with conscious ornament, not so much in order to win assent as to stimulate attention and gratify the taste. Here it may be defined as the art of ornamental composition" (p. 14).

Beginning in the late 1870s a more consistent attitude toward rhetoric began to appear. The books were still a good deal more abstract than they later became, but there was much less interest shown in trying to establish rhetoric as a science, either expressly or by implication. Instead, the practical function of rhetoric was recognized much more widely. Until the early 1890s most writers still spoke of "laws" and "principles" as though they were dealing with "rhetorical science," but they seldom made an overt claim that the field is a science, and in fact often tried to give their books a "practical" cast. Though they did not make a clean break with the earlier approach, these men were reacting against the purely theoretical conception of rhetoric that was a part of the disciplinary attitude toward education. As the older educational philosophy collapsed, rhetoric gradually changed to meet the new conditions.

A. S. Hill, for instance, in *The Principles of Rhetoric* (1878),[9] said rhetoric is "the art of efficient communication by language. . . . It is an *art*," he declared, "not a science: for it neither observes, nor discovers, nor classifies; but it shows how to convey from one mind to another the results of observation, discovery, or classification; it uses knowledge, not as knowledge, but as power" (p. iii). John F. Genung's definition in *The Practical Elements of Rhetoric* (1886),[10] perhaps the best known definition in this period, was "the art of adapting discourse, in harmony with its subject and occasion, to the requirements of a reader or hearer" (p. 1). A more informal definition was offered by Alfred H. Welsh in his *Complete Rhetoric* (1885),[11] where he called it *"the art of enabling those who have something to say, to say it to the best advantage"* (p. 5). Brainerd Kellogg in *A Text-Book on Rhetoric* (1880)[12] called rhetoric "the art of arts" (p. 3) and declared that, since he had kept in mind constantly the fact that the student was to acquire an art, he had emphasized throughout his book the necessity for actual practice in writing (p. 6).

It is true that these books, though showing signs of the reaction against the older abstract rhetoric, still had by no means made a complete break with the past. By the mid-1890s, however, the break had become fairly complete. Again, developments in rhetorical theory paralleled developments in education: it was in the 1890s that the elective system finally triumphed over the disciplinary ideal with its required curriculum and its outmoded psychology. One of the clearest signs of the extent of the reaction against the older view of rhetoric was the attitude of rhetoricians toward defining their subject. The careful definitions, the discussions of whether rhetoric is an art or a science or both—in the last decade of the century these almost vanished from rhetoric textbooks.

In several books published in the closing years of the century there was a distinction drawn between the terms rhetoric and composition, a distinction that had been made earlier by Henry W. Jameson in his little book called *Rhetorical Method* (1879).[13] Thus Fred Newton Scott and Joseph V. Denney published in 1897 a book called *Composition-Rhetoric*,[14] in which rhetoric was defined as "the theory of the pupil's practice . . . the explicit statement of principles which are implicit in all successful elementary composition" (p. iii). Rhetoric, that is, was being used in a sense which comes close to what was meant by earlier writers when they spoke of the "science" of rhetoric;

composition was being confined to the "art" of rhetoric, or the actual practice of writing. G. R. Carpenter restricted the terms in the same way: "we use the term 'rhetoric' with reference to formal or systematic instruction in the theory of expression, parallel to instruction in formal or systematic grammar, and the term 'composition' with reference to instruction and practice in the art of expression, i.e., essay writing and similar exercises."[15] The books that took the trouble to distinguish in this way between the two terms invariably confined themselves to a minimum of theory and made copious provision for actual writing by the student.

Other writers, of whom Arlo Bates was typical, defined only composition. In his *Talks on Writing English, First Series* (1896),[16] Bates said, "Composition is the art by which ideas and mental impressions are conveyed in written language" (p. 5). Many men offered no direct definition. A. G. Newcomer, in *Elements of Rhetoric* (1898),[17] said that "Practical or Applied Rhetoric and the Art of Composition are convertible terms." He added, "While this treatise is called a rhetoric, in conformity with established practice, the word composition will be more frequently used, as serving to convey more directly its chief aim, which is constructive rather than critical or scientific" (p. 1). Scott and Denney's *Elementary English Composition* (1900)[18] and Henry G. Pearson's *Freshman Composition* (1897)[19] contained no definitions of either composition or rhetoric, and in fact the word "rhetoric" never appeared in the books; only "composition" was referred to. The earlier argument over whether rhetoric is an art or a science was practically ignored after 1893. G. R. Carpenter introduced a brief informal discussion of the matter in his *Exercises in Rhetoric and English Composition (Advanced Course)* (1893),[20] but he was almost alone in giving any attention to it. The writers of the middle and later nineties were overwhelmingly in favor of regarding rhetoric as an art—as "composition." The fact that they so rarely felt called upon to defend this view suggests that it was taken for granted in this period. Rhetoric no longer presumed to be a "mental science," composed of immutable laws worth learning in and for themselves. On the contrary, in keeping with the "practical" emphasis that had become so prominent in education by the 1890s, rhetoric was looked on as a set of practical injunctions valuable almost wholly for their application to the production of actual writing.

RELATIONS

Until nearly 1880 the American rhetoricians were usually careful to indicate the place of rhetoric in relation to other disciplines—an essential preliminary when each subject in the required curriculum had its own particular function to fulfill in the process of disciplining the mental faculties. It was desirable also because, in these years when rhetoric was usually thought to be a separate "mental science," a distinctive field had to be marked out for it and bulwarked against the encroachments of such other disciplines as logic, grammar, psychology, and ethics. The most plausible way to do this was simply to show in what ways rhetoric is indebted to these other subjects, yet manages to preserve its own identity and function.

Henry Day admitted that rhetoric is related to logic, ethics, esthetics, and grammar, but he cautioned that it should not be considered a branch of any of them. Rather, it presupposes them and works in accordance with their principles (p. 6). John S. Hart, in A Manual of Composition and Rhetoric (1870),[21] paraphrased Campbell: rhetoric depends on grammar for the laws of language and on logic for the laws of thought (p. 13). Bascom mentioned grammar, logic, and elocution, which respectively govern the combination of words into correct expressions, test the validity of thought, and guide delivery and enhance its effect (p. 14). Francis Theremin's book Eloquence a Virtue (1850, 1859),[22] freely translated from the German by W. G. T. Shedd, insisted that all the laws of rhetoric are derived from a single basic "science"—ethics. Religious influence on higher education was of course strong in these years, and Theremin's book, which is almost a text on homiletics rather than rhetoric proper, is striking evidence of this influence. Theremin admitted certain relations between rhetoric and both poetry and philosophy, but he concluded that "Rhetoric, considered as the theory of Eloquence, is a part of Ethics, and . . . Eloquence itself is an ability to exert influence according to ethical laws,—that is to say, is a *Virtue*" (p. 69). A large part of the book was devoted to defending this view.

Several other writers, in these years when "mental science" was popular, stressed the relations of rhetoric with psychology. "The philosophy of rhetoric," wrote Bascom, "is the reference of its rules to the principles of mental and moral science on which they are dependent. . . . Whether composition is sought as a means of expression or of persuasion, its end is reached in mind, and mind gives the governing principles" (pp. 14–15). Hope declared that the principles of rhetoric are those of human nature itself (p. 1). Hepburn's view was similar: the process of communication "is subject to fixed laws inherent in the mind . . ." (p. 14). The man who gave the most detailed attention to the relations between rhetoric and mental science, however, was D. J. Hill in *The Science of Rhetoric*. Hill's avowed aim was expressed in the title of the book; he wanted to systematize rhetorical "laws" into a coherent science. All discourse, he said, aims at effecting a change in the mind of the person addressed. This change is produced by ideas, and "These ideas are effective in producing the change only when they are assimilated to the dominant ideas of the mind addressed" (p. 37). The mental changes that are brought about by this process take place according to certain laws; most of the book consists of an exposition of these laws, which are based on Sir William Hamilton's system of psychology—the "mental science" of the 1870s. Hill mentioned other relations between rhetoric and logic, grammar, esthetics, and elocution, though only logic and psychology figured prominently in the book. Hill's effort to make rhetoric a science depended, in fact, on the psychological basis he furnished for rhetorical phenomena.

In the 1880s, as the elective system and curriculum expansion began to break down the traditional relations among academic subjects, there was less attention given to trying to determine the exact place that rhetoric occupies among related disciplines. Most of the writers in these years followed Campbell in mentioning logic and grammar, and only a few included ethics and esthetics. The discussions were usually perfunctory.

T. W. Hunt, one of the few men in the 1880s who still argued that rhetoric is a distinct mental science, mentioned grammar, logic, ethics, esthetics, and mental science as being related to rhetoric;[23] but his book was not typical of the time. Neither was John G. R. McElroy's *The Structure of English Prose* (1885),[24] which listed all these fields except mental science; McElroy's book was admittedly based on Day's *Art of Discourse* and as a result showed many of the emphases common in the 1850s. Another anachronism was J. H. Gilmore's *The Outlines of Rhetoric*,[25] first printed in 1877 for Gilmore's own use at the University of Rochester but taken over and reissued in 1891 by a large publisher. Gilmore illustrated his conception of the relations of rhetoric by a diagram: at the base was psychology ("The Germs of Thought"); above this was logic ("Thought developed"); then came grammar ("Thought expressed"); then rhetoric ("Thought communicated"); and finally, at the apex, elocution ("Thought orally delivered") (p. 9).

Except for these three men, who were hardly typical, the writers after 1880 were intent on what seemed to them more practical aspects of doctrine. Rhetoric was becoming more concrete, and such theoretical distinctions seemed unimportant. In the last decade of the century the tendency became even more marked. The relations of rhetoric to other fields of study were simply ignored. From the textbooks there could be inferred certain relations with grammar and (rarely) with psychology, but there was no explicit discussion. Such detailed treatments belonged to the older and outmoded tradition of philosophies of rhetoric, which in the nineties had become identified with a theory of education no longer popular.

SCOPE: THE RHETORIC OF ORAL DISCOURSE

In the years after 1850 when the change was being made from the British rhetorics to American works, there was much uncertainty over the place to be assigned to oral rhetoric. Blair had practically ignored oral discourse; Campbell had tried to consider both oral and written productions; and Whately, more conscious than either Blair or Campbell of the classical tradition of rhetoric, had given more emphasis to spoken composition. The American writers, during the time when they were trying to break away from the dominance of the British texts and fashion their own theory, were almost equally divided among these three positions.

Men like Day, Theremin, Hope, and Bascom, who represented the oral emphasis, did so for different reasons. Day, for example, seems to have felt that oratory was the master type of prose composition and that other forms such as history, essay, treatise were all derivatives of it. Oratory, he declared, is the "only pure form of discourse" because it presupposes an actual audience which is to be influenced by the discourse. He believed, therefore, that rhetoric should restrict itself to oratory, since other species are *"abnormal* [26] forms of discourse, and want some element which is to be found in proper oratory." But if the rhetorician expounds the principles of true oratory, he will also have explained the principles of these abnormal types of composition, for they are offshoots from it (pp. 26-27). Theremin, Hope, and Bascom seem to have preferred to stress oral rhetoric because it, more obviously than written composition, aims at an "outward end," at an effect on the minds of hearers. Being clergymen, these men would naturally believe this aim very important. Bascom, for example, though he said he was opposed to limiting rhetoric to oratory alone, showed very little interest in other types of composition. The reason for this was that he believed there were three departments of the human mind—understanding, emotions, will—and these departments corresponded exactly with the three main types of composition. Prose (non-oratorical) addresses the understanding, poetry the emotions, and oratory the will (pp. 21-22, 23). But poetry and non-oratorical prose do not have an "outward end" like oratory; they do not seek to influence action (pp. 36, 53-54). Therefore, though Bascom gave a few pages to both poetry and prose in the section devoted to the ends of composition, the largest section (on means) was concerned almost wholly with oratory.

Among the early rhetoricians who emphasized written composition were Hart, D. J. Hill (*Elements*), DeMille, and George Payn Quackenbos in his *Advanced Course of Composition and Rhetoric* (1854).[27] All these men showed a strong influence from Blair and retained his belletristic emphasis. Hart, for example, recognized that oratory is a legitimate part and indeed the original concern of rhetoric, but said he would omit from his book all that is peculiar to oratory. His reason was that oratory had long since "branched off into a separate study"—a reference to the popularity of the elocution movement (p. 13). The only further mention of oral rhetoric consisted of a little over four pages, where oral discourses of all sorts were touched on. Hill's book, which, unlike his *Science of Rhetoric*, was intended as a practical textbook rather than a scientific treatise, contained a good deal of the eighteenth century belletristic material—the beautiful, the sublime, the witty, the pathetic, and so on. It leaned heavily toward written composition, with special discussions of descriptions, narrations, and various forms of letters. Orations were mentioned, but they got eight pages as compared with over fifteen for letters.

Distinct claims for oral rhetoric diminished for a time after 1880. Books published in this decade nearly always made some mention of oratory—usually as one of the various types of composition—but it was seldom more than a perfunctory gesture. The main interest of the authors was written productions. There were several reasons why this was so: the nearly universal monopoly of instruction in speaking held by the elocutionists; the rapidly growing importance of the written word as literacy spread and mass publications mushroomed; and the increasing interest in college instruction in literature. One of the very few defenses of spoken rhetoric in these later years is found not in a textbook but in a short article outlining a course in public speaking given at Amherst. H. A. Frink, author of the article and professor of logic, rhetoric, and public speaking at this college, restricted rhetoric to "the forms of composition adapted to public delivery," though he wished to include in this class those compositions which, though they may not actually be spoken, yet "must have the directness, force, and pointedness of oral address. . . ." "Literature proper," Frink said, "which appeals to the thought, the imagination, the sensibilities, simply through the eye, is but slightly subject to the rules of rhetoric. The essential elements of literary power and beauty are indefinable, illusive; and are not to be communicated by formal instruction."[28]

Oral rhetoric usually did not appear in any form in the books published between about 1893 and the end of the century. Elocution was still thriving, though it was beginning to be challenged by new courses in public speaking conceived on a somewhat broader basis than gestures and vocal intonations. Between the two of them, however, they monopolized the field of oral rhetoric. Thanks especially to the Harvard Reports and the furor they caused, the attention of both schools and colleges was centered predominantly on written composition, and with an intensity never approached since. These are the years when the "daily theme" became a regular fixture of rhetoric courses on the theory that only constant practice would arrest "the growing illiteracy of American boys." The trouble with this theory, plausible as it may have been, was that the combination of swelling enrollments, small composition staffs, and unprecedented masses of student writing resulted in an impossible situation. It was not surprising, therefore, when about 1900 a few writers again began to urge the importance of what was now called "oral composition." The reasons advanced in its support were often sound enough: Scott and Denney's *Elementary English Composition* protested "the isolation of written from spoken discourse. The artificial separation of two things which naturally belong together takes the heart out of both of them" (p. iv). But the reason why "oral composition" suddenly became so popular—especially in the high schools, where the teacher-student ratio was even more discouraging than in the colleges— is not hard to guess. Here was a way to reduce somewhat those mountains of daily themes, yet still give some training in "composition." As the new century advanced, oral rhetoric appeared with some frequency in composition textbooks, though the majority still confined the field to written composition.

SCOPE: BELLES LETTRES AND LITERATURE

As one would expect from the strong imprint that Blair's *Lectures* had made on rhetorical activity in America, most of the

American rhetoricians of the third quarter of the century, when the British works were finally being supplanted by native texts, included within the province of rhetoric material that later writers considered to belong more properly to esthetics, belles lettres, or criticism. This sort of material found its way into rhetoric texts and courses not only because of Blair's example, however, but also because until about 1880 there was no other place to put it; literature had still not become an independent subject in the curriculum but was instead a sort of appendage to rhetoric.

Several of the earlier American writers—Quackenbos, D. J. Hill (*Elements*), and Hart—included in their books discussions of the nature and pleasures of taste, the imagination, the sublime, the beautiful, the ridiculous, very much in the manner of Blair. These writers, and others as well, included also a section on prosody and on the types and forms of verse—lyric, epic, dramatic, pastoral, and so on, also after Blair's example. Day and E. O. Haven (*Rhetoric*, 1869)[29] had only the discussion of poetic types and omitted prosody. Bascom, dividing man's mental powers into the understanding, the emotions, and the will according to the scheme of mental science, admitted poetry as a legitimate concern of rhetoric because it appeals to one of the three chief human faculties, the emotions. In point of fact, however, his chapter on poetry covered only four pages, since he regarded oratory as the most important type of composition. In *The Science of Rhetoric* D. J. Hill omitted all mention of belletristic matter—"These topics belong strictly to Aesthetics. . . . It is as reasonable to discuss the nature of *truth* or of *right* in a text-book on Rhetoric, as to admit the discussion of Taste, Beauty and Sublimity" (p. 5). In the *Elements*, however, Hill rather inconsistently included a full treatment of criticism, taste, beauty, sublimity, and the rest. Two other men, Hepburn and Hope, barred poetry from the province of rhetoric, though they were exceptional in this period for doing so. Hepburn, defining rhetoric as "the Science of the Laws and Forms of Prose," drew a number of distinctions between prose and poetry to show why the latter is not a proper concern of rhetoric; the most important of these were that poetry, unlike prose and oratory, does not try to influence the minds of readers or hearers; it makes a freer use of imagination; it idealizes reality; it tries consistently to awaken the emotion of the beautiful; and, finally, it is usually in meter (pp. 13-14). Hope left poetry out of his scheme of rhetoric on the grounds that it conduces neither to conviction nor to persuasion, which he regarded as the two aims of rhetoric (p. 2).

As the independent study of literature gained in popularity in the 1880s, rhetoric was allied more closely with this study. In a sense it was an extension of the belletristic tradition in rhetoric, but it expressed itself in more modern terms. The formal discussions of taste, beauty, sublimity, wit, and pathos that had been so common in the books of the sixties and seventies became much less frequent. Welsh's *Complete Rhetoric* and Charles Coppens' *A Practical Introduction to English Rhetoric* (1886)[30] are just about the last rhetoric textbooks to mention them—and these two books, compared with others from the same years, were anachronistic in more ways than this. A good many of the other books from the eighties and early nineties stressed the relations of rhetoric and literature, and the matter was discussed in numerous articles published in the early educational journals.

A considerable number of books in the 1880s did, however, retain the sections on prosody and types of poetry. But as the nineties advanced, these features became for a time less common in rhetoric textbooks. The impact of the Harvard Reports, the great popularity of the "daily theme," the emphasis on practical application centered the attention of most authors of rhetoric texts on simple prose composition. And literature, meanwhile, was of course doing very well for itself without the aid of rhetoric. George R. Carpenter's *Elements of Rhetoric and English Composition,*[31] published in 1900, did include brief sections on poetry and versification (pp. 121-138), and so did Scott and Denney's *Composition-Literature* (1902)[32] (pp. 367-384). The aim of the latter book, however, was somewhat different from that of the usual rhetoric text—"to make the pupil's work in composition and his reading of the English Classics more helpful to each other" (p. iii). The book was, in fact, almost an anthology. But these books belong to the next century, when the reforming zeal that had motivated the great attention to theme-writing in the nineties was beginning to lose its force.

In the first dozen or fifteen years of the new century, as composition instruction—and rhetorical theory—became increasingly routinized, discussions of prosody and often of types of poetry appeared more frequently again in rhetoric texts. The public indignation that had in the nineties forced teachers to give their exclusive attention to writing had now subsided. When no miraculous results had been immediately forthcoming from daily themes, rhetoric as an academic subject had lost status; in the new century no one seemed to care much what was done in the composition course. The contrast between this lackadaisical attitude and the critical attitude of the nineties is seen clearly in the grudging note that Scott and Denney prefixed to the second edition of their *Composition-Rhetoric*, published in 1897: "In response to an earnest desire, persuasively expressed, on the part of certain teachers of English, there is added to this edition an Appendix containing a brief statement of the Types of Discourse . . . of Figures of Speech, and of Poetry. It is the opinion of the authors, however, that between the matter of this Appendix and the original plan of the work the connection is very slight. They trust that no secondary teacher will teach these things to his pupils as a substitute for exercises in composition" (p. vii).

In the eighties and nineties, as rhetoric tried to ally itself more closely with the popular new study of literature, some rhetoricians urged the value of rhetorical analysis of literary works. Only a few people protested that "The union of the soul with truth is not effected by the process of pulling sentences asunder limb by limb, and assorting the members in piles of verbs, nouns, phrases."[33] Many more insisted that a main function of rhetoric is, through close analysis, to open the road to enjoyment and understanding of literature. James M. Hart declared in 1891, "I believe that the professor will achieve the best results, first, by dismissing every purpose or expectation of making *writers* of his students, second, by opening their eyes to the characteristics of style in men who *are* writers."[34] Welsh said in his *Complete Rhetoric* that "while rhetorical study possesses a high value as a means of cultivating reflective habits and of refining the writer's style . . . its great end is to increase the reader's power by affording a way toward a better discernment of the beauties in which he takes delight, and hence, through improved imagination and taste, toward a higher stage of intellectual enjoyment" (pp. v–vi). J. Scott Clark, in an article called "The Art of English Composition," offered a list of eleven questions on style to be used by students in analyzing a piece of literature. The nature of these questions can be estimated from the following specimens: "Is the author's vocabulary large?" "Does he violate Purity by coined words, foreign idioms, grammatical errors, &c.?" "Is he precise?" "What is his predominant rhetorical figure?" "Is he pointed?" "What proportion of Anglo-Saxon words does he use?"[35] Theodore W. Hunt's *Studies in Literature and Style* (1890)[36] was almost a book of literary criticism. It showed a strong influence from Taine; but, being restricted solely to the stylistic aspects of literature, it was much narrower than Taine's work. It consisted of a classification of types of style and their exemplification in English literature, together with critical discussion.

A more constructive approach was John F. Genung's little *Handbook of Rhetorical Analysis* (1888),[37] designed to accompany his *Practical Elements of Rhetoric*. It was a small anthology of literary selections, with analytical questions referring the student back to the *Practical Elements*, intended to help the student discover for himself the reason behind the rule. In Genung's theory of rhetoric there were three essentials: theory, examples, practice. The *Handbook*, being designed to supply the second of these, was probably the first of the freshman reading anthologies that have now become so indispensable a part of the composition course. "This book is frankly committed," said Genung, "to the conviction that it is much better to discover a thing than to be told it, even though one does not discover so much" (p. viii). This book contained twenty-six selections from a variety of nineteenth century writers, divided into the same two main divisions as the *Practical Elements*—style and invention. The questions concerned choice of words, kinds of diction, figures of speech, the sentence, the paragraph, and so on, under style; and under invention, the arrangement of material, and Genung's five forms of discourse—description, narration, exposition, argumentation, and persuasion. This method of analysis, in which the student himself goes directly to the literature and tries to deduce "his own rhetoric" instead of being confronted with the finished principles in a textbook, was what Genung sometimes referred to as the "laboratory method" of teaching rhetoric. The *Handbook* was, then, a laboratory manual.

This sort of approach showed the influence of science—specifically, of scientific method. Another example of this influence, and a more pronounced one, was L. A. Sherman's *Analytics of Literature* (1893), subtitled *A Manual for the Objective Study of English Prose and Poetry*.[38] In this book, which seems to have been intended for use in regular literature courses rather than in courses in rhetoric, Sherman tried to discover the "elements" of literature—the "common constituents and factors which, in different frequency and degrees of potency, make up the very diverse effects" of the styles of various poets and prose writers (pp. ix–x). Sherman's methods, which were quite similar to some of those used today by analytical critics, consisted chiefly of what would now be called "close reading," together with statistical analysis.

Some of the results of his studies of English prose style are worth summarizing. He found, for instance, that sentence-length (in words) had steadily decreased in English prose. He presented figures showing that this was the result of a decreasing number of predications per sentence down through the centuries. The fewer the predications per sentence, the easier a style is to read, since there are fewer qualifying details for the reader's mind to take account of. Just as children tend to speak at first in coordinate sentences, or elements with no subordination, so the early writers had a higher proportion of coordinate sentences. As prose became more sophisticated, subordination increased. Sherman pointed out that oral style uses shorter sentences than written, and generally expresses less complex thought; there is a relation between sentence-length and complexity of thought.

Prose before the Romantic movement had used very long sentences, but since 1800 the length of sentences had been steadily decreasing. In other words, written style had been approaching more closely to oral style. This can be seen also in what he called the new articulation of clauses. Oral style (and the style of all good poetry from the time of *Beowulf,* he said, had been essentially oral) uses fewer conjunctions and relatives than ordinary written prose. Modern prose, however, by reducing these connectives, was coming close to oral style. Sherman predicted that this tendency would continue, that written and oral styles would steadily become more similar.

W. T. Brewster's *Studies in Structure and Style* (1896)[39] was still another book of analysis, but closer in approach to Genung's *Handbook* than to Sherman's *Analytics*. It was, however, less mechanical and considerably more penetrating than Genung's text. The book included seven modern English essays by such writers as Arnold, Newman, Ruskin, and Stevenson, together with separate sections analyzing the structure and the style of these essays. Brewster's conception of style, which was rather narrow because he saw it as something with which structure had nothing to do, kept his style analyses from being very profound. He seems to have recognized this, for he regarded the analyses of structure as much more important. The style analyses followed a uniform pattern for all seven of the essays: a brief discussion of the purpose of the style, and a fairly detailed examination of the stylistic technique. The latter was divided into a consideration of words and of sentences; Brewster believed that paragraphs and larger units were more significant for structure than for style. The analyses of structure were less rigid. Most of them began by determining the purposes of the essay, then pointed out the particular principles of structure involved, and concluded with an exposition of the plan of organization. Both principles and plan were treated in such a way as to show their relation to the author's specific purpose—an emphasis that was not apparent in Genung's book. The intention behind this sort of analysis, as G. R. Carpenter said in an introduction to the *Studies*, was not only to familiarize the student with good prose literature but also to give him an "appreciation of order in the expression of thought, and the power of expressing thought in an orderly fashion . . . " (p. xi).

Though Brewster believed that stylistic analysis is less rewarding than analysis of structure because its effects are "more subtle and elusive" (p. 245), Fred Newton Scott at the University of Michigan taught for many years a course specifically in the principles of style. Scott's view of style had considerably more latitude than Brewster's, and it was based on the assumption that style is not necessarily elusive. In a little pamphlet entitled *The Principles of Style* (1890),[40] intended for use in this course, Scott distinguished between what he called the lower rhetoric and the higher rhetoric. In the former the student learned rules and possibly went beyond them to the discovery of some general principle of which the rules were particular applications. The higher rhetoric, however, called for the exercise of imagination and feeling by the student; it led him beyond the bounds of what were usually thought to be the limits of rhetoric. "'Step over this line,'" says the ordinary rhetorician, "'and you get into the region of the vague. Rhetoric cannot account for the finer effects of literature. There is an indescribable bloom, a charm'—and so on" (p. 5). Scott did not agree. He thought blooms and charms are describable; their investigation is one of the concerns of the higher rhetoric. His separate course on "Prose Rhythms" was a good example of his conviction.

To Scott, mastery of the higher rhetoric meant an increasing concreteness in the student's conceptions—"All the new sap of feeling and imagination that collects with the study of the Higher Rhetoric, should flow back into the hard abstractions of the Lower to give them richness and ease." The student will for the first time come to realize "that whatever is not a piece of his own personality can be nothing but . . . a pasteboard box to hold abstractions" (p. 7). It was the cultivation of this "rational and sensitive personality" that was the main object of the higher rhetoric. The more highly developed this personality was, the more discriminating and accurate a person's taste would become. Masterpieces of style were, for Scott, simply perfect expressions of personalities that deserved to be expressed.

In other words, Scott not only was convinced that literary effects, no matter how subtle, are capable of being studied and explained, but he believed that it is the particular office of rhetoric to make this study. Rhetoric for Scott was a broad humanistic discipline, not merely a set of barren formulas studied by freshman classes. This wide conception of rhetoric, together with Scott's curiosity about "blooms and charms," made his graduate program in rhetoric at Michigan a center of original thought.

Scott saw rhetoric as a discipline closely related to literary criticism; in fact, for him there was no sharp dividing line between the two subjects: they interpenetrated. But Scott stood alone. For nearly all other men of the time, rhetoric was a much narrower and more pedestrian subject that was wholly identified with teaching young people how to write in such a manner as to avoid social censure. Men like Brewster and Genung did, it is true, try to introduce the study of literature into the rhetoric course, but their motive was the practical one of trying to "show how it is done"; students were supposed to improve their own writing by such study. And as rhetoric steadily became more isolated in the curriculum, more restricted to a single narrow purpose, literary criticism moved in and took away from it its terminology, its methods of analysis, even its legitimate aims. Perhaps the best example of this was C. T. Winchester's *Some Principles of Literary Criticism* (1899),[41] which was much more a book of rhetorical analysis than one of literary criticism. To the present day, rhetoric has never fully recovered the ground lost then.

Subject Matter and Logic

CHAPTER FIVE

INVENTION, or the finding of suitable material for discourse, has been one of the main rhetorical categories since the very beginning of rhetoric itself. And, because of the original emphasis on rhetoric as persuasion or argument, invention has usually been involved more or less closely with logic. Aristotle, with his emphasis on logic and rhetorical "topics" or "common-places," devoted a considerable part of the first two of the three books in his *Rhetoric* to the finding of suitable arguments. Cicero and Quintilian, who regarded rhetoric as a master discipline embracing all others, developed systems of "status"; that is, sets of leading questions for the orator to ask himself in order to investigate the limits of the subject and to turn up appropriate material. When, however, rhetoric declined during the period of the Second Sophistic in Rome, invention was deemphasized in favor of style, which became the ruling concern. From then until the time of Campbell there were fluctuations in the relative positions of style and invention, though in general style remained uppermost. Campbell—and, fifty years later, Whately—agreeing with Aristotle that rhetoric is "an offshoot from logic," stressed invention heavily. Blair, however, with his interest in belles lettres and style, insisted that invention lies outside the proper field of rhetoric.

INVENTION

Until about 1875, American rhetoricians, partly because they were reflecting the disagreement in the British rhetorics, exhibited nearly all varieties of opinion toward invention. Some excluded it as Blair had done, some accepted it in the manner of Whately and Campbell, still more tried with varying success to effect a compromise between the two extremes. None felt that he could ignore so important a question, for the formal approach to rhetoric in these years almost required that some sort of attitude be taken toward all major items of traditional theory. Typical of the first group, who ruled out invention, were D. J. Hill (*Science*) and Theodore W. Hunt. "Invention," said Hill, "implies the production of some particular kind of thought, conditioned by the nature of the subject-matter. What propositions are to be maintained by the lawyer, the theologian, the scientist, or the critic, must depend upon the facts of law, theology, science, and criticism. The methods of investigation are different in the various departments of thought. Hence no truly useful rules can be given on this subject" (pp. 3-4). Hunt, in an article called "Rhetorical Science" published in 1874, admitted that for the ancients, who had regarded rhetoric as "the universal science," the high place given then to invention was perhaps justified. But, since he believed the entire ancient scheme of rhetoric had been wrongly based (it had not placed enough emphasis on ethics), he felt free to drop invention: ". . . the materials of thought are necessary pre-requisites to the existence of rhetoric as a science, or its operation as an art. As to what the sources are, whence these materials are derived, it is not in point here to determine, further than to say that they are derived from all conceivable sources other than Rhetoric itself. . . ."[1]

Hope, Quackenbos, John S. Hart, and Haven took a middle ground, usually admitting that actually the materials of thought lie outside the province of rhetoric, but at the same time devoting more or less space to fairly traditional discussions of invention. Haven (and D. J. Hill in the *Science*) quoted with approval John Stuart Mill's statement that "'Invention, though it can be cultivated, can not be reduced to rule; there is no science which will enable a man to bethink himself of that which will suit his purpose. But when he *has* thought of something, science will tell him whether that which he has thought of will suit his purpose or not.'"[2] Hart said that as to the chief functions of invention, "it is not in the power of mere rhetoric to supply what is needed. Invention, except in its lowest and most mechanical details, is not a thing to be taught. It is a part of one's native endowment, and of his general intellectual accumulations." Nevertheless, Hart added, he thought it possible for rhetoric "to help considerably the beginner in the use of such materials as he has." The ancients, and some of the moderns, had given a great many rules to govern invention. Hart would not present "such a learned array of barren formulas, which, at the best, are only perplexing to the beginner in the art of composition, as they are useless to the expert." Instead, Hart intended to give some practical examples to show how invention actually proceeds (p. 294). He began with the simplest subjects ("Paper," "Water") and proceeded to more complex ones ("Fear," "Memory"). Hart's method was essentially one of simplified "status." The subject of "Paper," for instance, was accompanied by a series of guiding statements: general appearance of paper, color, forms in which it comes, materials it is made of, uses, etc. A sample composition on paper was included (pp. 295–296).

Day, Hepburn, and DeMille all admitted invention without apology. Day, in fact, claimed as one of the chief distinctions of his book that he was restoring invention to its rightful importance. Invention is "the very life of an art of rhetoric," since "It respects the soul and substance of discourse—the thought which is communicated" (p. 40). Day defined invention as "the art of supplying the requisite thought in kind and form for discourse," and said that it includes invention proper (the actual supply of the thought) and arrangement or disposition. Day justified his placing of arrangement as a subhead under invention (for the ancients it was a separate category) by saying there are really only two parts to rhetoric—thought and expression—and since arrangement is obviously not a coordinate head with these it must fall under thought, i.e., invention (p. 42). Day's actual discussion of invention was long (it took up half the book) and exceedingly complex; it was a striking example of the abstract and theoretical approach to rhetorical doctrine that was typical of the fifties and sixties. According to Day, the immediate objects of discourse are explanation, confirmation, excitation, and persuasion (pp. 48-50). The problem of invention in compositions governed by each of these aims was taken up in turn. The first of them, explanation, is ruled by four laws: unity, method, selection, completeness (pp. 60-62). The processes of explanation are narration, description, division, partition, exemplification, and comparison and contrast (pp. 67-69). Each of these processes was discussed separately.

Some idea of the nature of these discussions can be gained from a brief glance at the treatment of division, which is typical. Division is "that process of explanation which exhibits the theme through its specific or similar parts." The theme must be grasped as a generic whole consisting of species, varieties, and individuals. It will be either simple, referring to outward and sensory objects; or it will be abstract, referring to "internal and spiritual" objects (pp. 83-84). Division, like the other five processes of explanation, will be governed by the laws of unity, selection, method, and completeness. Unity "requires that the theme be a single class, and that all the parts in each set be given by one principle of division" (a page and a half of discussion) (pp. 84-86). Selection demands that "such attribute of the theme be selected as the principle of division, and that such subdivisions shall be given as shall best subserve the particular design of the discourse" (a page of discussion) (pp. 86-87). Method "requires that the subdivisions, or the lower grades of parts, be presented under the higher species to which they respectively belong" (nearly two pages of discussion) (pp. 87-88). Finally, completeness "requires that all the parts which make up the class under the assumed principle of division be presented; and that such successive subdivisions be given as the purpose or occasion of the discourse may prescribe" (discussed in only half a page) (p. 89). Confirmation, excitation, and persuasion later were each taken up in turn, rigorously analyzed, and the particular problems of invention presented by them explained in the most exhaustive fashion.

DeMille had a section in his book entitled "Method" under which he included both invention and disposition. He defined method as "the choice and arrangement of the subject-matter of composition, as distinguished from style, which is the manner of its expression in words" (p. 294). Invention proper was treated briefly. DeMille divided it into two kinds: "accumulative invention," which depends on research, study, observation, or testimony; and "creative invention," which relies on "the inventive powers of the mind." The latter is essential to fiction. In most productions, however, the two kinds are generally mixed (pp. 304-309). DeMille said no more of invention; he had a fairly long discussion of status but classified it under arrangement rather than invention (pp. 309-314). Hepburn had a chapter on invention, in which he urged meditation and reading as aids. Systematic meditation may be helped by the classical system of topics, though he cautioned that they are subject to abuse (pp. 34-43). Unlike Day and DeMille, he considered disposition as a separate head, in the manner of the ancients. The discussion of invention in George W. Hervey's *A System of Christian Rhetoric* (1873) is striking: he believed "all true preachers of the Gospel are the successors of the prophets" (p. 3), and may therefore draw on the Holy Ghost for divine inspiration to help them in invention. The Holy Ghost will not only furnish the materials of a sermon "on occasions when we have no time for preparation," but will also determine the arrangement of them (p. 74). Hervey did not rely exclusively on the Holy Ghost, however, though he did give directions for putting oneself in a proper condition to receive inspiration. He had a chapter on invention, the most prominent feature of which was a set of 27 topics quoted from one of the church fathers.

After the late 1870s, very few writers ruled out all discussion of invention. As the amount of writing required in the classroom slowly began to increase in the seventies and eighties, nearly all rhetoricians came to feel that either the teacher or the textbook had some responsibility to help the student find and organize material. A. S. Hill and T. W. Hunt were exceptional in continuing to insist on the purely theoretical point that, considered logically, the material of a discourse lies outside the proper sphere of rhetoric. In Hunt's theory of rhetoric, style was dominant. His 1874 article on "Rhetorical

Science," referred to above, had made it clear that he believed invention is not a legitimate part of rhetoric. "Let it, first of all, be accepted as indisputable that the *materials* of our thought are already at hand, furnished outside of and apart from any agency of Rhetoric" (p. 663). In *The Principles of Written Discourse* (1884) his opinion had not changed, as his definition of discourse showed: "Given the Materials of Thought and a Definite Object in view, Discourse is such a *selection* and *adaptation* of these materials and their *presentation* in such a form as best to secure the Definite Object" (p. 153). The book itself was concerned with style and forms of writing, though it is true that Hunt's desire to raise rhetoric to a science by basing it on mental philosophy kept the book from being a stylistic treatise of the earlier sort. A. S. Hill said in the introduction to his *Principles of Rhetoric* that "Rhetoric applies to any subject-matter that can be treated in words, but has no subject-matter peculiar to itself. It does not undertake to furnish a person with something to say; but it does undertake to tell him how best to say that with which he has provided himself" (p. iv). There was no treatment of invention in the book.

The remaining men in this middle period all admitted invention. Welsh, for instance, in his *Complete Rhetoric* treated it under choice of subject, determination of status, accumulation of material, disposition, and amplification (pp. 154-157). Gilmore divided rhetoric into three "departments," one of which was "inventive rhetoric." His main heads were choice of themes, accumulation of material, and arrangement of material. Each of these was further divided. Under choice of themes, for instance, Gilmore said a theme should be real, fresh, original, unified, not too broad, and "adapted" (pp. 27-29). Material is accumulated by reflection, reading, discussion, analysis (pp. 30-32). Coppens, in *A Practical Introduction to English Rhetoric*, said that "The first requisite for success in any composition is that the writer have clear and correct ideas on the matter to be treated." He would therefore "premise a few exercises on the acquisition of thought" (pp. 9-10). These exercises were "object-lessons" of the sort devised by Pestalozzi. They concerned names of objects, parts of objects, qualities of objects, etc. The student was asked to examine objects, their parts, qualities, and list what he observed. An example: "*An apple* has stem, peel, pulp, juice, veins, eye, dimples, core, seeds, seedcase" (p. 14). This sort of exercise was designed, Coppens said, to "cultivate habits of attention," "lead to greater distinctness of perception," "store the mind with useful knowledge," "cultivate a taste for what is real," and so on (p. 11). Later in the book, when he came to speak of "Essays," he introduced an abridged version of the classical system of "topics" to help the student collect material (pp. 182–189).

McElroy declared in *The Structure of English Prose* that he had "tried to exhibit the laws of Rhetoric in their entirety,— not the laws of Style alone, but also those of Invention. However we may quibble about that word *Invention* in its rhetorical sense, Rhetoric does teach other laws than those of Form; and these laws must be exhibited, if the art is to be taught fully" (p. iii). The discussion of invention, however, covered only 47 pages; that of style took up 231. McElroy's section on invention was little more than an abridgment of Day's discussion in *The Art of Discourse*. After a few preliminary pages on "The Theme," the rest of the section divided into Day's four modes of discourse: explanation, argument, excitation, persuasion.

Kellogg's *Text-Book on Rhetoric* claimed to give great importance to invention, "that most important element in discourse of any kind. Thirty lessons, more than a third of the whole number, are devoted to this." Strictly speaking, said Kellogg, neither rhetoric nor anything else can teach the student to think, but "he can be brought into such relations with his subject as to find much thought in it, get much out of it, and he can be led to put this into the most telling place in his oral and written efforts" (p. 5). Kellogg's method of teaching invention was based on the sentence as the unit of thought. Invention was defined as "that which treats of the finding of thought for single sentences, for continued discourse" (p. 19). He followed this definition with a page and a half on the mechanism of thought and concluded that "A thought is produced by the fusion of at least two ideas" (p. 21), ideas being "impressions, or images, or pictures, of things" (p. 20). He illustrated a "thought" by a simple sentence ("Birds fly") and then launched into the subject of invention by showing how a simple sentence may steadily be made more complicated by the addition of other elements. As he said in the preface, "the author leads the pupil up through the construction of sentences of all conceivable kinds, from the simplest to the most intricate—transformed by substitution, contraction, and expansion—through the synthesis of sentences, in their protean forms, into paragraphs, and through the analysis of subjects and the preparation of frameworks, to the finding of thought for his themes," (p. 5). Exactly how these exercises in sentence construction and analysis contributed to the finding of thought Kellogg never made quite clear. We have only his statement in the preface that they did.

Though Genung's treatment of invention in *The Practical Elements of Rhetoric* was the fullest of any of these later authors, he limited the scope of this rhetorical category. "All the work of origination," he said, "must be left to the writer himself; the rhetorical text-book can merely treat of those mental habits and powers which give firmness and system to his suggestive faculty, and the principles and procedures involved in the determination of any literary form" (p. 8). The act of literary invention is composed of three separate processes: finding material by observation or thought, selecting from this material, and finally arranging what has been selected. Only the last, he said, is really teachable, and it was this on which he centered his attention. He had a chapter of some twenty-four pages on mental habits and aptitudes that conduce to finding material—observation, mental alertness, wide tastes and interests, habits of seeking order and clearness, various sorts of reading, etc. Following this was a chapter more than twice as long, in which there was a very full discussion of arrangement, disposed under the main heads of determining the theme, constructing a plan, and amplifying the outline. The treatment was detailed, even minute. The five remaining chapters in the section (it covered more than half the book) were devoted to invention in each of Genung's five main forms of discourse—description, narration, exposition, argumentation, persuasion.

In the 1890s, when the amount of student writing required

became staggering, these older methods of coping with the problem of what to write about no longer seemed satisfactory. Urging the student to cultivate thoughtful and reflective habits of mind, and giving him directions for analyzing a subject once it had been decided on, did not seem to be very helpful. What was needed was a more concrete approach. A few writers, however, clung to the older theories. A. S. Hill in his 1895 revision of *The Principles of Rhetoric*[3] made a number of changes to bring the book into line with the progress of rhetorical theory since 1878, but his attitude toward invention remained unshaken: rhetoric has nothing to do with finding the material of discourse. Genung in *The Working Principles of Rhetoric* (1900)[4] had the same two major divisions into style and invention that he had had in his 1886 volume, and he treated invention by splitting it up among the forms of discourse as he had done before. William B. Cairns followed Genung's example pretty closely in both his *Introduction to Rhetoric* (1899)[5] and *The Forms of Discourse* (1896).[6] E. E. Hale, Jr., though his *Constructive Rhetoric* (1896)[7] differed in most respects from Genung's books, said nevertheless that "The answer to the question, How shall I get together and arrange what I am going to say? goes, in books on Rhetoric, by the name of Kinds of Composition"—that is, narration, description, exposition, and argumentation (p. 10).

Among nearly all the other books after 1893, however, there was a distinct tendency to face the problem of invention more realistically than had often been done in the past. The word "invention," it should be remarked, practically disappeared—only Genung and Cairns still used it. But no matter whether it was called "The Student's Equipment" or "What to Say" or "How to Find Material," in all these discussions there was an attempt to give the student really practical assistance in finding substance for his daily themes. This assistance took the form, usually, of including lists of specific theme topics much like those still found in composition textbooks today.

COMPOSITION TOPICS

The assigning of specific topics for compositions, whether oral or written, has been a common pedagogical practice from the time of the Roman rhetoricians. It is one of the simplest and most practical ways to solve the problem of invention in the sort of composition exercises required in school. The American rhetoricians between about 1850 and 1875 who wrote textbooks for the lower schools were quick to recognize this. While the authors of college-level texts were offering complicated philosophical discussions of invention in the abstract, the writers of more elementary texts were trying to meet the difficulty on a humbler but more concrete level. Lists of composition topics appeared commonly in such elementary textbooks as G. P. Quackenbos' *First Lessons in Composition* (1851);[8] William Swinton's *School Composition*, (1874);[9] and James R. Boyd's *Elements of English Composition* (1860).[10] They also appeared in books intended to be used in both secondary schools and colleges—Quackenbos' *Advanced Course of Composition and Rhetoric*, D. J. Hill's *Elements*, and John S. Hart's *Manual*. The composition subjects themselves were, however, poorly adapted to the abilities and level of maturity of the students. A few examples will serve to suggest their general character: "Evanescence of Pleasure" (Swinton), "The Domestic Life of the Ancient Egyptians" (Boyd), "Man and Government, as Found in the Savage, the Pastoral, the Agricultural, and the Commercial, State" (Quackenbos, *Advanced Course*). One of the last books to list this sort of subject was Jameson's *Rhetorical Method* (1879), which contained some 390 topics of which the following are typical: "Curiosity," "Paul at Athens," "The Mills of the Gods," "Ruins of Time," "Youth, Mammon, and Old Age," "The Dice of the Gods Are Loaded."

Though Jameson's book was one of the last to include such subjects, earlier books containing them were apparently in use throughout the eighties; for as the amount of student writing increased and as more serious attention was paid to composition work, objections against this sort of topic became strenuous. A. S. Hill, for example, declared in 1888 that "I know of no language—ancient or modern, civilized or savage—so insufficient for the purposes of language, so dreary and inexpressive, as theme-language in the mass." The reason for this, he felt, "has been the practice of forcing young men to write on topics of which they know nothing—topics, moreover, that present no salient point for their minds to take hold of."[11] J. Scott Clark objected to compositions in which the student presented "a set of dreary platitudes on some such over-broad expository theme as Music, Pride, Selfishness, Ambition, Education, 'The Greatness of Our Country,' &c. . . . An actual test, based upon a large number of printed high-school rhetorical programmes, shows that over 90 percent of the themes are of this indefinite character."[12] Ernest W. Huffcut asked of his fellow teachers, "Which one of us would like to stake his literary skill upon an essay on Honesty?" Yet immature students were asked to write on this and similar subjects, with the result that "the pupil writes words, words, words. . . ."[13] Huffcut suggested that all such composition subjects be consigned "to the limbo of Dr. Quackenbos' 'Rhetoric'" (p. 15).

Several suggestions were made for the improvement of composition topics. The influence of Pestalozzi and Herbart was apparent in Huffcut's statement that "the requirements must be adapted to the experiences and attainments of the pupil" (p. 13). The composition teacher, he added, must select something in which the student is interested. "Let it be a subject about which he knows something. Let it be specific, concrete, not too broad in its scope, and capable of simple and direct treatment" (p. 16). Of the four kinds of composition—narration, description, exposition, argumentation—exposition is the most difficult, yet most of the topics to which Huffcut was objecting demanded expository treatment. He recommended, therefore, that students begin with narration, which he thought the easiest of the four (pp. 16–17); elementary classes might proceed to description, but not beyond (p. 20). Clark said the four sorts of composition practicable for secondary school pupils are description, narration, argumentation, and paraphrasing from verse to prose. He suggested beginning with descriptions of familiar objects, advancing to personal narratives, and then going on to the other kinds. He believed exposition should be omitted.[14]

Genung, in describing his course in rhetoric at Amherst, said fluency with the pen should be the first aim, and therefore appropriate subjects were essential to the success of the class.

He began with "subjects requiring simple observation or imagination," and later introduced "subjects requiring exercise of thought." He followed the order description, narration, exposition, argumentation.[15] J. M. Hart, in a rhetoric course at Cornell, had his students write solely on literary topics. He was opposed to subjects that relate to fields outside the main sphere of English studies: "Our English course should be reserved for the discussion of facts and principles needful to the understanding of English authors."[16] This idea, as well as several of the others just mentioned, are still met from time to time in professional journals or at professional meetings—and usually such notions are presented as though they are something entirely new and revolutionary.

In the nineties, the reaction away from the old types of composition subjects became almost complete. Formal discussions of invention dropped out of nearly all books in this decade, and lists of theme topics were moved in to fill the vacuum; but they were topics of a new sort. A. G. Newcomer, in his *A Practical Course in English Composition* (1893),[17] after cautioning the student against choosing abstract subjects, adages, etc., for themes, offered a single rule for guidance: in what he writes the student must interest the reader. If he is to do this, Newcomer added, he must be interested himself in the subject he writes about; and topics of this sort are usually found within the student's own range of observation and experience (pp. 5-6).

This emphasis on personal observation and experience appeared in one form or another in most of the books—a sign that the Pestalozzian and Herbartian theories of adapting the difficulty of the work to the student's stage of development were generally accepted by this time. As Espenshade said in *The Essentials of Composition and Rhetoric*, the old-fashioned composition topics were far beyond the student's knowledge and ability. "The teacher who is guilty of assigning to his pupils such theme-subjects as 'Disease,' 'Comets,' and 'The Love of Fame' cannot reasonably complain if they conceive a hearty dislike for theme-writing" (p. 38). Like Newcomer, Espenshade believed the best composition topics would come from things the student knows best and is most interested in. He recommended "the habit of close and accurate observation" as one of the surest ways of having something to write about (p. 24), though he also mentioned two other sources of material—reading and research, and the writer's imagination (p. 40). Scott and Denney in *Composition-Rhetoric* said the student should ask himself what he is interested in, and what those who will read what he writes will find interesting. "If he can find anything in the world that will stand as answer to both these questions, he has a good subject . . ." (p. 41).

Several specific devices were used to help the student find appropriate material, the most common of which was lists of theme titles. Without exception, they were in sharp contrast with the similar lists found in earlier texts, such as those of Quackenbos and Jameson. Scott and Denney, in an appendix at the end of *Composition-Rhetoric*, suggested such topics as "Our newsboy," "How I learned to like good music," "Condition of the roads in this neighborhood," and "Teachers should be made a part of the Civil Service." Hale offered "The First Snowstorm this Year," "An Early Morning's Fishing," "A Twenty-mile Ride for the Doctor" (p. 22). Charles Sears Baldwin in *A College Manual of Rhetoric* (1902)[18] had topics like these as well as some calling for research: "The Trans-Siberian Railway," "The Resources of Arizona," etc. (p. 259). All the topics in the books after 1893 showed that an effort was being made to ask of the student only what he knew or could reasonably find out through limited investigation.

Joseph V. Denney, in a paper read in 1896 at a joint conference of the Michigan Schoolmasters' Club and the Association of Teachers of English of the North Central States,[19] criticized the fairly common practice of requiring the student to base all his compositions on his readings in English literature, since this provided training only in the critical essay. He also doubted the practicability of having the student draw on the subject-matter of other courses in his themes, a system that was then operating in some of the upper-division writing courses at Harvard. The likely result of this plan, he thought, would be that the writing would sound bookish and would lack originality (pp. 6-7).

Denney recommended that a considerable part of the student's composition work be based on experience and observation, but he added that even more important than the actual choice of subjects was the way in which they were phrased.

> If our object is to train the power of seeing and expressing relations, of grasping in imagination the meaning and total significance of a number of details, the statement of the topics should, if possible, suggest a typical situation in real life. And if we wish to enlist the personal interest of the writer in his work, the statement of the topics should suggest a personal relationship to the situation, of the one who is to write. Moreover it should suggest a particular reader or set of readers who are to be brought into vital relationship with the situation. . . . The composition that suggests a problem for solution calls into activity all of the resources of the pupil (p. 7).

Instead of asking the student to write a description of his city, Denney suggested that the teacher tell him to write it as though he were a property owner trying to induce a retired farmer to come live in the city. The advantages of this sort of subject were that it presented a real social situation such as the student might actually encounter later on; it provided the student with criteria by which to judge his material, his diction, and arrangement according as they served to accomplish the purpose in hand; and it made criticism of the composition more vital, since everything in the theme would be weighed to see whether it helped or hindered the writer's object. This put criticism on "a more reasonable foundation" (p. 8).

The problem, then, of finding subject-matter began in the 1890s to take on the characteristics that discussions of the subject still have today in most composition textbooks. The student was told to write about things that interest him, he was encouraged to draw on his own experiences, subjects were made sufficiently concrete and restricted so that the student had a fair chance of discussing them competently, and he was urged to keep the idea of an actual reader consistently before him as he wrote. These tendencies were due to several conditions. One was that the unsatisfactory results of the older systems of invention and the old generalized theme subjects were commonly recognized; another was that, since students were being asked to do much more writing in this period than earlier, attention was necessarily focused more sharply on the problem of how to provide enough substance for the increased writing; finally, the belief that the student's capacities and interest should be considered is a direct outgrowth of the new study of pedagogy which, in the 1890s, revolutionized teaching methods.

LOGIC

Logic, traditionally allied with rhetoric, is so closely related to discussions of invention proper that it may be best to include it here. Almost none of the earlier writers omitted logic entirely. Nearly all gave it more or less space, and always in connection with the finding and arranging of arguments. D. J. Hill in *The Science of Rhetoric* recognized that the great importance of logic in argument came close to placing argument outside the sphere of rhetoric and within that of logic instead. He criticized those rhetoricians who had so abandoned argument and said that there is a distinction between the logical and the rhetorical methods of treating the matter.

> Logic deals with the laws of thought as thought; Rhetoric deals with the laws of altering or producing conviction. The problem of Logic is, with certain propositions as premises, what conclusion may we draw in accordance with the laws of thought? The problem of Rhetoric concerning argument is, given, a certain conclusion, how may we confirm it to the mind of another? Logic gives us the *test* of arguments; Rhetoric gives us the rules for making them effective. With this distinction, argumentation forms an important part of Rhetoric (p. 107).

Hope made a somewhat similar distinction. Logic is concerned with the rhetorical process of argument only in judging the validity of arguments. The actual finding of arguments to bring about proof is the province of rhetorical invention;

but invention, if it is to be sound, must be conducted according to the laws of logic. "Hence the relation of Logic to Rhetoric is very intimate, viz: that of judging how far arguments are valid, or otherwise; and, if not valid, of pointing out the reason of their invalidity, by showing how they cross the laws of thought, implicated in conviction" (p. 8). Day found that rhetoric is related to "the three mental sciences" of esthetics, ethics, and logic, but is not a branch of any of them. Rhetoric depends on ethics for the end of discourse, on esthetics for the form, and on logic for the matter (pp. 6–7). Logic supplies "the various forms of the True" as elements of discourse (p. 9). DeMille made substantially the same distinction between the functions of logic and rhetoric with regard to argument that Hope and Hill did: rhetoric finds suitable arguments and arranges them properly to prove a point; logic judges these arguments. "Rhetoric is thus concerned with composition. Logic with criticism" (p. 347). This distinction seems to have come from Whately.

The actual treatment of argumentation in these books consisted usually of a detailed analysis of types of arguments (a priori, a posteriori, from analogy, testimony, authority, and so on), types of reasoning (deductive and inductive, direct and indirect, regular and irregular, probable and necessary), modes of refutation, the syllogism and the enthymeme, and many subdivisions of these terms. The substance apparently was drawn chiefly from Aristotle and Whately, though specific credit was rarely given, and various changes of emphasis make it difficult to identify sources exactly. DeMille seems to have been alone in drawing on John Stuart Mill's Logic; he devoted a couple of pages to an exposition of Mill's "Four Experimental Methods of Inquiry": method of agreement, method of difference, method of residues, and method of concomitant variations (pp. 350–351). Like so many other rhetorical categories in the texts of these years, argumentation and logic were treated with great elaborateness. Rigorous training in logic was, of course, thought to be one of the most efficient ways of disciplining the intellect; and, in fact, a course in logic was usually required for graduation from college. Hence the detailed treatments of logic in these books.

In the textbooks of the eighties and early nineties, when the disciplinary ideal of education was beginning to break down, logic became somewhat less prominent. Barrett Wendell in his *English Composition* (1891)[20] and Brainerd Kellogg in *A Text-Book on Rhetoric* omitted it entirely, Wendell probably because he had no occasion to speak of argumentation and Kellogg because his treatment of oral discourse (where logic customarily appeared) was sketchy and superficial—nine types of oral discourse taken up in as many pages (pp. 198–207). Charles Coppens also omitted logic from his *Practical Introduction to English Rhetoric*, perhaps because he discussed argumentation in a companion volume on oratory.[21] All the other books from these years mentioned logic—always in connection with argumentation or persuasion—but only two men, A. S. Hill and Genung, gave it really detailed treatment.[22] All the discussions aimed at showing the student how to find and test arguments, how best to arrange them, and how to refute opposing arguments. The tone was still formal and academic. Whately seems to have furnished the pattern for the more ambitious treatments, though Hill drew also on John Stuart Mill.

In the middle and later nineties, discussions of logic became more informal—there was less pressure for using it as a staple of mental discipline. In the average textbook that made room for the forms of discourse, such as Newcomer's *Practical Course* or Carpenter's *Elements*, there was some discussion of framing the proposition, of types of reasoning and methods of proof, but little more. Like most other points of rhetorical doctrine, the treatment of argument was simplified. Scott and Denney's *Composition-Literature* disposed of the subject simply under proposition, arguments, tests of arguments, and arrangement and amplification. The tone was informal and nontechnical. Baldwin's *College Manual* was somewhat unusual both in giving more than the ordinary amount of attention to logic and in presenting a really systematic view of proof, refutation, and other processes involved in argument. This emphasis may perhaps be attributed to Baldwin's familiarity with classical rhetoric, in which logic of course played a large part. The most ambitious treatment of logic was in G. P. Baker's *Principles of Argumentation* (1895),[23] a book devoted entirely to the subject of argument.

A new and less prescriptive approach distinguished Gertrude Buck's *A Course in Argumentative Writing* (1899).[24] Rather than exhibit to the student all the machinery of formal logic, Buck relied on the inductive method. She believed "the student should be asked to dissect out logical formulae for himself from his own unconscious reasonings, using them, when discovered, to render those reasonings more exact" (p. iii). The book was full of informal exercises that tried to help the student accomplish this. Furthermore, since the student was being asked to observe some of his own mental processes, Buck felt it necessary to bring in a certain amount of psychology. She said in the preface that everyone recognized the logical basis of argument, but few had realized that there is a psychological basis underlying logic. Since, therefore, logic had been "cut off from its deepest roots," it had become a set of dry formulas apparently unrelated to living thought. In her book she had tried, she said, to show the student that his "unconscious reasonings" are natural expressions of thought. In the book "Each argument is referred not only to its logical but to its psychological antecedent, so that the maxims and formulae, usually regarded by the learner as malign inventions of Aristotle, represent to our student rather the ways in which real people really think" (p. v).

Buck's book was rather exceptional—and so, for that matter, was Baker's. The general tendency of most books in the closing years of the century was to get rid of anything that looked too abstract and formal, too reminiscent of the older rhetorics with their elaborate machinery. Since formal logic could scarcely avoid looking like this, most writers played it down. Another and perhaps more important reason why logic lost the prominence it had enjoyed in earlier books was that, whereas in the middle years of the century logic had been one of the staples of the required curriculum, the advent of the elective system and the consequent expansion of the curriculum had displaced logic from its favored position. It no longer seemed as important as it once had.

UNITY, COHERENCE, EMPHASIS

Probably one of the best-known—and certainly one of the longest-lived—points of rhetorical doctrine to appear in America in the nineteenth century is the familiar triad of Unity-Coherence-Emphasis. For thirty or forty years after the time of its formulation in the early 1890s, it was a feature of nearly all composition textbooks published. It is not uncommon, in fact, to find these terms even today in books just off the press. Though the terms have their origins in the lists of stylistic qualities inherited from the eighteenth century, and varied and refined upon in the nineteenth, they belong more properly to a discussion of subject-matter rather than of style. The reason is that they are, essentially, criteria to determine the selection and arrangement of material, and in the twentieth century they supplanted, to some extent, the earlier discussions of invention and disposition.

The origins of these terms can be traced back at least as far as Blair's set of stylistic qualities that apply to sentences: clearness and precision, unity, strength, and harmony. Later writers, in their discussions of the sentence, often did no more than repeat Blair's terms. Men like Richard Green Parker, G. P. Quackenbos, James R. Boyd, and John S. Hart were examples, though it should be mentioned that Hart added "emphasis" to the list. In 1866 the Scottish rhetorician Alexander Bain insisted on two essentials for the sentence: unity, and an important position for important elements (what was later called "mass" or emphasis). This matter of the position of sentence elements again came from Blair, who had cautioned that one should "dispose of the capital word, or words, in that place of the sentence, where they will make the fullest impression," and added, "For the most part, with us, the important words are placed in the beginning of the sentence" (pp. 146, 147). For paragraphs (a subject not treated in Blair) Bain again required unity, as well as clearness of connection among sentences (consecutiveness), proper subordination, clear reference, and parallel construction for parallel ideas. Several of these ideas were included within the later term "coherence." In 1874 William Swinton mentioned unity, variety, and coherence as requisites for sentences. A. S. Hill said that the same principles that regulate the construction of sentences apply equally to the construction of paragraphs: structure should follow the order of thought (should "cohere," in other words), the order of climax should be used, and the chief ideas or words should have the most prominent place. J. Scott Clark said paragraphs should have unity and sequence.[25] Genung in the same year (1886) prescribed unity, and distribution of emphasis for sentences; and unity, continuity, and proportion for paragraphs.[26]

All these ideas and terms had become a part of the rhetorical climate by 1890. Barrett Wendell was the man who made a selection from among them and gave to the terms he selected the application that was to make them so attractive to later writers. It is true that Wendell's terms were unity, coherence, and *mass*. George Rice Carpenter substituted the word "emphasis" for "mass" in 1893, thus putting the three terms in their final form;[27] but this is a minor detail. The principles themselves were formulated by Wendell. In his *English Composition* Wendell remarked that the prevailing fault of nearly every textbook on rhetoric that he had seen was the "appallingly numerous" suggestions to govern the act of writing. "It took me some years," he said, "to discern that all which have so far come to my notice could be grouped under one of three very simple heads, each of which might be phrased as a simple proposition.

> Various as they are, all these directions concern either what may be included in a given composition (a sentence, a paragraph, or a whole); or what I may call the outline, or perhaps better, the mass of the composition,—in other words, where the chief parts may most conveniently be placed; or finally, the internal arrangement of the composition in detail. In brief, I may phrase these three principles of composition as follows: (1) Every composition should group itself about one central idea; (2) The chief

parts of every composition should be so placed as readily to catch the eye; (3) Finally, the relation of each part of a composition to its neighbors should be unmistakable. The first of these principles may conveniently be named the principle of Unity; the second, the principle of Mass; the third, the principle of Coherence (pp. 28–29).

Wendell applied these three "principles of composition" to sentences, paragraphs, and whole compositions, but the degree to which they applied to each of these was to some extent regulated by what he called "good use." His discussion of good use, based generally on Campbell, is long and detailed, but it may be summarized something like this: Language is a medium of communication solely because it represents a set of agreements among the users of the language as to the meanings to be attached to certain symbols, oral and written. This "great fact of common human consent" is what he called good use. If one departs from it too widely, he runs the risk of not being understood. In regard to words, good use decrees that the three canons of Reputable, National and Present must govern one's choice, and the power of good use here is "absolute." In sentences good use inhibits the free application of the principles of composition. A determined effort to place important words invariably in important positions, for instance, "is deliberately to alter the natural order of our words; and to alter the natural order of our words in an uninflected language is to strain, and often to violate, the authority of good use" (p. 101). Good use does favor sentence unity, and gives a qualified assent to sentence coherence—qualified because the effort to keep the relations of words and constructions unmistakably clear sometimes violates the normal word-order prescribed by good use. In the paragraph and the whole composition, unity, mass, and coherence may be applied with no appreciable interference from good use. These larger units are not bound by syntax and idiom as sentences are and therefore the writer may dispose the component parts in the way that will best satisfy the requirements of the principles of composition. Wendell's theory is summed up in this passage:

Modern style . . . I believe to be the result of a constant though generally unconscious struggle between
good use and the principles of composition. In words,
of course, good use is absolute; in sentences, though it
relaxes its authority, it remains very powerful; in paragraphs its authority becomes very feeble; in whole compositions, it may roughly be said to coincide with the
principles (p. 39).

This theory of the conflict between the principles of composition and good use found little support among later rhetoricians, but the principles themselves became popular almost
immediately. For a time, however, the formula appeared with
some variations. Espenshade, and Newcomer in the *Elements*,
for example, were not content with just the three terms; Newcomer added "proportion" to them, and Espenshade added
"proportion," "selection," and "variety." Arlo Bates, whose *Talks
on Writing English* is the result of lectures delivered like Wendell's at the Lowell Institute, kept Wendell's original form of the
terms: Unity, Mass, Coherence. He admitted a heavy debt to
Wendell in this and in other points of theory as well.[28] Baldwin,
both in the *College Manual* and in *The Expository Paragraph and
Sentence* (1897),[29] used Carpenter's modification of the terms. So
did Pearson in *Freshman Composition*, and both he and Baldwin
followed Wendell in applying the terms to the sentence, the
paragraph, and the whole composition, though they used a different order.

Pearson showed perhaps a stronger attachment for Unity-
Coherence-Emphasis than anyone else. The passage in which
he defended these principles is worth quoting:

The basis of authority for the principles of Unity,
Coherence, and Emphasis lies in the fact that they represent what the common experience of mankind has
found to be the best way of expression . . . . Gradually
evolving from the attempts of writers of all kinds, certain general principles have become clear, and made
their value evident as guides for a man who wishes to
put his thoughts in language that shall do his work

exactly and forcibly. With the constantly growing realization of the worth of these principles of composition,
came stronger and stronger support for them, as repre-
senting an experience more widespread. Thus the ob-
servance of these principles is now obligatory, because
they stand for the general processes of thought as prac-
tised by all men.

Under these circumstances, it is the business of the
young writer to accept the principles of composition
without question (p. 7).

The neatness and simplicity of Wendell's scheme recommended it in a time when the complex rhetorical terminology of an earlier period was being reduced to fewer and fewer
heads. It is important to notice that Wendell's formula did not
represent any real departure from the traditional method of
categorizing various parts of the rhetorical process and regarding composition as the sum of a certain number of abstractions.
All Wendell had done was to reduce the number of terms
and devise a *rationale* for his list that allowed it to be applied
to every unit of composition larger than the single word. The
plan looked both practical and simple, two powerful endorse-
ments in the nineties and in the new century as well. After
1900 Unity-Coherence-Emphasis became nearly as ubiquitous
as the "Four Forms of Discourse."

Considering the great influence of the formula it is
strange that no more than one attempt seems to have been
made to evaluate it critically. In 1918 H. B. Lathrop wrote an
article on the subject[30] in which he showed that coherence is
really an aspect of unity, and emphasis an aspect of coherence;
thus instead of three separate and coordinate principles there
is only one. Lathrop condemned these abstractions for having encouraged a mechanical approach to writing and for
ignoring the fact that a composition is organic and functional.
Lathrop's criticism apparently made no impression, however, for Unity-Coherence-Emphasis continued to thrive for
a good many years after 1918.

The Forms of Discourse

CHAPTER SIX

I
N PRECEDING centuries, rhetoricians had often classified composition according to its literary form—epistle, romance, treatise, dialog, history, and the various poetic forms of lyric, pastoral, dramatic, etc. This plan persisted for a time after 1850 but soon died out. A much more important scheme of classification was what later came to be known as the "Forms of Discourse," one of the two or three most influential items of rhetorical doctrine that appeared between 1850 and 1900. This classification was adopted almost universally in the 1890s and continued to dominate rhetorical theory well into the 1930s. In spite of its great significance, however, no attempt has so far been made to determine its origins.

The Scottish rhetorician Alexander Bain (1818-1903) claimed that he himself had formulated the plan. Bain was very influential in rhetorical activity in the second half of the nineteenth century, not only because of what he did to popularize the forms of discourse, but also because he was the first man to present a systematic treatment of the paragraph; in addition to this, his scheme of classifying figures of speech was perhaps the most popular of all the many such systems that existed in the last thirty years of the century. Bain's rhetorical theory was contained in *English Composition and Rhetoric*, published in 1866.[1]

Bain announced on the first page that the second part of the book would deal with "the different Kinds of Composition."

Those that have for their object to inform the Understanding, fall under three heads—*Description, Narration, and Exposition*. The means of influencing the Will are given under one head, *Persuasion*. The employing of language to excite pleasurable Feelings, is one of the chief characteristics of *Poetry*.

The Will can be moved only through the Understanding or through the Feelings. Hence there are really but two Rhetorical ends (p. 19).

Really, Bain divided discourse into five varieties, since he included poetry. The division he made was based on an oversimplified sort of faculty psychology that one would not expect from Bain, who was also a pioneer in applying physiological data to psychology. His explanation of how the will can be moved is subject to the same criticism: it came directly, in fact, from Sir William Hamilton.[2] Bain's account of volition in *Mental Science* (a shorter edition of his two chief volumes on psychology) was much less simple.[3] It is curious that Bain, one of the most advanced psychologists of his time, made so few applications of psychology to rhetoric. Associationism, with its emphasis on mental processes rather than static faculties, would have had a very healthful influence on rhetorical theory in this period, and no one would have been better fitted to point out the relations than Bain. He failed to do so.

Regarding the types of composition themselves, Bain had, apparently, come close to formulating them some years before. In 1849 he had written a paper on rhetoric for a popular encyclopedia, *Chambers's Information for the People*. In his *Autobiography* he remarked that in this article "Description was for the first time made a distinct form of composition, having laws of its own. Exposition was carried out from the point of view of the logic of Science."[4] Later, when he came to speak of writing his *Composition and Rhetoric*, he said:

> Under the kinds of composition, Description for the first time found a place; and as it so happened that this lends itself to the enunciation of specific rules and principles, it was, in consequence, received by Professor

Masson and others as an integral portion of the department of kinds of composition. History or Narrative was
much less manageable, but, nevertheless, was amenable
to considerations that, when stated, could not be re-
fused. The topic of Exposition was also fertile in suggestive hints, growing out of the very essence of scientific
form. . . . It was the branch of Oratory or Persuasion
that brought into the foreground the more valuable and
ambitious portion of the ancient rhetoric. . . . The remaining department of Poetry was simply reduced to
definition, to which was added a statement of its leading
conditions (p. 279).

It seems pretty clear from this that so far as Bain himself was
concerned, he believed he was the originator of this particular
set of categories. The matter is not that simple, however. All
these terms had been floating around for years. Several rhetoricians had come close to putting them together in this pattern
before 1866 and one or two had actually succeeded.

Rhetoricians from the time of Aristotle have liked to classify and categorize; regardless of how widely they may have differed on their views of rhetoric itself, this tendency is perhaps
the one thing that just about all of them have had in common.
We need go back no farther than Campbell, though, in order to
trace the history of this particular set of abstractions. Campbell
seems to have been the first to make a clear division of types of
discourse according to the mental faculty to which each was
addressed. His fourfold division was into compositions that en-
lightened the understanding, pleased the imagination, moved
the passions, or influenced the will (p. 23). Though he mentioned "narration, description, argumentation" in the introduction to the *Philosophy of Rhetoric*, it was just a passing reference
in a discussion of prose and poetry (p. 18); the terms were not
made formal types of composition in the text of the book. It
might be remarked that Lord Kames earlier in the eighteenth
century had had a chapter on narration and description, though
he had treated them as parts of particular literary types, history
and epic.[5] Campbell seems to have laid the real groundwork,

however, by distinguishing different kinds of composition according to purpose. Blair mentioned that the purposes of eloquence are to instruct, to please, or to persuade (pp. 316–317), but this was probably no more than a variation of Cicero's and Quintilian's formula of proving (or informing), winning sympathy, and moving.

The American rhetorician Samuel Newman stated in 1827 in his *Practical System of Rhetoric* that "Writings are distinguished from each other, as didactic, persuasive, argumentative, descriptive and narrative. These distinctions have reference to the object, which the writer has primarily and principally in view." Newman's "didactic" is what later would be called exposition: "Didactic writing, as the name implies, is used in conveying instruction; the common text-books used in a course of education are examples" (p. 28). The distinction Newman made between persuasion and argumentation was Blair's—persuasion aims at inducing action through the will, argumentation tries merely to convince the understanding. Bain, it will be remembered, used the term persuasion rather than argumentation, but the question of which to use—or whether, like Newman, to use both—was not settled finally until the opening years of the twentieth century. In effect, Newman anticipated Bain by some forty years; the important thing, however, is that the classification did not take hold in 1827 but was delayed until the seventies.

In his *Aids to English Composition* (1844) Richard Green Parker had the same categories as Newman but he added one more—the pathetic (pp. 300–301). Henry Day six years later listed explanation, argumentation, excitation, and persuasion as the ends of all discourse, and among the processes of explanation he included both narration and description.[6] Quackenbos in the *Advanced Course* (1854) said that "The parts of composition, whether Prose or Poetry, are five; Description, Narration, Argument, Exposition, and Speculation. Either of these may separately constitute the bulk of a written production; or, they may all, as is frequently the case, enter, in a greater or less degree, into the same composition" (p. 348). He did not consider them as separate species, as was the tendency later, but as constituent parts. His "Exposition" seems, from his definition of it, to have been the same as Newman's "didactic": "*Exposition* consists in explaining the meaning of an author, in defining terms, setting forth an abstract subject in its various relations, or presenting doctrines, precepts, principles, or rules, for the purpose of instructing others." He cited a treatise on grammar as an example. Speculation was defined as "the expression of theoretical views not as yet verified by fact or practice." He did not distinguish between argument and persuasion, merely saying that argument is a statement of reasons for or against a proposition, "made with the view of inducing belief in others" (p. 354). Boyd's *Elements of English Composition* (1860) contained a sort of omnibus list including description, narration, letters, essays and dissertations, orations, arguments, and poetry (pp. 301 ff.); it is evidence of the fact that these terms were in the air, and all that was needed was an influential writer who would form them into a system and give them currency. The man was Bain.

The first American rhetorician after Bain to make use of this division of forms of discourse seems to have been A. D. Hepburn in his *Manual of English Rhetoric* (1875). Since Hepburn defined rhetoric as "the Science of the Laws and Forms of Prose" (p. 13), he of course omitted Bain's separate heading for poetry; he also substituted argumentation for persuasion. He did not anywhere admit any indebtedness to Bain—few writers of the period felt any strong compulsion to acknowledge borrowings—though his extended treatment of the paragraph was prima-facie evidence that he knew Bain's book and had drawn on it. "The matter of discourse," wrote Hepburn, "is of different kinds. In communicating knowledge, we may have an object to describe, an event to narrate, a general notion to explain, or a proposition to prove. Description, Narration, Exposition, and Argumentation are therefore the elements, or elementary forms, of all discourse. . . . These elements are combined in different ways and modified according to the purpose of the writer" (p. 24). From these modifications arise various classes of prose: dialog and epistolary, didactic, historical, and oratorical. Of the four main divisions of Hepburn's book, the third was given entirely to the four elementary forms, description, narration, exposition, argumentation. Whereas Bain had made his distinctions among the forms on the basis of the mental faculties addressed, Hepburn classified them according to "the objects of thought."

> The objects of thought can be reduced to two classes; viz., individual objects and general notions.
>
> Individual objects are of two kinds. Either they are simultaneous wholes; i.e., those whose parts exist at the same time, whether individual things existing, or conceived to exist in space; as, this tree, house, etc.; or particular mental states and qualities of which we get a knowledge by consciousness;—or they are successive wholes; i.e., those whose parts are not presented as existing at one time, but which arise in successive periods of time; as, for example, a storm, a battle, the life of a man—in general, all changes in the internal and the external world.
>
> General notions are formed by comparison and generalization; they have no one object precisely corresponding to them, but are applicable to an indefinite number of objects; as, tree, man, house.
>
> We may consider individual and general notions in themselves, or we may endeavor to show that two or more of them are related (p. 162).

In direct correspondence to this classification, said Hepburn, we have the four elementary forms of discourse: "1. Description, or the exhibition in language of the parts of a simultaneous whole. 2. Narration, or the exhibition of the parts of a successive whole. 3. Exposition, consisting in the explication of general notions and propositions formed from them. 4. Argumentation, by which the truth or falsehood of a proposition is evinced." He added that "There can be no connected discourse without one or more of these forms. In a composition in which several of them enter, one will predominate, giving character to the whole" (pp. 162–163). He then took up each of the forms separately and in considerable detail, with rules and suggestions for style, organization, variations according to specific subject, etc.

Among the other earlier American rhetoricians, only one included the four forms of discourse after the plan of Bain. He was D. J. Hill, in *The Science of Rhetoric*, which appeared in 1877, two years after Hepburn's book. Hill was not an original thinker; his *Elements of Logic* (1883)[7] was simply a revision of Jevons' *Logic*, and his *Elements of Psychology* (1888)[8] leaned heavily on Bain, Maudsley, Sully, Spencer, and a host of other writers. The same was true of his two books on rhetoric. The *Elements of Rhetoric and Composition*, which came out a year after *The Science of Rhetoric*, was a very derivative book, being heavily indebted to Blair, Campbell, and the older writers in general. The *Science* showed evidence of an acquaintance with Bain in the classification adopted for figures of speech, though Hill announced it as if it were an original idea. The discussion of the paragraph in this book might have been drawn from either Bain or Hepburn; but there can be little doubt that Hill's discussion of the forms of discourse came from Hepburn, though again no admission of indebtedness was made.

Like Hepburn, Hill used the term argumentation instead of Bain's persuasion, but the significant fact is that Hill adopted Hepburn's classification according to kinds of ideas. "All our ideas," said Hill, "may be distributed under two heads: (1) ideas of individual objects; and (2) general notions." Then he went on to give exactly the same explanations that Hepburn had given (pp. 73–74). It must be said that Hill's statement of these classes of ideas and of their corresponding forms of discourse was somewhat neater and more precise than Hepburn's, and his subsequent discussions of each of the forms were recommended by a very exact categorizing of subtypes and by numerous "laws" stated with great assurance. It is possible, therefore, that Hill had more to do with the later popularity of the four forms than Hepburn—there is no evidence that Hepburn's book was ever reprinted, whereas Hill's was reissued at least twice, once in 1883 and again in 1905. Bain's direct influence continued, of course, since his book was widely used as a text in America; many of the later formulations, in fact, used Bain's heading of persuasion instead of Hepburn's and Hill's argumentation.

In the books of the middle period—late 1870s to early 1890s—Bain's classification still did not win out clearly, though it appeared in one form or another in several influential books, and some of the headings were found in nearly all the texts. Wendell was alone in not offering any system of classification. Jameson, Coppens, and Kellogg used more or less traditional categories; Coppens, for instance, listed epistolary composition, narration, description, essays, dialogs, novels, history, and poetry. Hunt in *The Principles of Written Discourse* had a scheme based on Hamilton's theory of mind: intellectual (including exposition and argumentation), emotional, and persuasive (p. 209). Gilmore and McElroy adopted more or less exactly Henry N. Day's rather complex system. McElroy, for example, divided discourse by form into prose and poetry; by character into oratory, representative discourse, romance, and poetry; and by purpose into explanatory, argumentative, excitatory, and persuasive.[9] Much of this was also in Gilmore, though he mentioned that representative discourse includes description, narration, and exposition (pp. 19–21). Both followed Day quite closely in saying that the processes of explanation (Gilmore called it "enlightenment") are definition, description, narration, analysis, exemplification, and comparison.[10]

A. S. Hill had sections on narration and description, and on argumentative composition, with persuasion as a subhead under the latter.[11] The difference between argument and persuasion is that argument appeals to the understanding, and persuasion to the will through the emotions. Ultimately, of course, as mentioned above, this distinction goes back to Blair, but it received strong support in the nineteenth century from Sir William Hamilton's theory that the will (the object of persuasion) could be moved only through the understanding and the emotions, in that order. Clark listed description, narration, exposition, "Persuasion or Argumentation," and versification as the departments of composition.[12] He apparently considered persuasion and argumentation synonymous, though most others did not. Clark gave nearly a hundred pages to a discussion of these several types. Welsh's list was composed of description, narrative, exposition, and argumentation (pp. 178-209); his treatment of exposition was distinguished by an enumeration of the modes of expounding: definition; obverse iteration (a sort of reverse definition—showing what something is by telling what it is not); examples; illustrations; and inferences, applications, and consequences (pp. 191-194). In the nineties many of these were to appear as methods of developing the expository paragraph.

Genung's section on invention was composed largely of separate chapters on the inventive process as applied to five forms of composition: description, narration, exposition, argumentation, and persuasion. These are "the particular forms that invention adopts, as it has to deal with material of various kinds, and the extension and combination of these forms in the leading types of literature."[13] The different sorts of material with which these five forms deal are "observed objects" (description), "events" (narration), "generalizations" (exposition), "truths" (argumentation), and "practical issues" (persuasion).

Nothing particularly new was added in these years to the earlier discussions of the forms of discourse. The desire to classify and categorize was present—as it nearly always has been—but there was still no general agreement as to the system of classification to be adopted. The popularity and influence of A. S. Hill's and Genung's books, however, and to a lesser extent of Clark's, helped to give currency to Bain's scheme, or a modification of it.

It was in the 1890s that the "Forms of Discourse," either four or five in number, finally triumphed and became the dominant organizing principle behind most of the textbooks in rhetoric. Of some twenty-eight books that have been examined, dating from 1893 to 1906, only four made no mention at all of these categories. One of them, A. S. Hill's *Foundations of Rhetoric*,[14] was not properly a rhetoric but a book on usage; three hundred of its three hundred and sixty pages concerned words and sentences. The other three—Pearson's *Freshman Composition*, Carpenter's *Exercises*, and Newcomer's *Elements*—were based on a different plan of organization: the whole composition, the paragraph, the sentence, and single words, taken up in that order; Pearson and Carpenter applied Wendell's formula of Unity-Coherence-Emphasis to each successively. The whole scheme, in fact, was a variation of the plan used by Wendell in his *English Composition*. Scott and Denney's *Composition-Rhetoric* and Espenshade's *Essentials of Composition and Rhetoric* did not mention the forms of discourse in the text proper, but both had appendixes containing composition subjects classified under the forms. The second edition of *Composition-Rhetoric* also had a special appendix defining the forms of discourse, but it was, like the appendixes on versification and figures of speech, added under protest (see p. vii).

About half the remaining number of books listed five instead of four types of discourse, persuasion ordinarily being the fifth. This followed the plan of Genung's influential *Practical Elements of Rhetoric*. A fair representative of this type of book is William B. Cairns' *The Forms of Discourse* which, after fifty pages on style, gave the remaining three hundred to narration, description, exposition, argumentation, and persuasion.

A compromise between the four and the five forms plan appeared in Genung's *Working Principles of Rhetoric*, the 1900 revision of his *Practical Elements*. Genung discussed the usual four forms, but whereas in his 1886 volume he had listed persuasion as a coordinate head, in 1900 he divided argument into debate and oratory. His fundamental beliefs had not changed— he was merely changing terms and organization: "The literary type to which oratory predominantly belongs is the argumentative; but the imperative cast of its theme causes the argumentation to assume a modified, more impassioned character, which we term persuasion; instead of moving in the formal lines of logical reasoning it may on occasion have the tone and order of emotion and appeal" (p. 643). Genung added that oratory deals with truth that has a personal application—"it contemplates more or less nearly an outcome in will and conduct" (p. 643).

C. S. Baldwin, in his *College Manual of Rhetoric*, divided prose composition into "logical" and "literary," the former including under it exposition and persuasion, the latter narration and description. His twofold division was based on a distinction between

> composition for business, for those common ends which are the only concern of most men in writing; and composition for pleasure, for that expression of individuality which is the concern of the few and which is the impulse to art. The former, being ultimately determined by logical relations, may be called logical composition; the latter, being controlled less by logical relations than by artistic, may be called literary composition. The progress of logical composition is from proposition to proposition, and may be so measured in summary; the progress of literary composition has a different measure of its own. The former is covered by the rhetoric of the ancients. For the latter, since they had comparatively little prose composition, except histories, outside of the former, the ancients had no separate body of theory; but since in their principles of the drama verse is not considered as an essential element, some of the fundamental aspects of our second class are developed at length in the ancient poetics (pp. 1–2).

Baldwin cautioned that one should not think of these two classes as more than "convenient abstractions," since "Business and pleasure are not terms mutually exclusive, nor logic and art"; the distinction has practical value, however, in serving as a basis of discussion. Each of the two classes has a type and a subtype. "The type of the former class, the main business of composition, is persuasion, the winning of assent; but necessarily combined with this, and also appearing separately, is exposition. The type of the latter class is narration, story-telling; but necessarily combined with this, and also appearing sometimes, though not often, separately, is description" (p. 2). The twofold division, Baldwin admitted, had certain points of resemblance with DeQuincey's "literature of knowledge and literature of power," but he believed it differed from DeQuincey's scheme "in dividing, not literature by its effect upon the reader, but composition by the method of the writer" (p. xiv).

It will have been noticed that Baldwin substituted persuasion for argumentation in his list of the forms of discourse—he
was the only one at this time who did so. He defined persuasion as "that kind of composition which seeks to win assent. It
is trying to make you believe, or even act, as I wish" (p. 60).
This was the original and whole meaning of rhetoric, he
pointed out, and he added that in a sense it still included most
uses of language. "For the common concern with words is to
win assent and action," whether it is words used by an orator, a
travelling salesman, or a newspaper (p. 61). This appeal for
assent, he said, is to feelings or to reason. But even modern
psychology had not yet produced anything specific enough to
help one in knowing exactly how to appeal to feelings effec-
tively—"There is no art of human nature, nor any science."
The best way to acquire skill in this is through "sagacity, coming only by experience" (p. 61).

Baldwin attacked the usual distinction between argument
and persuasion—again, the only man who did so. Persuasion
may appeal to feeling and to reason, but we should not over-
simplify. "We are not so crudely twofold that it is easy to find
feeling without reason, or reason without feeling. Pure reason
is rather a notion than a fact of human nature; and all great
orators have acted accordingly. Feeling, again, hardly ever has
way among civilized people without at least some show of reason" (p. 63). In any event, he said, the distinction between
appeal to feeling and appeal to reason is impracticable since "in
most persuasion the two have always been inextricably com-
mingled."

> It is sometimes said that the object of persuasion is
> action; the object of argument, conviction. But convic-
> tion is not sought for itself, except in exercises purely
> academic; it is sought only as a means of persuasion.
> Outside of pure science, how many pieces are there of
> pure conviction without intent to persuade? Certainly
> the aim of argument is to convince; but it is not an
> ultimate aim, nor gained by a process sharply distinct in
> practice from that other, the appeal to feeling. Feeling

and reason are appealed to, not separately, but together; and all the means of appeal are included in the idea of persuasion. Thus argument is not something distinct from persuasion; it is a part of persuasion (p. 64).

The reason why other rhetoricians—and Baldwin himself—gave much more room to the materials and processes of argument than to those of persuasion was simply that appeals to the feelings could not be analyzed as completely and satisfactorily as those to reason. Thus most discussions of persuasion, regardless of the usual distinction between persuasion and argument, were based on an analysis of logical processes.

Baldwin's substitution of persuasion for argument was due in part no doubt to his wide knowledge of the history of ancient rhetoric, when the discipline was regarded as the art of persuasion. His familiarity with the works of the classical rhetoricians was unrivaled in this period. The second half of his book was a long "Appendix," which, while including suggestions for composition assignments, contained very full references to the works of the ancients not only to buttress specific points in his own theory of rhetoric but also to bring before the student the "ultimate sources."

The forms of discourse were found in other books in the form they assumed typically in scores of books later: narration, description, exposition, argumentation. Typical examples were Hale's *Constructive Rhetoric* and J. M. Hart's *Handbook of English Composition* (1895).[15] Scott and Denney, it will be recalled, reluctantly added an appendix on the forms of discourse to the second edition of their *Composition-Rhetoric*. It is rather surprising, therefore, to find evidence of the forms not only in their earlier *Paragraph-Writing* but also in the later *Composition-Literature* and *Elementary English Composition*. In *Paragraph-Writing* the types of paragraph structure were given as expository and argumentative, and descriptive and narrative. The same book classified types of student essays into descriptive, narrative, expository, and argumentative. In the *Elementary English Composition* four of the six chapters that made up the book concerned the four forms, and about half of the *Composition-Literature* was taken up with the same material. Evidence of how the four forms of discourse soon swept all before them is seen in the 1911 revision of *Composition-Rhetoric*, [16] where not only were they admitted without protest but they occupied some 250 pages—more than half the length of the book.

It is not possible to point with certainty to one particular man who was responsible for putting the types of discourse into their final form of narration, description, exposition, argumentation. Up to 1905 there was an almost equal division between writers who listed four forms and those who made a fifth of persuasion. It is likely that Baldwin's attack on the difference between argument and persuasion—even though he preferred persuasion himself—weakened the case for argument and persuasion as coordinate heads. Certainly the decline of faculty psychology had something to do with it too. Arlo Bates may have contributed to establishing not only the pattern of four forms rather than five but also to installing argumentation for persuasion. In his *Talks, First Series*, he had two chapters each on exposition, argument, and description, and four on narrative. Before these came a separate chapter entitled "Classification," in which he argued that persuasion has no place among the forms of discourse.

> Persuasion, in the strict sense of the term, is of course not a kind of composition, but a quality of style. An argument, an exposition, a narrative, must alike be persuasive to succeed in winning the reader. Indeed, persuasion is a quality essential to all art. In the sense of being that which leads others to submit their personality to the artist, it is necessary to painter, musician, sculptor, and architect, no less than to writer. As used to designate a department of composition, persuasion has been that which addresses, which appeals to the passions directly. The term is not a happy one, since it would seem that the vocative—the mood of address—might include denunciation, or invective or praise, as well as persuasion (pp. 123–124).

Bates attributed the presence of persuasion among the forms of discourse to an earlier desire "to provide a place of dignity for oratory." Earlier—"in the days of our forefathers"—oratory was held in high esteem, "and it was evidently felt that there should be a separate department for it in formal rhetoric. Persuasion as a division of composition seems to have been provided for oratory, much as a sinecure is established for a court favorite. . . ." Now, however, with platform eloquence out of fashion, exposition and argument are recognized to cover the whole ground (p. 124). Whatever this may reveal of Bates's knowledge of the tradition of persuasive rhetoric, it is likely that the argument helped in some measure to cast out persuasion as a separate form of discourse. Even Baldwin, in books published later in the new century, abandoned his fight for persuasion and substituted argument.

A by-product of the popularity of the four forms was the appearance of textbooks devoted to only one of them. One of the first, as well as one of the longest lived, was George Pierce Baker's *The Principles of Argumentation*, a revised edition of which came out as late as 1925. It was a massive work, heavily logical, and extremely careful in making minute discriminations in kinds of evidence, validity of witnesses, etc. Persuasion was the subject of a separate chapter, where oral presentation of the argument was discussed. Other examples of this sort of book were Gertrude Buck's *A Course in Argumentative Writing*, C. S. Baldwin's *The Expository Paragraph and Sentence, A Course in Expository Writing* (1899),[17] by Gertrude Buck and Elisabeth Woodbridge, and *A Course in Narrative Writing* (1906)[18] by Gertrude Buck and Elisabeth Woodbridge Morris.

Baldwin's little book was not very important, but the other three listed above showed several differences from the standard rhetorical doctrine of the time. They were based, it is true, on the forms of discourse, but Buck's interest in psychology and in the scientific method gave them a new cast. Her book on argumentation made a striking contrast with Baker's. Where his was heavy and formal, presenting to the student at the outset all the machinery of logic in systematic array, Buck (as mentioned earlier) helped the student to arrive at the essentials of logic inductively by encouraging him to observe his own mental processes. Buck's interest in psychology colored her definition of argument: "The act of establishing in the mind of another person a conclusion which has become fixed in your own, by means of setting up in the other person's mind the train of thought or reasoning which has previously led you to this conclusion" (p. 3). This should be contrasted with Baker's definition: "the art of producing in the mind of another person acceptance of ideas held true by a writer or speaker, and of inducing the other person, if necessary, to act in consequence of his acquired belief" (p. 7)—a definition that does not show *how* argument accomplishes its purpose.

The *Course in Narrative Writing*, by Buck and Morris, was distinguished from other treatments of narrative chiefly by its emphasis on the fundamental structure of narrative rather than on more superficial aspects of narrative style that grow out of this structure. The *Course in Expository Writing* had an even more individual character, which again was due to Buck's interest in contemporary psychology. Exposition was approached through description. The reason is something like this: Buck assumed the basis of our knowledge is sense-impressions. Description is a substitute for actual sense-impressions, presenting to others the way things appear to us. But sense perceptions are only the first stage of experience; as we reason about the impressions conveyed to us by our senses we begin to classify and relate them to the rest of our store of experience and thus arrive at a more complete realization of the world around us. In other words, we form the raw materials of sense-impressions into judgments (p. 56). When we wish to convey not merely the record of sense-impressions (which would be pure description) but our interpretation of or belief regarding these impressions, then we use exposition—which is still description, but serving another purpose. Such description "has ceased to be a final end and has become a means" (p. 63). It will often be impossible to distinguish exactly between description and exposition, since they are only different aspects of the same process; consequently, the methods of both are substantially the same: both develop from the general to the specific. It is perhaps because of the close relationship that Buck saw between exposition and description that she did not publish a separate book on descriptive writing.

Other new theories of description appeared in a special study by Frank E. Bryant entitled *On the Limits of Descriptive Writing Apropos of Lessing's Laocoon*,[19] another in F. N. Scott's series of *Contributions to Rhetorical Theory*. Like Buck, Bryant had studied under Scott at Michigan, and he showed the same interest as Buck in experimental psychology. Bryant believed that there are three main stages in the presentation of ideas: simple presentation; explanation or interpretation; and argument and persuasion. Description and narration fall under the head of simple presentation, and since they have nearly the same methods and purposes they often mingle. The only significant difference between them involves action; action is essential to narrative and not to description, though description may portray action "if the action is duly subordinated and does not bring about a significant change in the object" (p. 25). Bryant also agreed with Buck that description, being chiefly a type of presentation, is closely allied with exposition and indeed includes much that is commonly thought to be expository.

Bryant pointed out that description embraces all kinds of sense-impressions, not merely the visual. But experimental psychology had shown that there were great differences among individuals as to what sort of sensuous imagery they perceive most clearly.

> A person who is a good visualizer,—that is, one who sees the appropriate picture arise in the mind's eye whenever he hears the name of an object,—is naturally of the opinion that other people must be similarly constituted. The good visualizer finds it hard to understand how those who are without the faculty can think at all. Nevertheless there are many persons who have no visual images worthy of the name. They perform all their mental processes —remembering, thinking, imagining—in other ways. The differences in this respect are so marked that men

may be classified under various types according to the nature of their mental imagery. Some persons imagine chiefly in terms of sight, others in terms of sound, others in terms of muscle sensations, etc. (pp. 26-27).

A descriptive writer should be keenly aware of these differences, because they mean that no description using only visual images, for example, will be realized with the same vividness by all readers. To some it will be vivid, to others it will "do no more than to present information" (p. 30). The descriptive writer should, therefore, appeal to as many senses as possible, not only because of the heterogeneous nature of his audience but also because other psychological experiments had suggested that appeals to one sense reinforce those to another. Bryant cited William James's experiment in which bits of color so far off as to be unidentifiable had at once been recognized when a tuning-fork was sounded near the ear of the subject; inaudible sounds had become audible when various colored lights were directed into the subject's eyes. Bryant admitted that so far as he knew there had been no experiment testing the effects of different kinds of mental imagery on each other, but he believed the principle might hold true for images as well as for direct sense-impressions.

Lessing in the *Laokoön* had recommended a sort of progressive description, one in which there was some sort of motion; he had based this on his belief that language, which is a process in time, is better fitted to portray action than rest. Bryant agreed that movement is an important quality in most good description, but not for Lessing's reason. He suggested two others: "First, motion enters not only largely but almost inseparably into many forms of experience; and secondly, though this needs confirmation, most persons seem to be somewhat motor in imagination, and therefore ideas expressing motion are almost universally realized in their own sensuous forms, and in this realization bring up, at least faintly, other sensuous impressions with which they are very closely connected" (p. 31).

The other important limitation of description is one common to literature itself: the fact that, unlike the plastic and graphic arts, it must work exclusively by means of symbols. The reliance on symbolism has one great advantage, since it extends the scope of literature to include the whole range of human experience. But there are several disadvantages. One is that literature can never be as sensuously intense as other arts; it must present its material obliquely through symbols rather than directly through sense-impressions. Another is that the same symbol will not create the same image in the minds of different people; the image each person gets will be colored not only by the dominant type of imagery in which his mind works, but also by past experience and associations. If the descriptive writer has only to direct the mind of a reader to an object with which the reader is already sensuously familiar, the writer will not have much trouble: "writer and reader have a common basis in experience." Where objects not familiar to the reader are described, there will not be much difficulty if the object is simple. In other cases there may be real confusion. The problem is made more acute because not only are the images actually aroused in the reader's mind likely to be different from those the writer intended, but each image aroused may bring with it unrelated images that have centered around this image because of some fact of the reader's past experience. For these reasons literature—and description, of course—cannot compete with painting, for example, "in intensity and universality of impression," nor is narrative equal in these ways to drama heard and seen on the stage, nor descriptions of music equal to actually hearing music. The weakness "is found in the element of symbolism in the instrument of expression" (p. 35).

Description, therefore, "generally does no more than to convey the essential truth of the object portrayed" (p. 36). The image that is aroused in the reader's mind is not the same one that was in the mind of the writer; the two images share only essential characteristics. The power of description, however, lies in connotation: "Since every word calls up associations, a few well-chosen descriptive epithets and phrases may suggest a picture that seems as complete and lifelike as reality" (p. 36).

In summary, then, it may be said that the forms of discourse became almost universal in books written after the early 1890s.

In many they provided the organizing principle for the entire book or for a large part of it. There was a nearly equal division between books that listed four forms and those that listed five, the fifth nearly always being persuasion. C. S. Baldwin classified discourse into four forms, but substituted persuasion for argumentation; his defense of persuasion was based chiefly on his intimate knowledge of the tradition of persuasive rhetoric. Arlo Bates argued for four forms instead of five, but differed from Baldwin in preferring argumentation to persuasion. Both writers probably contributed in some degree toward establishing the formula that finally won out: narration, description, exposition, argumentation.

The reasons why the four forms became so popular toward 1900 and after were concerned chiefly with the narrowing of rhetorical theory and its increasing rigidity. Except for the brief period in the early and middle nineties when serious attempts were made to evaluate the teaching of rhetoric and to redirect it into more vital channels, the prevailing tone of rhetorical theory throughout the nineteenth century had been abstract and almost purely academic. When the Harvard Reports centered attention on superficial correctness and thus helped to extinguish the new and more fruitful ideas that were beginning to appear, the abstract tone quickly reasserted itself. Such convenient abstractions as Unity-Coherence-Emphasis and the forms of discourse were ideally suited to the purposes of instruction in a subject that had been cut off from all vital relations with other subjects in the curriculum and, in a sense, from life itself. They demanded no change in traditional habits of thought, they were few and easily remembered, and if one did not look at them too critically they had an apparent plausibility.

In the late 1890s texts began to appear that were devoted entirely to just one of the forms of discourse. The most interesting of these, the ones of which Gertrude Buck was either author or co-author, were distinguished by original thought and by an awareness of developments in psychology and science. The stimulating influence of Fred Newton Scott at Michigan was apparent not only in the distinctive character of Buck's texts but also in Bryant's discussion of descriptive writing, a discussion that attempted to modify the principles of literary description that had been established by Lessing and had been commonly accepted since the eighteenth century. Bryant's theory, however, like nearly all of the really vital ideas that appeared in these years—and there were not many—had no perceptible influence on accepted rhetorical doctrine. It was too unfamiliar, requiring too basic a reorientation of traditional thinking, to win any support. Besides, by the time Bryant's study appeared, rhetoric had lost all status; teachers of a subject that, in its debilitated form, was regarded as valuable only insofar as it could eliminate mechanical errors from freshman writing would not be a receptive audience for ideas that were either radically new or that questioned long accepted beliefs.

The effect of the forms of discourse on rhetorical theory and practice has been bad. They represent an unrealistic view of the writing process, a view that assumes writing is done by formula and in a social vacuum. They turn the attention of both student and teacher toward an academic exercise instead of toward a meaningful act of communication in a social context. Like Unity-Coherence-Emphasis—or any other set of static abstractions concerning writing—they substitute mechanical for organic conceptions and therefore distort the real nature of writing. Besides all this, they are an oversimplification, assuming that a composition consists of certain distinct ingredients that are, one might say, chemically pure, and that will be found to exist either in their pure state or in certain intentionally contrived combinations and proportions. Their dominance, especially after 1900, had much to do with maintaining the stereotyped character of composition instruction for at least three decades.

The Communicative
Function of Rhetoric

CHAPTER SEVEN

RHETORIC in its most vigorous periods has always paid close attention to the requirements of an actual audience. This means that language is regarded as the medium of human communication, and rhetoric as the art which shows how to make this communication most effective. The language itself, the organization of thought, the selection of material, the style, all these must be adapted to the particular audience being addressed. This awareness of an audience keeps rhetoric functional and vital. In times when the estate of rhetoric has been low, invariably the communicative function has been lost sight of, and the discipline has become the art of ornamented language, or merely an academic exercise. The great years of rhetoric in Greece and Rome were periods when rhetoric was used to prepare men to take an active part in public life. The period of the second Sophistic in Rome saw rhetoric reduced to the level of a school exercise or a vehicle for social display, in which ornamentation was the chief goal.

The period 1850–1900 in America certainly cannot be called one of the great eras of rhetoric, even though there was a brief flash of more vital activity in the closing years of the century. The subject was too heavily academic during most of this period to allow it much vigor. In no part of rhetorical doctrine can this be seen so clearly as in the matter of audience awareness—that is, the recognition of rhetoric as the art of communication. In the first twenty or thirty years after 1850, before treatments of oral rhetoric had become perfunctory, there was perhaps a somewhat sharper consciousness of the existence of an audience than there was later in the 1880s, though this consciousness was confined to a relatively few men and even with them it could hardly be said to have been a dominating principle.

Of all the earlier men, Henry N. Day probably had most to say of the necessity for adapting discourse to an audience. Day believed that oratory is the master type of all composition since it most nearly fulfills the essential conditions of discourse: "a mind addressing, a mind addressed, and the act itself of addressing."[1] The special law of oratory, he said, is "that it ever respect the mind of the hearer, and regard it as present to be influenced by the discourse" (p. 27). Therefore when Day gave instructions for selecting the general theme of a discourse he warned that four things must guide the selection: suitability to the mind of the speaker himself, to the occasion, to the mind addressed, and to the purpose of the discourse (pp. 45–48).

His classification of discourse according to its various ends—explanation, confirmation, excitation, persuasion—implied a purpose and the proper means of accomplishing it. This was especially clear in his sections on the last three of these, where a more pronounced reaction from the audience is called for than in explanation. In his discussion of style, he listed one set of stylistic qualities that are determined by the nature of the audience, though it is true that not much came of this because the idea of stylistic adaptation got lost among such abstractions as clearness, energy, beauty, propriety, tone. With so well developed a sense of audience in oratory, Day seemed curiously unaware of a communicative purpose underlying other types of composition. Poetry and ordinary prose ("representative discourse") he looked on as devoid of any intent to influence the reader (pp. 28–29).

Hope and Theremin, two other men who were more concerned with oral rhetoric than with written, showed a sharper audience awareness than most. Hope, agreeing as he did with

Whately that the important aims of rhetoric are conviction and persuasion, obviously had to keep an audience well in mind. Theremin had a chapter on "The Law of Adaptation" in which he considered the means of adapting a discourse and the justice of those means.[2] His strong ethical bias kept an audience in view through a good part of the book, but the effect was somewhat blunted by his desire to prove all aspects of oratory virtuous or conducive to virtue.

D. J. Hill in *The Science of Rhetoric* gave an appearance of stressing communication through his psychological approach to rhetoric—chiefly in the section of the book where he discussed the "Laws of Mind." In the introduction Hill said that discourse tries to produce some sort of change "(1) *in the mind*, (2) *by means of ideas*, (3) *expressed through language.*" Therefore rhetoric, the "science of producing mental changes," must take into account three sets of "laws": those of mind, of idea, and of form (p. 39). These three categories constituted the main divisions of the book. The long section on laws of mind, based almost wholly on Hamilton's neat classification of mental phenomena (knowing, feeling, willing), contained Hill's rules for influencing an audience. But the rules were so numerous, so abstract and academic, that they were useless as guides to actual practice. The real defect in Hill's theory was that he was not interested in communication at all, but rather, by expressing rhetorical principles and processes in terms of "mental science," in making rhetoric itself into a full-fledged mental science like logic, ethics, and esthetics and thus fit it more neatly into the prevailing philosophy of education. Another defect, for which one can hardly blame Hill, is that his scheme was based on an oversimplified account of the psychological phenomena involved in communication.

There were in these earlier books several discussions of audience psychology patterned more or less on the similar section in the second book of Aristotle's *Rhetoric*. DeMille, for instance, in *The Elements of Rhetoric* had a chapter on "The Desires" in which he distinguished "animal" (hunger, thirst, sleepiness, and so on) and "mental" (self-preservation, self-esteem, ambition, avarice, desire for knowledge). Each of the mental desires was discussed in a paragraph. The next chapter was on "The Affections," which comprise parental, filial, fraternal, conjugal; friendship, esteem, veneration, gratitude, patriotism, philanthropy; moral affections (concerning duty and honor); and religious affections. There was a third chapter on "The Passions," which were duly classified, and two more chapters on "The Literature of the Desires, Affections, and Passions," and "Forms of Expression Associated with the Emotions and Passions" (pp. 430-455). The management of this subject by Hope and Day was not greatly different.

This sort of approach was, like Hill's, plainly colored by the "mental science" theories of the time; in Bascom's *Philosophy of Rhetoric* the influence was even more apparent. Such treatments of audience psychology furnish a good example of the complexity of formal rhetoric under the disciplinary theory of education that prevailed in these years, as well as indicate how the learning of categories and classifications easily became an end in itself—these books were designed to be memorized and recited from in class. The application of all this complicated doctrine to a practical act of communication was never really made.

There was some talk of adaptation in several of the books, but not much came of it. Hervey, for instance, in his *Christian Rhetoric* had a chapter on "Adaptation" which opened auspiciously with a homily from Gregory the Great: "An instructor ought to consider what, to whom, when, in what manner, and how much he speaks" (p. 191). The chapter was concerned, however, with adaptation as it appears in the utterances of Christ, the apostles, and the prophets; with adaptation of a sermon to the letter and spirit of Holy Writ; and with a warning not to "adopt the prevailing taste as to *style*." The book of course concerned oral rhetoric, and the idea of a congregation was always more or less present; but Hervey seemed more concerned throughout with the preacher than with the preacher's flock. Hepburn in the introduction to his *Manual of English Rhetoric* spoke of the outward end of all prose (in contrast with poetry, which has none) (pp. 13-14); and he had a page and a half on adaptation of the discourse to the writer and to the reader (pp. 29–30). The subject was not brought up again, and there was no perceptible sign that it had influenced anything else in the book. Much the same can be said of D. J. Hill's *Elements*: a nod was given to adaptation in the first chapter (pp. 8–9), and no more was said of it. In the books of Quackenbos, John S. Hart, DeMille, and Haven not even this much was done. The whole subject of rhetoric was treated as though it were no more than an academic exercise and had no bearing on communication.

In the eighties and early nineties there was, except in two or three men, still no sharp awareness of rhetoric as communication; even in these few men, the awareness was blunted by an abstract and formal approach. Three men—Kellogg, Jameson, and Hunt—showed no perceptible consciousness of writing as something designed to be read. Jameson, in fact, even in his section on argumentation made not a single suggestion aimed at adapting such discourse to the nature and needs of an audience.[3] Coppens had a few paragraphs on the need for adapting one's choice of words to "the intelligence of readers and hearers" and to the subject, but he said nothing more. Welsh, Clark, and McElroy—in fact nearly everyone else who discussed persuasion, oratory, or argument—mentioned adaptation. This was to be expected, since both persuasion and argument were commonly looked on as oral forms, and oral delivery presupposes an actual audience that must be taken into account. Wendell's *English Composition* concerned only written rhetoric, and chiefly the stylistic aspects of that; but Wendell showed some concern for the reader in his frequent references to the effect a writer intends to produce. For example, it is on the basis of the desired effect that Wendell said questions of diction must be decided.

A. S. Hill's definition of rhetoric was "the art of efficient communication by language." Rhetoric "shows how to convey from one mind to another the results of observation, discovery, or classification; it uses knowledge, not as knowledge, but as power." Since it "implies the presence, in fact or in imagination, of at least two persons,—the speaker or the writer, and the person spoken to or written to," its rules are relative rather than absolute—"relative to the character and circumstances of those addressed."[4] After these remarks in the introduction, however, Hill did little more with the ideas. When he spoke of clearness in diction he did point out that a writer's language "*must* be understood," since "so far as attention is called to the medium of communication, so far is it withdrawn from the ideas communicated . . ." (p. 65). Besides this passage, and the section on persuasion, no more was said of the communicative aspects of rhetoric.

In Gilmore's *Outlines of Rhetoric* the sections on "Conviction," "Excitation," and "Persuasion" (based on Day) gave a number of suggestions showing that, at least in theory, an audience was being considered (pp. 55–91). When he spoke of "Choice of Themes" for discourse, one of the six requirements was that themes must be adapted to speaker, hearers, and occasion; they must, moreover, be adapted to each of these in four ways: physically, intellectually, esthetically, and ethically (pp. 28–29). The discussion was so brief, however, and presented so abstractly that little importance can be assigned it. Gilmore gave a little more space to adaptation of style—"the style varies with the theme, the audience, and the occasion" as well as with the individual writer or speaker (pp. 92–97)—and his detailed remarks on Clearness, Energy, and Elegance were directed quite often toward the effects these qualities have on a hearer or reader (pp. 97–138). Again, however, the approach was too theoretical to be of value.

Genung in his *Practical Elements* made more of adaptation and audience requirements than any of the other men. He defined rhetoric, in the first place, as "the art of adapting discourse, in harmony with its subject and occasion, to the requirements of a reader or hearer." He proceeded at once from this definition to a discussion of "Rhetoric as Adaptation," in which he emphasized the communicative function and steps that must be taken to facilitate it (p. 1). He spoke later of style as adapted to the thought, the reader, and the writer himself (pp. 17–19). His canons of choice in the discussion of diction were not Campbell's familiar Reputable, National, and Present, but instead "Accurate Use," "Present Use," "Intelligible Use," and "Scholarly Use." Of the third of these Genung said,

"The word must also be adapted to the reader; and in general the reader must be supposed not a learned man, but a man of average information and intelligence." He recommended, therefore, "ordinary popular usage" (p. 39). He had a separate section on "Diction as Determined by Object and Occasion," in which he took up differences between oral and written language (pp. 76-84). Figures of speech, which were viewed as devices to enhance effect, were classified according to a system based on effect—those promoting clearness and concreteness, and those promoting emphasis (p. 87). His chapters on argument and persuasion constantly referred to audience considerations. Again, however, as in the case of earlier writers, Genung's desire to erect a systematic theoretical structure of doctrine kept him fairly remote from a realistic appreciation of language as a social instrument.

There was, then, a good deal of talk about adaptation to an audience in Genung and Gilmore, some in A. S. Hill and Wendell, less or none in the others. Most of the men viewed rhetoric, consciously or not, as little more than an academic discipline. A good many of them, as we shall see, stressed the necessity for practice in writing, but the writing did not seem to be thought of as anything more than a school exercise. Even Genung and Gilmore, who on the surface seemed to see writing as communication, still organized their books around sets of abstractions or general rules that were to be mechanically applied. Gilmore, for instance, after insisting that style must be adapted, said that clearness, energy, and elegance are "essential to all good style" (p. 97). The manner in which he discussed each of these qualities may be judged from the headings of the section on "Energy": simple words, specific words, suggestive words, the smallest number of words consistent with clearness, such disposition of the parts of a sentence as will give prominence to the leading thought, periodic structure, euphemism (pp. 112-121). Genung did the same thing. For example, he did not use Campbell's tests for diction, but he substituted other abstractions of his own, each of which was followed by numerous rules. He said in the preface to his book:

Literature is of course infinitely more than mechanism; but in proportion as it becomes more, a text-book of rhetoric has less business with it. It is as mechanism that it must be taught; the rest must be left to the student himself. To this sphere, then, the present work is restricted: the literary art, so far as it is amenable to the precepts of a text-book and to the demands of a college course (p. xii).

It might be said that Genung and Gilmore gave lip-service to a purposeful view of rhetoric as real communication, but their actual discussions of rhetorical categories revealed a static, formalistic conception of writing. In spite of their protestations, they seem to have regarded writing as something that is done according to formula, and that is not directly connected with anything outside the rhetoric course.

After 1893 there was finally a general recognition that rhetoric is essentially the art of communication. The extent to which this function was recognized, however, varied a good deal. A. S. Hill merely repeated from his 1878 volume that rhetoric is "the art of efficient communication by language,"[5] but nowhere else in the book did he suggest that an audience was being considered. Genung, both in *The Outlines of Rhetoric* (1893)[6] and in the *Working Principles*, said a good deal about "adaptation," but never really came to grips with the problem of an actual audience. Cairns, whose two books were largely based on Genung's *Practical Elements*, did substantially the same thing. In the *Introduction to Rhetoric*, for instance, he had a long chapter on "Language Adapted to the Needs of the Reader," but he spent a large part of the space discussing the subject under a set of stylistic abstractions: economy, clearness, force, ease, unity (pp. 49–71).

These books were not wholly typical, however. They represented an earlier period, and different ideals. The other writers faced the problem of an audience more squarely. Arlo Bates, himself a former editor and the author of several novels, realized the necessity for putting oneself in the reader's place. In the *Talks on Writing English, Second Series* (1901),[7] he said, "The first assumption in writing is a reader." The fact is obvious, he admitted, yet it was regularly ignored by untrained writers; and "many men of no small reputation not unfrequently go on for page after page without the smallest notion of the person addressed. They are pleasing themselves by saying things, but they are not considering any reader who will be compelled by irresistible interest to heed these when said" (p. 23). The first thing to be taught a class in English composition, he declared, is that someone is to read what is written. Everything the student writes should be aimed at some definite person or group, and preferably the other students in the class rather than the teacher. "The pupil should write for his peers" (p. 24). The advantage of this practice is that when a specific reader is being addressed, everything said centers around the problem of how to say it best in order to get the idea in its fullness across to this reader. In addition, it facilitates revision; the writer must put himself in the place of the reader and make whatever changes the reader might demand. The same attitude was expressed by Scott and Denney in *Composition-Literature*: "the beginner should form the habit of putting himself in the place of his readers" (p. 4). The testimony of half a dozen professional authors was quoted in support.

Scott and Denney in *Composition-Rhetoric* and Newcomer in his *Practical Course* stressed the need for interesting the reader, and suggested that subjects which interest the writer are likely also to be of interest to the one who reads. It was for this reason that not only these two books, but many others as well, suggested composition topics that were close to the student's interests. These topics were intended to lead to writing that the author himself would find attractive, and that would be attractive to his classmates who might hear what he had written. It was an attempt to put the writing of themes into a social context and thus give it purpose. A number of specific devices were suggested to heighten the awareness of writing as a social activity. A contributor to the *School Review* urged that more class time be given to reading themes aloud, preferably by the author himself, in order to make "communication to an audience of our fellows a real and vital thing."[8] Joseph V. Denney, as mentioned earlier, suggested specific phrasing of composition topics so as to create an actual problem in effective communication.[9] In the preface to *Elementary English Composition* Scott and Denney said that ignoring the social function of writing leaves the student "in the attitude, and the spirits, of soldiers who are firing their ammunition into the void."

> This is to reject one of the most powerful of incentives to good writing. If a pupil can be led to see that of two ways of expressing one of his own wants, one is better than the other because it is more readily understood by the particular person addressed, or because it is more likely to secure a voluntary hearing, he has a new motive for examining his English and for learning more about it. Presented as a means of meeting definite social needs more or less effectively, of winning attention and consideration, the various devices of grammar and rhetoric make an appeal to self-interest which pupils can understand. They will learn the mechanical and grammatical details of writing, will be careful of their oral expression, and will acquire, through willing practice, one by one the necessary principles of discourse just as rapidly as they come to appreciate the value of these things to themselves as members of society (pp. iii–iv).

One of the means Scott and Denney used in this book to try to bring about a social awareness was assignments in oral as well as written composition, thus creating situations where the student, actually confronted by a live audience, found out through experience how important it was to keep audience interest in mind. The section on written composition began with several paragraphs on "The Reader," where the student was told that principles of organization, selection of material, the rules of grammar and punctuation all are important only so far as they make what is being said more clear or effective for the reader (pp. 41–42).

This emphasis on the social aspects of writing was carried farther by Scott and Denney than by any other authors in this period, but the tendency seems nevertheless to have been widespread. Gertrude Buck, writing in 1901 on "Recent Tendencies in Teaching English Composition,"[10] summed up the changes that had taken place since about 1890. First had come a reaction against the inculcation of formal rhetorical precepts and the whole idea of making a student write merely to exemplify certain laws of discourse. This artificial motive having been done away with, there followed the attempt to find real motives. The result was the use of theme subjects drawn from the student's experience and observation, and the aiming of all written work at a definite audience. Buck herself, as a Scott disciple, was in complete agreement with the new plan. "Yet every schoolboy has interests, if one but knew them—interests which, however trivial they may be in the teacher's eyes, are to him and his spiritual peers worth communicating. There is a real demand somewhere for the experiences which he is eager to impart. And until this supply and this demand are brought into relations with each other, there can be no genuine writing" (p. 374). The old system, which had stuffed the student with rhetorical formulas, had left him with "no particular desire to 'produce an effect of vivacity' on some unspecified and unimagined audience," nor had it given him an "insatiable longing" to write a paragraph having unity, coherence, and proportion (p. 376).

> The trend of every recent reform in composition-teaching has been toward a responsible freedom for the process of writing—a freedom from laws apparently arbitrary and externally imposed, a responsibility to the law of its own nature as a process of communication. Thus free and thus responsible, composition becomes for the first time a normal act, capable of development practically unlimited. The initial movement has been made toward teaching the student, in any genuine sense of the words, to write (p. 382).

There was, then, after about 1893 a consciousness that writing is not—or should not be—done in a social vacuum. The causes for this sudden awareness were several. It was to a considerable extent a reaction against the formal rhetoric of the earlier periods that looked less toward actual written production than toward memorizing laws of discourse to discipline the mental powers. The very practical character that education assumed in the nineties led to a more realistic view of rhetorical training, one that contemplated skill in writing for practical purposes. At the same time, the vastly increased amount of composition work demanded of students in this period made a more effective sort of motivation desirable; an obvious solution was to give writing a social context. Finally, the new study of pedagogy, with its interest in educational psychology, exerted an influence in this direction by stressing the importance of student interest. Hence textbook authors proposed theme subjects that were likely to be interesting to the student who wrote and to the students who heard what he had written. The intention was to make composition a purposeful activity.

Buck, when she listed the reforms that had taken place in the nineties, seemed to be speaking not only of rhetorical theory as it appeared in textbooks and periodical articles, but of rhetorical practice in the classroom as well. The somewhat hortatory tone of her article suggested, however, that these reforms were not yet complete in practice. There is no way of knowing for certain how far the average teacher of the nineties changed his methods of teaching and his whole attitude toward rhetoric under the impetus of the reform movement. It seems fairly safe to assume that sometimes he did, for there was a very genuine enthusiasm that accompanied the developments of these years.

Unfortunately, the enthusiasm did not last. At the very time when it was at its height, the "Four Forms of Discourse" were beginning to take on their final shape and become the organizing principle of textbooks and of composition courses. The "Four Forms," with their emphasis on mechanism and their isolation from a social context, were inimical to communicative rhetoric. So, for that matter—and for much the same reasons—was the Unity-Coherence-Emphasis formula that rose to prominence at the same time. Thus, when the fervor of the reform movement had passed, as it did about the turn of the century, rhetoric as communication began to decline. Once more the subject became academic, formal, and routinized; once more it was cut off from its vital function as the art that helps men communicate with each other.

The Paragraph

CHAPTER EIGHT

AS A SPECIFIC instance of the development of an item of rhetorical doctrine, the paragraph has unusual interest. It was first introduced into rhetorical theory during the period being considered here; it was amplified and refined upon until it assumed the proportions of a major category; and finally, after having been inflated to an importance beyond what was actually justified, it became stereotyped and rigid. Nothing new has been added to paragraph theory since the crest of its vogue in the 1890s, all later writers simply copying or paraphrasing the discussions of the paragraph in earlier books. It is, in this respect, an excellent example of what has happened to rhetorical theory generally since the end of the last century.

E. H. Lewis, in his *History of the English Paragraph* (1894),[1] the only historical study ever made of the subject, pointed out that English prose writers from the time of Tyndale had in their practice been more or less conscious of paragraph technique; in the writings of Sir William Temple in the seventeenth century the paragraph had already assumed something approaching its modern form (pp. 174, 172). As a distinct rhetorical category, however, the paragraph was not recognized until more than two centuries later. There was no mention of it made by Blair, Campbell, or Whately, nor by any other rhetorician until after the middle of the nineteenth century. This is remarkable, since a number of eighteenth century prose writers

(Addison and Swift, for example) were often meticulous in their paragraphing, relying on it in fact almost as much as on diction and sentence structure to achieve stylistic effects. The popular prose writers of the mid-nineteenth century, however—such men as Macaulay, Newman, Carlyle—with their fondness for a carefully patterned prose style, created a type of paragraph having such an obvious structure that recognition of the paragraph as a rhetorical unit was inevitable.

In 1861 Joseph Angus, an examiner in English language and literature at the University of London, included a brief discussion of the paragraph in his *Handbook of the English Tongue.*[2] Angus' remarks were not very systematic, and the whole discussion lacked focus; but it is plain from the numerous examples he quoted that he had arrived at his conclusions, tentative though they were, by an inductive study of actual paragraphs. Unlike later writers on the subject, Angus made no attempt to legislate, to lay down hard and fast rules; instead, he merely reported what he had observed. His definition of a paragraph illustrates this tentative approach: "A paragraph is a combination of sentences, intended to explain, or illustrate, or prove, or apply some truth; or to give the history of events during any definite portion of time, or in relation to any one subject of thought" (p. 401). The only major requirement for paragraphs, he said, is unity, which is as necessary to them as to sentences, though paragraph unity is "more comprehensive."

Also present was the germ of the topic sentence theory: "Properly a paragraph has *one* theme, which may be stated in the margin, or at the beginning, or at the close, or at both beginning and close: or which may be implied only and not stated" (p. 401). A paragraph having no one theme to discuss is not, Angus said, properly a paragraph at all, since it lacks the essential quality of a paragraph—unity. Angus offered numerous examples of paragraphs with the topic sentence in various positions—sentences quoted from Macaulay, Carlyle, Burke, and various writers of sermons. He gave no systematic list of modes by which paragraphs may be developed—these appeared a few years later—though he did quote several paragraphs that had been developed in particular ways: expansion

of topic sentence, illustration, combination of proof and illustration, "showing the results of the contrary," and a few others
less definite. He concluded his discussion with a few words
on various methods of connecting paragraphs—logical order
of thought, restatement of theme, connecting words, etc.—
together with examples of these devices.

Five years after the appearance of Angus' book, Alexander
Bain published his *English Composition and Rhetoric*. In his
Autobiography, Bain claimed that in this textbook both the
sentence and the paragraph "were elaborated upon first principles."[3] There was, actually, very little in his treatment of the
sentence that was new, the discussion being based mainly on
Blair and Campbell; the paragraph, which Bain said "had not
hitherto been even named as a department of Rhetoric,"[4] contained many of the observations that Angus had made earlier,
but they were presented much more fully and systematically.
Whether or not Bain drew on Angus' earlier discussion would
be difficult to say; there are no exact verbal parallels, and certainly the British prose writers of the time had furnished a
wealth of data that anyone might suddenly recognize and draw
conclusions from. At any rate, it was customary later in the
century to give Bain the credit for being the first to discuss
the paragraph systematically.[5]

From the examples quoted in the *English Composition and
Rhetoric*, it seems probable that Bain had, like Angus, studied
actual paragraphs and deduced certain typical traits from them.
He differed from Angus, however, in the way he stated the
results of his observations. Bain offered no tentative deductions;
he laid down hard and fast rules. Defining the paragraph tersely
as "a collection of sentences with unity of purpose," he presented six rules for paragraph construction: 1) each sentence
within the paragraph must have a clear bearing on what has
gone before; 2) parallel construction should be used for consecutive sentences expressing parallel thought; 3) "The opening
sentence, unless so constructed as to be obviously preparatory,
is expected to indicate with prominence the subject of the paragraph"; 4) each paragraph should be "consecutive"—that is,
each sentence should have its proper place in the paragraph;

5) the paragraph should have unity; and 6) "a due proportion should obtain between principal and subordinate statements." Each of these rules was explained and illustrated (pp. 142-152).

These six rules were of the greatest importance in the subsequent development of paragraph theory; most later speculation on the subject was based directly on Bain's statements and reflected their limitations as well as their virtues. Most of the rules, if one discounts the unequivocal expression of them, are rhetorically sound; but an examination of them will show that they pertain primarily to one sort of paragraph only—the expository paragraph developed on a logical pattern. This is especially clear in the third rule, which has furnished the basis for a great deal of dogmatizing on topic sentences. Why Bain chose to insist that every paragraph must have a topic sentence, and why this sentence must nearly always come at the beginning, is a little difficult to understand. Certainly contemporary writing offered plenty of examples of topic sentences placed elsewhere—and even omitted; Angus had had no trouble in finding instances.

Bain was, however, characteristically a dogmatic writer. He nearly always preferred to express himself categorically, seldom allowing any latitude for other interpretations. As for his obvious preference for the logical expository type of paragraph, perhaps as reasonable an explanation as any is that he was a professor of logic at the University of Aberdeen and would perhaps have had a bias for the sort of writing that proceeds from one logical proposition to the next in orderly fashion. Be that as it may, Bain's rules, as E. H. Lewis remarked, were instrumental not only in encouraging the belief that the sort of paragraph that opens with a topic sentence is "the only right kind," but also in causing composition teachers to advocate particularly the logical expository paragraph and to slight or belittle other sorts.[6]

Soon after the appearance of Bain's book in 1866, the paragraph began to be included in American rhetoric texts. In 1874 Swinton mentioned it in his *School Composition*, though briefly (p. 68). A year later Hepburn's *Manual of English Rhetoric* devoted an entire chapter to the subject, treating it in a manner which clearly suggested the later developments of paragraph doctrine in the 1890s. Hepburn defined the paragraph as "A connected series of sentences containing the development of a single topic. . . ." The laws governing the paragraph were listed as unity, continuity, proportion, and variety (pp. 147-153)—a list that seems quite obviously adapted from Bain's rules, though it is true Bain had not included variety. Hepburn also included the topic sentence theory but allowed much more latitude than Bain: though it is usually wise to state the theme of a paragraph "in a brief sentence toward the beginning," it may, in some cases, be left to the reader to infer; furthermore, it may appear sometimes at the end instead of the beginning, or to gain emphasis it may even be repeated at the end (p. 153). Hepburn's most important contribution, from the standpoint of later development of paragraph doctrine, was his theory that the paragraph "may be regarded as a discourse in miniature," so that the same laws that apply to construction of paragraphs apply also to construction of whole compositions (p. 147). This idea was used in the 1890s to justify a whole philosophy of composition instruction that made the paragraph the center of attention.

In *The Science of Rhetoric* (1877) D. J. Hill included several pages on the paragraph under the heading of "The Combination of Sentences." He did not offer a definition but did give several rules to conserve the "interpreting power" of the reader: progressive development, explicit reference, and a "theme," which may be either stated at the beginning or merely implied (pp. 198-202). Hill discussed the paragraph in more detail in the *Elements* the following year. Here there was a definition: "A paragraph is a group of sentences that are closely related in thought" (p. 71)—another variation on Bain's definition. The rules were about the same as in Hill's earlier book, though this time "variety" was added. Several examples were given of different sorts of paragraph development (pp. 72-77), though whether these were original with Hill or whether he borrowed them elsewhere cannot be determined. They included such methods as definition, repetition, contrast, illustration, etc.—a list that was added to later by other writers and that persists in nearly every discussion of the paragraph down to the present time.

After about 1880 the paragraph became an almost inevitable feature of composition textbooks, though for a time the amount of space given it varied considerably. Between 1879 and 1891 Gilmore seems to be the only man who failed entirely to mention it; his book, having been published originally in 1877, was of course untypical in other ways as well. Kellogg, Coppens, Clark, A. S. Hill, Genung, McElroy, Wendell—all these men gave more or less room to the paragraph in their texts. Hill added a new detail that was later made use of by Barrett Wendell: the same principles that govern the construction of sentences, said Hill, apply also to the construction of paragraphs. The principles themselves numbered three: the order of thought should be followed, the order of climax should be used, and important ideas or words should be given the most prominent places.[7] These again came from Bain; more interesting, however, is the fact that the first is really what Wendell later called coherence, and the third is substantially what he called mass (emphasis).

McElroy (like Hepburn earlier) made the point that paragraphs are compositions in miniature, and listed seven principles for paragraph construction drawn almost entirely from Bain (pp. 196–222). Genung's discussion in the *Practical Elements*, which Scott and Denney in 1893 called "the best that has yet appeared,"[8] stressed the composition-in-miniature theory, and insisted on topic sentences for most sorts of paragraphs. In cases where the use of a topic sentence would be awkward, the paragraph should still have "unity of impression," which may be tested by seeing whether or not the paragraph can be summarized in a single phrase or sentence (pp. 194–195). The laws applicable to paragraph construction are unity (this is the most important), continuity, and proportion (pp. 194–210)—identical with Hepburn's list, except for the omission of "variety." Genung did not propose to list all the possible kinds of paragraphs, but only those chief types where the purpose of the paragraph might cause basic differences in structure. He mentioned three varieties: "propositional"—the most common—in which "the subject is expressed in the form of a definite assertion, and then developed, by proof or illustration or some form of repetition";

"amplifying," frequent in narrative and description, and having typically no topic sentence; and finally, preliminary and transitional paragraphs (pp. 210-213). Genung's contribution was that he recognized and exemplified these different types of paragraphs which performed varying functions—something that no one before him had clearly done. In addition, he added to the accumulating list of terms that were applied to modes of paragraph development; his list, though not specifically introduced for this purpose, included such familiar terms as repetition, obverse (usually called, a little later, obverse iteration), definition, exemplification or detail, illustration, proof, result or consequence, enforcement (p. 199).

Barrett Wendell, who offered the fullest discussion of the paragraph up to 1891, also presented new theory. An entire chapter—one of eight in his *English Composition*—was given to the paragraph. Wendell, combining the ideas of Hepburn and A. S. Hill, declared that the same principles may be applied to sentences, paragraphs, and whole compositions—even entire books. He was speaking, of course, of his triad Unity-Mass-Coherence. Most of the chapter was taken up with a detailed consideration of the ways in which these criteria can be applied to paragraphs. What he had to say of unity was not out of the ordinary—this had become a commonplace—nor was the discussion of coherence unusual: "A paragraph is coherent when the relation of each sentence to the context is unmistakable" (p. 134). Wendell's remarks on "mass" in paragraphs, however, constituted his one original contribution to paragraph theory; and it, unfortunately, turned out to be of almost no practical value. His principle of mass, it may be remembered, meant that the important parts of a composition should be so placed as to catch the reader's eye readily. Mass in paragraphs, said Wendell, is extremely important. He offered the following definition of a well-massed paragraph: "A paragraph whose unity can be demonstrated by summarizing its substance in a sentence whose subject shall be a summary of its opening sentence, and whose predicate shall be a summary of its closing sentence, is theoretically well massed" (p. 129). He cautioned that he might have shown "dangerous dogmatism" in this statement, and that "No principle of composition is anywhere absolute." When the application of this principle results in perceptible artifice, then "good use" is violated and the principle should be abandoned (pp. 130-131). He believed, nevertheless, "that to-day no writer can intelligently follow any one principle with more certainty than that which shall encourage him carefully to mass his paragraphs" (p. 134).

This theory of the "well-massed paragraph" was far too rigid and unequivocal to make it of any value in actual writing. It cannot be applied to all sorts of paragraphs; and even in those where it can be used, following the formula exactly would result in monotony of structure. The results of observing this formula too closely were the subject of a complaint voiced in 1913 by a professor at the Massachusetts Institute of Technology: "If a man has taught composition any time these twenty years, he is marked. You recognize his method as far away as you can read his work. To conclude a paragraph with a summary is for him as unavoidable as to expel breath after inhaling. His style crawls over the page like an inch-worm, constantly measuring its heels up to its chin."[9]

It is probable that Wendell did not seriously intend that his rule for paragraph mass should be followed literally. The qualifying statements he added seem to suggest this, and certainly his own paragraphs rarely exemplified the theory. Wendell was a rather glib writer and speaker, with a fondness for turning a phrase or giving the impression that he was reducing the irreducible. There is a good chance that the theory of paragraph mass was a result of this penchant. Nevertheless, his discussion of the paragraph did direct more attention to the subject and did emphasize that paragraphs should have some sort of planned structure.

Very shortly after the appearance of Wendell's book the paragraph entered into the period of its greatest vogue. Its central position in rhetorical theory can be dated from the appearance of the first large edition of Scott and Denney's *Paragraph-Writing* in 1893.[10] After this year it became almost impossible to find a rhetoric text in which the paragraph was not discussed in great detail. Carpenter's *Elements of Rhetoric and English Composition* and the *Introduction to Theme-Writing* by Carpenter and J. B. Fletcher[11] did not mention it, but Carpenter treated it in some detail in his *Exercises in Rhetoric and English Composition.* Cairns ignored it in *The Forms of Discourse* (1896) and so did Newcomer in his *Practical Course in English Composition* (1893). In the *Introduction to Rhetoric,* however, which Cairns published in 1899, the paragraph appeared; it was also seen in Newcomer's later book, *Elements of Rhetoric* (1898). In the *Talks on Writing English, First Series* (1896), Bates merely suggested that paragraph analysis is a more useful exercise than sentence analysis (p. 31); in the *Talks, Second Series* (1901), he remedied the omission and gave one chapter to the paragraph and another to the topic sentence. In other words, by the opening of the new century the paragraph had come to be one of the main staples of rhetorical doctrine.

The influence of Wendell was prominent in many of the discussions. Typically, writers who followed his lead took up sentences, paragraphs, and whole compositions, applying to each in turn the Unity-Coherence-Emphasis formula or some variation of it. Examples were Baldwin (in both *The Expository Paragraph and Sentence* and *A College Manual of Rhetoric*), Pearson, Carpenter (*Exercises*), Newcomer (*Elements*), Espenshade. The revised edition of A. S. Hill's *Principles of Rhetoric* (1895) gave more space to the paragraph than the earlier edition had done, and this time Hill's abstractions that governed style (Clearness, Force, Ease, Unity) were applied specifically to the paragraph (pp. 230–238). It is likely that Hill got the idea from Wendell, who was his subordinate at Harvard.

The other strong influence in the paragraph doctrine of the 1890s came from Scott and Denney. Wendell and Genung did much no doubt to focus attention on the paragraph, but the idea of making it the center of composition training came from Scott and Denney—specifically, from their little book *Paragraph-Writing.* In the preface they said the aim of the book was "to make the paragraph the basis of a method of composition, to present all the important facts of rhetoric in their application to the paragraph" (p. iii). Their reason was that they had found the essence of learning to write lies in finding how to organize thoughts into units of discourse. There are three such units: the sentence, the paragraph, and the whole composition. The sentence is "too simple and too fragmentary" to be made the center of attention—practice in writing disconnected sentences is not very useful. The whole composition, on the other hand, is too long and too complex for the student to appreciate as a whole. In between lies the paragraph, ideally suited in length and difficulty to the purposes of instruction. It is governed by the same principles as the whole essay, yet shows them in small space so they may be readily detected and understood. The student has time to write more paragraphs than essays in a school term and therefore gets more practice in applying the principles. In the same way, the teacher can correct more paragraphs than longer compositions; and since the student is likely to make the same sorts of errors in paragraphs as in essays, the shorter unit may profitably be substituted for the longer (pp. iii-vi). (These one-paragraph themes recommended here fitted in well with the "daily theme" idea popular at the time.)

Scott and Denney defined the paragraph as "a unit of discourse developing a single idea. It consists of a group or series of sentences closely related to one another and to the thought expressed by the whole group or series. Devoted, like the sentence, to the development of one topic, a good paragraph is also, like a good essay, a complete treatment in itself" (p. 1). The main classes of paragraphs are the related and the isolated. The former is a unit of a longer composition, related to paragraphs on either side of it; the latter is a complete composition in itself. General laws of paragraphs are unity, selection, proportion, sequence, and variety; most of these terms had been applied to the paragraph by earlier writers—Bain, Hepburn, and Genung, chiefly—but no one had gathered them all together before.

The isolated paragraph was discussed under paragraph subject, types of development, effect of certain kinds of paragraph development on sentence structure, and types of paragraph structure. There was nothing particularly new in any of this. Scott and Denney listed the various possible positions of the topic sentence ("paragraph subject") and mentioned also that the theme of the paragraph may be only implied; but Genung had done this in the *Practical Elements*. Types of paragraph development were listed as repetition, definition, contrast, explanation and illustration, particulars and details, proofs, and enforcement (application); again, Genung had had most of these. The effect of paragraph development on sentence structure was something that had not appeared in just this way before, but the effects mentioned— inversion, parallel construction, repetition, subordination, punctuation—were all familiar items in rhetorical doctrine. A new turn was given to the discussion of types of paragraph structure by classifying these types according to the forms of discourse; hence Scott and Denney listed expository, argumentative, descriptive, and narrative paragraphs. The treatment of the related paragraph was also built around the forms of discourse, most of the section being composed of instructions for writing essays in each of the four forms.

Scott and Denney's contributions here were not, then, strikingly original in content; what the two men had done, however, was assemble and codify a considerable mass of ideas on the paragraph which now appeared for the first time in one volume. More than this, by urging the paragraph as the center of composition instruction they provided a sort of rationale for composition courses at a time when teachers, wincing under the strictures of the Harvard Reports, were searching desperately for some means of coping with an apparently insoluble problem. And as critics of high school and college English were forcing the adoption of the daily theme idea on the theory that more practice in writing was all that was needed, Scott and Denney's persuasive argument for one-paragraph themes fell on receptive and grateful ears. Here was a way for the overburdened composition teacher to survive with honor.

Scott and Denney did offer something new to paragraph theory in an appendix to *Paragraph-Writing*—a serious attempt to discover the psychological basis of the paragraph.[12] And in *Composition-Rhetoric*, which contained a full treatment of the paragraph, there was an attempt to establish a "kinetic theory of discourse" which argued that paragraphs develop organically from a germinal idea (pp. iv, 44). These ideas, however, though they might have done much to stave off or prevent the atrophy of paragraph doctrine had they been understood, were too new and unfamiliar to gain any acceptance or even to arouse any noticeable interest. The parts of Scott and Denney's paragraph theory that had the greatest and most lasting influence were those items that had largely originated with Bain and to which Scott and Denney gave a fresher expression and more attractive organization. Acknowledgments of indebtedness to *Paragraph-Writing* were almost a standard feature of rhetoric textbooks from within a year or two of its appearance up to 1915; as late as 1929, in fact, R. W. Pence mentioned it in the preface to his *College Composition.* [13]

But, like most pedagogical devices that have a wide vogue, the idea of the paragraph as the center of composition instruction led to abuse. People lacking the discernment and common sense of Scott and Denney carried the notion to extremes and forced paragraph doctrine itself into strained and rigid forms. A good example was Helen Thomas' *A Study of the Paragraph* (1912),[14] in which it was claimed that every paragraph is exactly like a geometrical proposition, consisting of the parts: given, to prove, proof, and summary. Even narrative and descriptive paragraphs were forced into this pattern.

Perhaps the most remarkable thing today about the theory of the paragraph is that nothing new has been added to it since the appearance of Scott and Denney's book. Looking through a dozen or so of even the most recent composition textbooks, one inevitably concludes that just about the only way in which one discussion of the paragraph is different from another is the particular examples quoted to illustrate development by definition, by example, by contrast, by repetition, etc. Definitions of the paragraph remain the same, the modes of development are unchanged, the same devices for paragraph transition are still enumerated—and in more books than one would expect, unity, coherence, and emphasis are recommended.

This curious atrophy seems to be the result of textbook writers' copying from each other rather than attempting to determine from good current writing exactly what sorts of paragraphs are being written, what their characteristics are, how they are being used, and so on. One gets the impression that these writers have been tied hand and foot by the older discussions of the paragraph, so that instead of approaching current writing with open minds, they examine it to find paragraphs developed by definition or comparison or details, and overlook those that do not fit the old patterns. It is this sort of uncritical preconception that has helped to freeze much of the American rhetorical theory in the form it had half a century ago.

It should be mentioned that in the 1890s a considerable number of rhetoricians began to include discussions of the whole composition in their books. In the earlier books the practice had been to consider words, sentences, figures of speech, and sometimes the paragraph, in that order. It is obvious that the authors of these books intended that complete compositions should be written, but they rarely gave any suggestions for constructing them. The chief exception was the rather frequent mention of the parts of an oration—exordium, division, narration, proof, etc. Genung in the *Practical Elements* gave some directions at the beginning of his section on invention to guide the student in organizing the material of a whole composition, but the first man to make a separate head of the complete discourse was Wendell in *English Composition*. He followed the order: words-sentences-paragraphs-whole compositions, applying to each in turn his "principles of composition," Unity-Mass-Coherence. Among the first to follow Wendell's example was G. R. Carpenter in his *Exercises in Rhetoric and English Composition*; he followed it exactly, preserving even the order that Wendell had used. In the same year (1893) Genung's *Outlines of Rhetoric* used this scheme of organization, though a chapter on phrases and another on style intervened between words and sentences. Genung did much the same thing again when he revised the *Practical Elements* in 1900.

A closer attention to the real nature of the writing process resulted in 1897 in a different order of these elements. Pearson's *Freshman Composition* in that year reversed the order, beginning with the whole composition, then taking up the paragraph, then the sentence, and finally individual words. Pearson was an instructor at the Massachusetts Institute of Technology, where he had found through practical experience that students could not appreciate the finer points of sentence and paragraph structure or the subtleties of effective diction until there had been some practice in writing entire compositions. As Arlo Bates said in an introduction to Pearson's book,

> In actual practice the learner does not write first words, then sentences, then paragraphs, and defer the attempt to produce a complete theme until he has mastered these. This is the manner in which he learns to speak, but when it comes to the study of composition as such, he begins by trying to make whole compositions,—often, of course, short ones, but complete as far as they go. Not until he is able to write simple themes with some proficiency is he in a condition to learn or to appreciate details. This every teacher of composition recognizes in actual school work; but, so far as I know, it is for the first time adopted as a theory in the following pages (p. ix).

Pearson's innovation was quickly adopted by a number of other men. It was found, for example, in Baldwin's *Expository Paragraph and Sentence* later in the same year, in Newcomer's *Elements* in 1898, Baldwin's *College Manual* and Scott and Denney's *Composition-Literature* in 1902, and Espenshade's *Essentials* in 1904. A. S. Hill's *Beginnings of Rhetoric and Composition* (1902)[15] did not discuss the whole composition, but the order of the other elements had become paragraph-sentence-word. This plan of beginning with the largest unit, then working down in turn to the progressively smaller units, remains the most commonly accepted pattern today.

The almost unanimous interest in the paragraph as well as the growing attention to the whole composition were evidence of a shift of emphasis in rhetorical instruction in the 1890s. Between 1850 and 1880, roughly, the emphasis tended to be on rhetoric for its own sake, rhetoric as a body of principles worthy in themselves of being learned without any necessary regard for actual writing. After the Harvard entrance examination in English had begun to make its effects felt—toward 1880—the emphasis was on rhetorical and mechanical correctness in the details of composition. In the early 1890s the ideal became, though temporarily, a sort of correctness of the larger units, correctness in the structure of the paragraph and the whole composition. This does not mean that mechanical correctness as a major aim disappeared. The Harvard Reports gave it a powerful impetus, and in the early years of the twentieth century the ideal of mechanical correctness gained a dominant position in rhetorical instruction that it has not wholly relinquished even today.

Style

ALTHOUGH the classical division of the rhetorical process was fivefold—invention, disposition, elocution (style), memory, and delivery—both in ancient times and later, rhetorical theory has gravitated chiefly around two poles: invention and style, matter and manner, substance and expression. In various periods in the long tradition of rhetoric one or the other of these emphases has been dominant, rhetoric usually being most vigorous when invention is stressed, and weakest when style is the center of attention. The rhetorical theory of eighteenth century England, on which so much of the rhetorical doctrine of nineteenth century American writers was based, was predominantly stylistic. Campbell, it is true, gave some space to invention, though more to style. The parts of his book that were most copied in the next century were the sections on usage—a stylistic matter. Blair, whose *Lectures on Rhetoric and Belles Lettres* was the most influential of any of the British texts, ruled out invention entirely on the grounds that it lies outside the scope of rhetoric. The emphasis of his book was, therefore, heavily stylistic.

A strong influence in keeping American rhetorical theory from being exclusively one of style was Whately's *Elements of Rhetoric*, which was at the opposite pole from Blair's *Lectures*. Since invention was, for Whately, the main concern of rhetoric, the popularity of his book was a salutary thing for American theory. Nevertheless, the emphasis in rhetoric texts in America to about 1890 was mainly on style; and even after that year, though treatments of style in the old sense tended to diminish somewhat in rhetoric textbooks, this was more because the field of rhetoric had by then become narrower than because the approach itself had been discredited. From 1850 to nearly the end of the century, the American writers argued endlessly whether invention is or is not a proper part of rhetoric; but they were unanimous in believing that about style, at least, there was no question.

STYLE

In no area of rhetorical theory did Blair cast a longer shadow than in that of style. Until nearly 1880 almost every American rhetorician patterned his discussion of the subject closely on Blair, whose definition of style—"the peculiar manner in which a man expresses his conceptions, by means of language" (p. 115)—furnished the model for nearly all other definitions. After about 1880 the definitions were rephrased a little more thoroughly, tending to become somewhat simpler and less formal. Genung in *Practical Elements*, for instance, after first saying that style is "manner of expressing thought in language," and adding that it includes giving thought "such skillful expression as invests the idea with fitting dignity and distinction" (p. 13), later offered a more compact definition: "Style is just the skillful adaptation of expression to thought" (p. 15). Essentially, this definition, though phrased differently from Blair's, represented a point of view that had changed slightly if at all.

Down to 1900, though to a somewhat less extent in the last ten years before that date, discussions of style retained the abstract emphasis given the subject by the British rhetoricians. These discussions were usually centered around the key terms found in Blair. It is true that the older classifications of types of style had nearly disappeared by 1850—only G. P. Quackenbos in the *Advanced Course* continued to speak of the dry, the plain, the neat, the elegant, the florid, and so on (pp. 262-267). Specific qualities of style, however, long remained a major concern of nearly all writers of the period.

Before 1880, during the years when formal rhetoric was flour-
ishing, Blair's list, or a variation of it, was an almost invariable
feature of American rhetoric texts. Quackenbos, for example,
in the *Advanced Course*, copied the list in full: purity, propriety, precision, clearness, strength, harmony, unity (pp. 270–
313). John S. Hart did the same thing but was even more literal
than Quackenbos, since he retained Blair's division between
qualities applicable to diction (purity, propriety, precision) and
those applicable to sentences (clearness, unity, strength, harmony—to which emphasis was added as a fifth) (pp. 68–86,
99–140). Hart, like many other writers in those years, did not
stop there. He went on to cite special properties of style—
sublimity, beauty, wit, humor—and discussed each of these
(except wit) in terms of numerous minor abstractions (pp. 188–
208). He also recommended special sets of abstractions to govern specific types of writing. News writing, for example, must
be characterized by accuracy, condensation, and perspicuity
(pp. 272–274). Oral discourses must have unity, adaptation (to
audience), and symmetry (p. 290).

Beginning about 1880, as the elaborate doctrine of the
earlier books started to go out of fashion, Blair's list of seven
qualities was superseded by Whately's shorter list of three:
perspicuity, energy, elegance. A. S. Hill adopted these terms in
1878, but changed the words to clearness, force, elegance.
Welsh, Genung, Wendell, and others adopted them as well,
though sometimes making substitutions as Hill had done. It is
important to notice that, in the first place, these terms meant
no break with the abstract approach to style—there were
just fewer of them—and in the second place, since Whately's
terms were based on the "mental science" view of the mind
(perspicuity addresses the understanding, energy the feelings,
and elegance the esthetic faculty), their popularity in the eighties and early nineties furnished another example of the persistence of eighteenth century ideas. There was in the eighties a
desire to simplify rhetorical doctrine, but not to change it
fundamentally.

Only one new idea appeared in the discussions of style in
American texts before 1880: Herbert Spencer's theory of

"economy." In the October 1852 issue of *The Westminster Review* Spencer had published an article called "The Philosophy of Style," in which this theory had been advanced. The essence of it is contained in the following passage from the article:

> Regarding language as an apparatus of symbols for the conveyance of thought, we may say that, as in a mechanical apparatus, the more simple and the better arranged its parts, the greater will be the effect produced. In either case, whatever force is absorbed by the machine is deducted from the result. A reader or listener has at each moment but a limited amount of mental power available. To recognize and interpret the symbols presented to him, requires part of this power; to arrange and combine the images suggested requires a further part; and only that part which remains can be used for realizing the thought conveyed. Hence, the more time and attention it takes to receive and understand each sentence, the less time and attention can be given to the contained idea; and the less vividly will that idea be conceived.[1]

To this rule of economy of the reader's attention Spencer referred nearly all aspects of style, from the choice of words (Anglo-Saxon derivatives are more economical of attention than Latin derivatives) to the use of figurative language.

Hepburn seems to have been the first American rhetorician to discover and make use of the theory, though in his *Manual of English Rhetoric* (1875) he merely listed economy as one of the qualities of style and quoted Spencer's article briefly (pp. 70-71). He did not elaborate on it. Two years later, David J. Hill, in *The Science of Rhetoric*, expanded Spencer's theory in great detail, devoting the last third of the book to the "Laws of Form," all of which he related to the principle of economy. These laws were discussed in terms of economy of interpreting power in plain language, economy of interpreting power in figurative language, and economy of emotions, the last being distinguished by an attempt to base Spencer's rule on Sir William Hamilton's theory of the emotions. As elsewhere in this book, Hill showed that his real purpose was not to formulate theory that would have a useful bearing on practice, but rather to erect a sort of metaphysical structure of principles and laws quite distinct from any application to actual writing or speaking. Hill's book probably marks, in fact, the farthest extreme to which the abstract approach to rhetoric was carried. Spencer's principle of economy, though a considerably more vital conception than most other abstractions popular in those years (it was, at least, audience-centered), was used by Hill merely as a device for rationalizing most of these other terms. The rhetoricians who followed did even less than this with it: they merely added it to their criteria of style as another term like perspicuity or harmony.

In the 1890s, as the field of rhetoric became narrowed to include freshman composition and little more, style began to take up much less room in rhetoric textbooks than it formerly had. The earlier books had typically been divided into two parts, one on invention and the other on style. It was still possible to find this sort of division in a few books after 1890, but they were not typical. Some books, such as Bates's *Talks, First Series* and Baldwin's *College Manual of Rhetoric*, still had separate headings on style, though these covered only twenty or thirty pages in contrast to the hundred or two hundred devoted to the topic in earlier books. Fletcher and Carpenter's *Introduction to Theme-Writing*, Carpenter's *Elements of Rhetoric and English Composition*, and all four of Scott and Denney's rhetoric texts not only had no division or chapter headed "Style," they did not even mention any of the usual stylistic abstractions.[2] The emphasis in these books was on substance rather than expression. In Scott and Denney's *Composition-Rhetoric*, for example, the chapter entitled "What to Say" was followed by one called "How to Say It," in which the old terms for qualities of style were replaced by a discussion of various types of sentences, choice of words, and "Imaginative Expressions." The last was notable for being a treatment of figurative language in which no individual figures were named. The whole chapter was focused on the effects that each of these several devices will have on a reader.

The majority of the books written in the last years of the century, though they gave less emphasis to style than had formerly been the custom, nevertheless kept much of the old abstract terminology. This was true not only of later books written by such men from the earlier years as Genung and A. S. Hill, but of men like Espenshade, Bates, and Newcomer, who were publishing for the first time. The old terms were usually brought in more incidentally (they no longer had a chapter devoted to each of them), but the abstract conception of rhetoric that they typified was still prominent in the minds of the writers using them. It was, again, the long shadow of the eighteenth century.

It has been suggested above that an important reason for the de-emphasizing of style in the rhetoric texts of the 1890s was the narrowing of rhetorical theory and the increasingly pedestrian nature of rhetoric instruction: when the study of rhetoric meant little more than the assigning and hurried grading of unending daily themes, there was little time or incentive to study any but the most elementary aspects of style, chiefly those that have to do with mechanical correctness. Another reason, however, for the lack of emphasis on style as a rhetorical category in these years was a result of the rise of the independent study of literature. As literature courses multiplied and assumed a secure place in the curriculum, the study of literary criticism became a staple in the new English departments. For a time, nearly all the men qualified to teach criticism were those whose training had been primarily in rhetoric; for several decades, in fact, the common practice, especially in smaller colleges, was to assign courses in rhetoric and in literature to the same teachers. As a result, courses in criticism simply expropriated those topics in rhetorical theory which had most relevance to the new study. Style, plainly, would have been one of the most attractive.

Winchester's *Some Principles of Literary Criticism*, which was really concerned much more with the rhetorical analysis of style than it was with literary criticism in the modern sense, is an excellent example of what had happened by the end of the century. More interesting in some respects, however, is T. W. Hunt's *Studies in Literature and Style*, published in 1890 when the transition was being made. Hunt tried in this book to

divorce style from the conception that regarded it as mere ornament, and demonstrate that style has intimate relations with the
substance of literature. Though in some respects the book is
quite similar to Winchester's, in another way it differs fundamentally. Hunt was a rhetorician who was trying to bring the
study of literature and literary criticism within the legitimate
scope of rhetoric; Winchester was also, really, a rhetorician, but
he had in effect turned the tables and annexed rhetoric to the
study of literature and literary criticism. As criticism broadened
and gained vigor later in the new century, it ceased to rely so
heavily on rhetoric. But rhetoric itself, narrowed and debilitated, was not only deprived of the vitality that closer relations
with literature would have given; it was not even able to reclaim
from literary criticism the concern with style that historically
had always been a rhetorical function.

FIGURATIVE LANGUAGE

Whenever in the history of rhetoric the stylistic emphasis has
been dominant—whenever, that is, rhetoric has been regarded
primarily as the art of embellishing language—figures of speech
have in such periods claimed a good deal of attention from
rhetoricians. American rhetorical theory almost throughout the
nineteenth century, though especially from 1850 to 1890, was
predominantly stylistic; it is therefore not surprising to find the
rhetoricians of these years much preoccupied with figurative
language. Like the discussions of other aspects of style in this
period, that of figures of speech showed little that was new.
It was based largely on traditional theories and was moreover
presented in the abstract manner of the British rhetorics. As a
guide to actual composition, most of this material was completely useless—a fact that was generally recognized toward the
end of the century.

Aside from the varying number of individual figures of
speech listed in the textbooks, there were three main problems
around which most of the discussions centered: the origin of
figurative language, schemes for classifying various figures, and
the function of figurative language. Through these forty years
there was, really, little basic disagreement about any of the three

problems—a measure of the generally uncritical attitude that these rhetoricians had toward the subject.

The usual answer to the question of the origin of figurative language was the traditional one advanced by Blair, though stemming originally from Cicero, from whom Blair had got it. Briefly, this theory was that figures of speech had first appeared in primitive times because of the poverty of language; later, in a more sophisticated era, when it was discovered that figurative expression gave pleasure, such language had been cultivated through choice.[3] The best and fullest statement of this theory was that of Barrett Wendell in *English Composition*. Figures of speech, said Wendell, are used well by two classes of people: savages, peasants, and children; and literary artists. Savages, children, and "untutored folks" have a limited knowledge,

> but what they know, they know pretty well. It is not often that they are called upon to recognize or to name any fact that is beyond the range of their daily experience. When they are so called upon, a double state of things arises: in the first place, the novelty of the idea they must name excites their interest, arrests their attention far more than would be the case with people who have new shades of thought a hundred times a day; in the second place, as the number of words at their disposal is relatively small, they are driven to describing this new idea in terms of comparison with something already familiar to them. And as the things already familiar to them are generally things that remain permanently familiar to everybody, their figures are figures that appeal to almost any human understanding they address (p. 250).

The effective use of figures by literary masters, continued Wendell, is due to the fact that these men, with their universal human sympathy and understanding, address themselves to the average man and therefore choose images that are meaningful to average people. Wendell believed that all writing "should on general principles be addressed to the average man,—not to this class or that." He found, therefore, that the literary use of figurative language is an especially clear illustration of the justice of this view, since "those figures which are obviously the best, and are admitted to be the best, are precisely those that people in general can best understand" (p. 258).

In devising schemes for the classification of figures of speech, the American rhetoricians showed both ingenuity and variety, though it was not till the nineties that anyone raised the question of the utility of such classifications. A common method of division was the one Quackenbos used in his *Advanced Course*: figures of orthography, etymology, syntax, and rhetoric (pp. 235-238, 246-252). DeMille, after citing eight different methods of classification used by earlier writers, found them all unsatisfactory and offered one of his own based on the "ends or aims of all figures of speech." These ends were three: clearness and illustration, heightened importance of the subject, and unusual emphasis (pp. 91-92). It turned out, however, that DeMille's classification was not so simple and logical as it first appeared, for the actual discussion ranged some 113 separate figures under such heads as "Figures of Relativity Arising from the Idea of Contrast," "Figures of Relativity Arising from the Perception of Resemblance," "Figures of Relativity Arising from the Idea of Contiguity," and so on. The discussion covered no less than eight chapters, the whole thing being an excellent example of the sort of metaphysical disquisition that later brought formal rhetoric into disrepute.

D. J. Hill in *The Science of Rhetoric* claimed that his plan of classification had been based on Aristotle's and Hamilton's "laws of association." He arranged figures into three groups: those of resemblance, those of contiguity, and those of contrast (pp. 203-204). As a matter of fact, this plan (which DeMille had also used) had been originated by Bain, from whom Hill made other unacknowledged borrowings as well. Neither Hamilton nor Aristotle had had anything to do with it. In his theory of psychology Bain had divided the powers of the mind into three categories: the feeling or sense of difference (discrimination), of agreement (similarity), and of retention (memory).[4] In his *Composition and Rhetoric* he arranged about ten figures under the analogous heads of similarity, contrast, contiguity, since he said they refer to the operations of the understanding or intellect.

He was left with about eight figures that would not fit into these categories. Hill, however, managed to get the very same figures (except "Innuendo," which he omitted) all under similarity, contiguity, or contrast. It was this scheme of Bain's that was to prove the most popular during the rest of the century. It was not until 1896 that Edward Everett Hale, Jr., had the temerity to write in his *Constructive Rhetoric* that this classification is of very little value to the student learning how to write. The classification of figures is of much less interest than their use. "The painter does not class his colors according to their origin, having the animal, the mineral, the vegetable in separate groups" (p. 251).

Among rhetoricians from the time of the ancient Greeks there had always been a general agreement that the function of figures of speech is to add ornament to language, a belief that carries with it the assumption that figures are external to the matter of a discourse and are added by prescription to gain an intended effect. American rhetoricians followed tradition in this as in most other aspects of style: nearly all of them— DeMille, John S. Hart, Day, D. J. Hill, Genung, Wendell, A. S. Hill, to name only the chief—believed figures are mechanical devices used to enhance thought. Even in the nineties, when only one writer (Newcomer) said plainly that he regarded the function of figurative language as primarily ornamental,[5] men such as Espenshade, Bates, and Carpenter continued to recommend the manufacture of figures in cold blood. "We must now glance at two mechanical devices for securing Force," wrote Carpenter. The first of these was "Emphasis or Climax," the second was figures of speech.[6] Similarly, Bates in the *Talks, Second Series* wrote, "In this search for comparisons the first step is to decide exactly what is to be the office of the figure. The exact point of likeness to be brought out must be entirely clear in the mind of the seeker, and with this as a measure he may try each idea which presents itself" (pp. 163–164). Perhaps the most explicit example of this approach was contained in Genung's *Outlines of Rhetoric*, where specific rules were offered to guide the writer in knowing what figures to use for what effects (pp. 149–153): "For trenchant assertion, use interrogation." "For illustrative value, use simile." "For vigor of conception, know the value of hyperbole." "For lively realization, use exclamation."

There were very few objections to this theory of the use of figurative language. One of the dissenters was Hepburn, who, in spite of the early date of his book (1875), often showed himself in advance of his time. Most rhetoricians, Hepburn said, thought of figures merely as ornaments to make a composition more pleasing; they "may be used or rejected at pleasure." Hepburn did not agree. Instead of being something that can be turned out on demand, figures "are the natural, and therefore necessary and universal forms, in which excited imagination and passion manifest themselves." It is true, said Hepburn, that figures are a departure from the normal unimpassioned forms of expression; but they *are* the norm of excited feeling (p. 93). Few other writers agreed with Hepburn.

In the early nineties, as rhetorical interest in style narrowed toward mere mechanical correctness, and as a large part of the machinery of the old abstract rhetoric was jettisoned, treatments of figures of speech were pruned drastically to bring them into line with the new emphases in education. The exhaustive lists and classifications of figures were among the first things to go. Such lists had reached their zenith, as far as American rhetoricians were concerned, when George W. Hervey, who felt that the subject of figurative language had been slighted by modern theorists, included in his *System of Christian Rhetoric* (1873) an appendix containing no fewer than 467 figures of speech. The other extreme was reached in 1897 when Scott and Denney in *Composition-Rhetoric* had the courage to point out that figures are not really essential to good prose style at all—"Many eminent writers dispense with them almost entirely." They added that "The only recipe for producing good figures is for the pupil to become deeply interested in his subject. If his mind is given to producing figurative images, the images will come unsolicited. If such images do not come of themselves, it is better to get along without them" (p. 223).

This was a more realistic attitude toward the subject than had so far appeared, though plainly it did nothing toward solving the essential problem of the nature and function of figurative language. The only serious attempt to do this was made by Gertrude Buck, who in 1898 received her doctorate of philosophy in rhetoric from the University of Michigan. Her dissertation on metaphor, prepared under the guidance of Scott, was distinguished sharply from all previous discussions of the subject by an attempt to use the data of experimental psychology in shedding light on the origin, nature, and use of this figure. The chief results of her studies were published in two numbers of Scott's series *Contributions to Rhetorical Theory*, appearing under the titles *Figures of Rhetoric: A Psychological Study*, [7] and *The Metaphor — A Study in the Psychology of Rhetoric*. [8] The latter, being considerably longer and more detailed, was the more significant of the two.

The purpose of her study of metaphor, Buck said, was to show, by means of data from contemporary psychology, that metaphor is not a mechanical device as rhetoricians had assumed but instead a "biologic organism." [9] She began by attacking the traditional assumptions that poverty of language had led to the origin of metaphor and that its widespread use was due to the human love for ornamentation. The contemporary British psychologist James Sully, she noted, had observed in his studies of child psychology that small children use a species of metaphor. One child may call any luminous object "moon"; another may use the term "key" for any small, shiny, metallic object; still another may call anything put on the head a "hat," even though it may be a hairbrush. Buck believed this same lack of clear perception and differentiation is the source of "radical metaphor" in primitive peoples, whose characteristically figurative mode of expression had been remarked at least from the time of the Renaissance. The primitive human, like the small child, is not conscious of making a metaphor; the two objects which he uses the same metaphorical term to cover are actually seen by him as one undifferentiated object. Psychologically, radical metaphor is "a survival from a primitive stage of perception, a vestige of the early homogeneous consciousness" (p. 15). Radical metaphor had not come, then, from poverty of language, but "from poverty or immaturity of thought." Two objects are at first seen indistinctly as one because of poorly developed perceptive powers. Later, as perceptions become more distinct, the two objects emerge as separate entities, and it is discovered that the term earlier used to apply to them both is "metaphorical." This conscious recognition of metaphor is, then, a sign of intellectual progress by the race.

> The perception of a radical metaphor, it may be said, is society's recognition of the fact that an idea has quite outgrown its habitual form of expression. When uttered the expression was sufficiently differentiate for the embryo thought; now the thought has grown into discriminations unrecorded by the word. The result is a tension within the expression itself which brings to light its diverse meanings and demands relief. This is accomplished usually by a gradual movement in the direction of limiting this word to one of its tugging significations, and remanding the other meaning to a different phrase (pp. 17–18).

The ordinary distinction that had been made between radical and poetic metaphor, Buck said, was that the former is more or less unconscious and the latter a conscious attempt to create a certain effect by substituting one word for another. Radical metaphor *is* spontaneous, she believed, though in a more fundamental sense than had been realized. Poetic metaphor presents a different problem, one not solved by the usual view of it as a device consciously employed for effect. Buck attributed the fact that rhetoricians had believed metaphor is used for effect on the reader or hearer to the tradition of rhetoric as persuasion—a view that makes effect on an audience paramount. Yet the metaphor that has been made solely for its effect on the reader is, she felt, different from the metaphor that seems to spring spontaneously from the writer's mind in the heat of composition. The difference is that between a theory of literature that aims only at effect on an audience, paying no attention to the fidelity with which the true ideas of the writer are expressed; and a theory that aims at what Buck called "communication," one in which both the conceptions of the writer and the needs of the reader are kept in mind. Theories of literature that are based exclusively on either the writer (self-expression) or the reader (persuasion) are one-sided. The communication theory is not. Both reader and writer are equally concerned in the literary process.

Buck attributed the origin of poetic metaphor to essentially the same process that produces radical metaphor, the only difference being in the speed with which the process operates. Radical metaphor is no metaphor at all for the primitive man who makes it; its metaphorical character is a later discovery by others. The same thing happens to a child in civilized society who at first, because of indistinct perceptions, makes "metaphors" but who in a few months is able to see the separateness of the several objects before named as one. The process is still more rapid in a civilized adult, who may momentarily confuse the separate identities of two objects but in a matter of a second or less will perceive the difference.

> The sophisticated modern, when he gives utterance to perception before it has developed out of the homogeneous stage, is making a radical metaphor just as truly as does the savage or the child. No two things are concerned in his thought, but only one. There is, in the ordinary sense of the word, no metaphor. The speaker has simply represented in words his own undifferentiate consciousness (p. 33).

A good example of poetic metaphor, said Buck, is the lines in Emily Dickinson's poem "The Snake" in which the poet says she saw

> . . . a whip-lash
> Unbraiding in the sun,—
> When, stooping to secure it,
> It wrinkled, and was gone.

"Her lazy impression of a something long, brown, slender and convolute," continued Buck, "had already separated out of its mass the idea of 'whip-lash,' with others, such as that of a snake, just stirring into consciousness, when, 'stooping to secure it,' of a sudden 'it wrinkled, and was gone,' so that the dormant idea of 'snake' sprang at once into full view and the figure was complete in which a snake is, according to the rhetorical dictum, 'compared' to a whip-lash" (p. 34).

Therefore, Buck concluded, poetic metaphor is merely the representative of an intermediate stage of the writer's perception and is not a conscious process at all. It is "a straightforward attempt to communicate to another person the maker's vision of an object as it appeared to him at the moment of expression . . ." (p. 35). Rhetoricians, she said, had made the error of not going beyond the simultaneous presence of the two elements in a metaphor to the first stage in which the two were perceived as one. For this reason they had tried to account for the simultaneous presence of two images by the fact of their resemblance, and attributed to the writer a conscious pairing of similar things for the purpose of giving pleasure to the reader. Buck believed her own theory of poetic metaphor had an important advantage over the traditional one of the rhetoricians in that it conceived metaphor not as a mechanical device "like a box, whose parts, gathered from different sources are put together to make the whole," but instead as "the result of a vital process, more like a plant or an animal, whose members grow from the same source, out of a homogeneous mass into a clearly differentiated structure" (p. 35).

In the rest of her study Buck made other contributions to the theory of figures. She pointed out, for example, that simile is a more sophisticated figure than metaphor; it represents the stage at which the two conceptions are beginning to draw apart and be recognized as separate. The connection that is still visible between them is indicated by the words "like" or "as." Beyond simile, Buck added, there comes only plain statement; things are recognized clearly for what they are.

Whereas rhetorical theory had usually been content merely to say that metaphor "gives pleasure" to the reader, Buck tried to analyze its effects more carefully. She suggested three possible reasons. One is that a metaphor gives the reader an opportunity to perceive unity in variety—pleasurable because pleasure involves symmetry and harmony, and the discovery of unity in diversity means the imposition of these qualities on material that previously lacked them. Another reason is that the activity set up in the reader by a metaphor is not purely cerebral but has physical repercussions too—a catching of the breath, muscular tension, and so on. When the metaphor is resolved, the tension suddenly relaxes and a feeling of relief and pleasure follows. Finally, metaphor gives pleasure because it provides symmetrical and harmonious activity for physical functions. The force of metaphor, Buck suggested, is due to the process the reader's mind goes through when he encounters a metaphor. First, she said, the reader "vibrates between the two disconnected images aroused by the figure, next perceives vaguely the primeval unity out of which they both had emerged and, having secured this, may repeat the original process by which the metaphor grew in the mind of the writer" (p. 50). Because metaphor compels the reader's mind to follow the processes of the writer's mind and thus possibly traverse ground that is wholly new to him, metaphor is consequently much more powerful than plain statement, which allows the reader's mind to move along channels familiar through common agreement as to meanings of the words employed.

Buck's discussion of metaphor was concluded by an examination of two kinds of "bad metaphor"—conceits, and mixed metaphors. The former are bad because they have been consciously constructed. They do not arise from a single original conception as true metaphors do, but instead have begun when the writer notices a resemblance between two things and mechanically combines them. It is the reverse of the process in the poet's mind. The effect of a conceit on the reader is usually disappointing because when the reader tries to trace the elements of the figure back to their single root he finds he cannot; the resemblance is obscure, unessential, or tenuous, and the reader cannot believe that the writer ever really saw the two as one. "The writer is convicted of falsehood to his own vision of things" (p. 64). As for mixed metaphor, Buck observed that, to the person who makes it, it is never mixed; it is mixed by a hearer or reader. If the maker of a mixed metaphor realized it were mixed, he would not use it. It occurs when a writer, "having used a metaphor, carries it in thought to plain statement and proceeds to develop this plain statement, which he has not expressed, by means of another metaphor, whose images jar with those of the first, or by means of a plain statement inconsistent with one of the images in the preceding metaphor. The rapidity with which the figure is reduced to a literal idea and the writer's forgetfulness of its earlier estate serve to bring about the mixture" (p. 67).

Gertrude Buck was undoubtedly ahead of her time. So radically different an approach to one of the rhetorical staples could not be assimilated by rhetoricians contemporary with her. More important, her theory if accepted would have eliminated any justification for discussions of figures in rhetoric textbooks except for the purposes of analyzing literature, and even there such discussions would have limited utility unless they were entirely reoriented along the new lines. The substance of Buck's theory is that figures are *not* mechanically produced; when they are they become mere conceits. The conclusion therefore is that definition, classification, or other pedagogic devices will not of themselves enable a person to make effective figures. If, as Scott and Denney remarked in *Composition-Rhetoric*, a writer becomes sufficiently engrossed in his subject, and if his mind works readily in images, the figures will appear of their own accord; he will be powerless to prevent them. But they are not something that can be taught by rule.

Buck's theory does not, perhaps, sound as revolutionary today as it did when it was first broached. There are few defenders now of the idea that was the object of her main attack: that style and substance are separate entities, that figurative language is external to the notions being expressed and can be added by prescription in order to embellish the composition. It is possible too that parts of her theory, based on the psychology of half a century ago, are no longer valid in the light of later research into mental processes. Certainly she was sometimes guilty of oversimplification, as in the notion that the only reason why a small child may make a "radical metaphor" is that he does not yet perceive the differences between the two objects

he is designating by the same name; an equally valid explanation would seem to be that he may be aware that the two
objects are different, but he simply does not yet have separate
words for each of them. That is, the reason might as well be
vocabulary deficiency as indistinct perception.

Be that as it may, Buck deserves much credit for her
courage in brushing away the accumulated dust of well over two
thousand years and for making an earnest attempt to attack the
subject of metaphor from a wholly new point of view, bringing
to bear on it the most recent and most pertinent information
she could find, even though that knowledge was drawn from
another discipline. In a period when rhetorical theory was becoming steadily more isolated from other fields of knowledge,
Buck's attitude was unusually and commendably independent.

Diction, Usage, Grammar

CHAPTER TEN

THROUGHOUT the period 1850–1900, discussions of diction and usage remained traditional, being based largely on the earlier treatments of Blair and Campbell. Toward the end of the century, these discussions became more detailed and specific, though characterized by dogmatic expression and capricious standards of judgment. Until rather late in the century, grammar did not appear in rhetoric textbooks designed exclusively for college use. The reason was that the study of grammar was generally considered to belong to the lower schools; by the time a student got to college, it was at first assumed he knew the rules of grammar. Later, as college enrollments rose and as students were required to do more writing in college rhetoric courses, the fact that the lower schools had not fully succeeded in teaching grammar became painfully evident. Since no separate course in grammar existed in the college curriculum, room had to be made in the rhetoric course for such instruction, and as a result the writers of rhetoric texts began in the eighties to include grammatical material in their books. This innovation declined briefly in the nineties, during the height of the paragraph vogue, but quickly rose again—and with such vigor that rhetorical material was almost crowded out. In only a few instances were there any signs that the scientific study of language had influenced any of the discussions of grammar; instead, they were based mainly on the work of eighteenth century prescriptive grammarians. As a result of this emphasis on grammar and mechanics, rhetorical instruction in the early years of the twentieth century came to be dominated by an ideal of superficial correctness, of conformity to rules chiefly for the sake of conformity.

DICTION AND USAGE

As in discussions of other aspects of style, American rhetoric texts between 1850 and 1900 showed a strong influence from the British rhetorics in their treatments of diction and usage. Campbell's doctrine of reputable, present, and national use, for example, was found almost universally throughout the period and in fact continued to appear in books published well into the twentieth century; probably its most recent appearance has been W. Cabell Greet's statement in *The American College Dictionary* that these criteria have governed choice of pronunciations in the dictionary.[1] Campbell's list of offenses against "grammatical purity" was also popular—barbarisms, solecisms, improprieties, obsolete words, coinages, etc.—as well as his headings of choice, number, and arrangement of words. Blair's main contribution was his three stylistic qualities that produce perspicuity in words: purity, propriety, precision.

The earlier American writers usually combined these two sets of ideas, the most common arrangement hinging on the fact that both Blair and Campbell had used the term "purity." Thus such writers as D. J. Hill, Quackenbos, and John S. Hart listed Blair's terms purity, propriety, precision, but the headings under purity were not Blair's but Campbell's.[2] Nearly all the other earlier American books used this scheme in one form or another. Day was the only one who criticized Campbell's doctrine of usage—he insisted that usage is subordinate to "grammatical science"—but the edge was taken off his criticism when he followed it with an orthodox statement of the reputable-national-present theory as well as Campbell's list of violations of good use (pp. 259–264).

A. S. Hill in the 1878 edition of *The Principles of Rhetoric* made Campbell's headings of choice, number, and arrangement of words the organizing principle of a considerable part of his discussion of diction, and also included Campbell's theory of usage. Barrett Wendell, who often borrowed ideas from other people and gave them a new application, expanded Campbell's concept of good usage so that it became an important part of his theory of style: the conflict between good use and the "principles of composition" (Unity-Mass-Coherence). Genung in the *Practical Elements*, though he also drew on Blair and Campbell, tried to give the material a new appearance—another instance of his desire to retain traditional ideas but give them a different pattern or expression. His discussion of diction was under four heads: choice of words, characteristics of poetic diction, characteristics and types of prose diction, and diction as affected by purpose and occasion. Under choice of words he listed four essentials, which were really a variation on Campbell: accurate use, present use, intelligible use, and scholarly use. In the rest of his discussion some old terms were renamed, a few new ones introduced, but there was no real departure from the traditional attitude since abstractions were still the center of attention.

In the nineties, though Campbell's three canons of good use appeared somewhat less often, his list of violations of good use was as popular as ever. Ordinarily it took the form of cautions about using new words, old words, long and short words, solecisms, etc. There were a few attempts to break away from some of these. Newcomer, for example, in *Elements of Rhetoric* declared in the preface that he had tried to avoid mentioning such things as provincialisms and barbarisms because of the difficulties they presented. "Judgment is difficult, legislation well-nigh impossible. Besides," he added, "it is in these matters that individuality of style chiefly lies . . . ." (p. iv). Discussions of obsolete words, Newcomer felt, were only "dead matter" in a rhetoric text. "No student ever writes obsolete words." If they are to be studied, they belong not in a course in rhetoric but in one in English literature. Newcomer's section on "Words and Phrases" was divided into three parts: "Relation to Thought," "Relation to Structure," and "Relation to Style." Though these headings suggested a fairly original treatment, actually they were broken down into various abstractions in the old manner.

"Relation to Thought," for example, was discussed under "Unequivocalness," "Precision," and "Familiarity"; "Relation to Style" under "Tone," "Vigor," "Beauty."

As the ideal of mechanical correctness in writing took on more importance in the nineties, rhetoric texts began to include alphabetically arranged glossaries of faulty diction. Such glossaries were found in Newcomer's *Elements*, Genung's *Outlines*, Espenshade's *Essentials*, and Scott and Denney's *Elementary English Composition*. A. S. Hill's *Foundations of Rhetoric*, though it had no glossary, covered at great length in the body of the book the same sort of material that was found in the glossaries. The germ of this kind of thing had existed in Campbell, who in his discussion of solecisms, barbarisms, archaisms, and so on, had, in spite of his statement that good use is the sole authority, made numerous pronouncements on individual usages—pronouncements that were often both arbitrary and dogmatic. In the nineties and on into the new century such discussions of usage were even more dogmatic and usually showed a strong element of personal caprice. Hill in *Foundations*, for instance, had nine chapters on "Words and Not Words," those words which he did not approve being simply "not words." A few examples will suggest Hill's criteria. The sentence "Congress *claimed* that the idea of Indian nationality had vanished" was corrected to read "Congress acted on the theory that," etc. Hill added, "The word 'claim' has been misused for at least two generations" (p. 111). "A beautiful doll came out and *gestured* solemnly" was changed to "A beautiful doll came out and gesticulated solemnly" (p. 115). The same sort of thing appeared in Genung's *Outlines*: "RECOLLECT, REMEMBER. We remember when an impression remains on our mind; we recollect when we call something to mind" (p. 325). "NO GOOD, NO USE, not to be used without of; as, 'The thing is no good,'—say of no good" (p. 321). "NEAR-BY, not to be used as an adjective; as, 'a near-by church'" (p. 320). "CELEBRITY, the abstract noun, not to be used in the sense of a celebrated person; as, 'A great celebrity is to preach tomorrow'" (p. 306). It was this sort of *ex cathedra* legislation on matters of usage that helped to prepare a receptive climate for

Edwin C. Woolley's *Handbook of Composition* (1907),[3] perhaps the most popular and certainly one of the longest-lived composition textbooks that have yet appeared in this country.

Discussions of diction and usage throughout the entire fifty years from 1850 to 1900 were, then, little more than revisions and recombinations of eighteenth century British doctrine. The fixed canons for determining good usage, and the sets of critical abstractions to be employed as yardsticks in choosing words, were features of the earlier systematic rhetoric that remained fairly constant no matter what other changes or excisions were made in the older theory. Some of the other areas of doctrine that remained substantially unchanged through the whole period did so in part because there had been no original investigation leading to results that would seriously have challenged the accepted beliefs: style is a case in point. In the area of usage, however, there was a wealth of important new data being supplied by the scientific study of language. It is a measure of the degree to which rhetoric was isolated from other disciplines— even one so closely related as linguistics—that no use whatever was made of this material.

GRAMMAR

The college-level rhetoric texts before about 1875 paid almost no attention to grammar. It was believed that rhetoric presupposes grammar in the same way it presupposes logic; it makes use of the data furnished by each, but does not include the subjects themselves. Grammar was, in fact, not considered a proper part of higher instruction, but instead something that belonged exclusively in the lower schools. Rhetoric, in these years, was a sort of metaphysical subject that, because of its difficulty and complexity, was more suitable to the colleges than to the high schools and academies. The abstract character of rhetorical doctrine at this time—the failure to require application of the rules and precepts to actual writing done by the student—meant that the grammatical deficiencies of the student were not highlighted; college courses in rhetoric could, therefore, omit instruction in grammar without causing any serious inconvenience.

In the rhetoric texts for the lower schools, grammatical and rhetorical material regularly appeared side by side in the same book. More than half of Quackenbos' *First Lessons in Composition*, intended for use in grammar schools, was taken up with catechetical lessons on grammar. Richard Green Parker's *Aids to English Composition* (1845) and James R. Boyd's *Elements of English Composition* (1860) were books of the same type, though much more compendious than Quackenbos' *First Lessons*. This sort of text appears to have been very popular for many years. By 1868, for instance, Parker's *Aids* had gone into a twentieth "edition" (probably printing); Quackenbos' *First Lessons*, reprinted as late as 1883, sold over 200,000 copies.

These were not, however, the usual sort of text for grammatical instruction. More customary were the formal grammars such as Lindley Murray's two-volume *English Grammar*,[4] which presented in great detail the sort of systematic study of the subject that was often urged as an excellent means of disciplining the mental powers. For the first quarter of the nineteenth century the field was pretty well dominated by Murray's text. In 1823, however, Samuel Kirkham published *A Compendium of English Grammar*,[5] which soon began to enjoy considerable popularity; by 1829 it had already reached an eleventh edition (revised and enlarged), and was now called *English Grammar in Familiar Lectures*.[6] A forty-third edition appeared in 1837, a fiftieth in 1840; the book seems to have been reprinted for the last time in 1857. By then, Samuel S. Greene's *Treatise on the Structure of the English Language* (1846)[7] had appeared and was gaining in popularity.

There were no doubt other popular texts in these years as well, but these three are especially interesting because, though they advocated various methods of study, they show how the basic conception of grammar instruction as analysis remained almost unchanged throughout the century. The first volume of Murray's text consisted primarily of etymology, in the old sense of kinds, modifications, and derivations of words; and of syntax. This material was given in the form of rules, followed by examples and discussion. The rules were to be memorized. The second volume was made up of exercises in parsing (orthographical, etymological, and syntactical) as well as exercises in punctuation and the correction of false syntax. The student thus had to memorize his way entirely through the text proper before the parsing began. Kirkham followed Murray closely in the content of his book but simplified the statements of the rules so as to make them more easily understood; and he made the important change of introducing exercises in parsing at the earliest possible moment so that new rules of syntax, for example, would be followed at once by exercises designed to secure the rules in the pupil's mind.

Samuel S. Greene did much to popularize "sentence analysis," a system that succeeded parsing. In his first book, *Treatise on the Structure of the English Language*, he reduced all sentence elements, whether words, phrases, or clauses, to five: substantive, verb, adjective, adverb, and conjunction. Then, using a system of notation that involved numerals and plus signs, he offered a plan of sentence analysis in which the symbols were used for the elements. In his later book, *Analysis of the English Language* (1874),[8] the system had become more complicated. There are, he said, two principal elements in a sentence (subject, predicate) and three subordinate (adjective element, objective element, adverbial element). If they are single words, they are of the first class; if they are phrases, they are of the second class; and if they are propositions, they are of the third. They may be simple, complex, or compound, and may be combined in a proposition in four ways: predicative, adjective, objective, adverbial (pp. 12–14, 16–17). To fit the new scheme Greene had a new sort of notation which was equally involved. The sentence "Those large red cherries tempt us," for example, in the new notation became: 3 a S P o (p. 23). The first stanza of Gray's "Elegy" became:

$$(S\ P).\ a\ a^2\ a'\ [and]\ a.\ S\ P\ \begin{cases} v \\ v^2 \end{cases} [and]\ .S\ P\ \begin{cases} v' \\ v^2 \end{cases} 2a'$$

$$[and]\ P\begin{cases} .o \\ o^2 \end{cases} and\ o^2\ (p.\ 291).$$

The final step in this process of development was the appearance of the familiar sentence-diagram in a book called

Higher Lessons in English (first published in 1878) by Alonzo Reed and Brainerd Kellogg.[9] The authors recommended the diagram by saying that it "will enable the pupil to present directly and vividly to the eye the exact function of every clause in the sentence, of every phrase in the clause, and of every word in the phrase—to picture the complete analysis of the sentence, with principal and subordinate parts in their proper relations." They added that "It is only by the aid of such a map, or picture, that the pupil can, at a single view, see the sentence as an organic whole made up of many parts performing various functions and standing in various relations. Without such map he must labor under the disadvantage of seeing all these things by piecemeal or in succession" (p. 8). The system of diagramming used in this book was substantially the same one that has been familiar to several generations of English teachers and students. The following diagram of the sentence "For us to know our faults is profitable" is a typical example (p. 95):

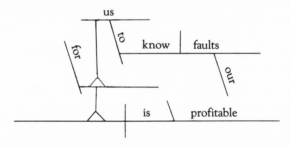

The Reed and Kellogg diagram was just a new device for accomplishing an old aim, an aim that had earlier been encompassed by parsing and analysis. The emphasis remained on the analytical rather than the synthetic approach.

In the late seventies and on through the eighties, grammar began to assume more importance in rhetoric textbooks on the college level. The reason for this was that, as efforts were made to move away from the old abstract rhetoric which seldom had led to actual writing by the student, more emphasis was placed on the necessity for frequent practice in composition. The more students wrote, however, the more glaring seemed the deficiencies in their knowledge of grammar. One of the first results of the realization that college students were graduating from the lower schools without a mastery of grammar was the imposition of the Harvard entrance examination in English, which soon was copied widely throughout the country. A main purpose of these examinations was quite frankly to force the lower schools to do a more effective job of teaching grammar. Until that should come about, a number of authors of rhetoric texts began to include material on grammar in their books. A. S. Hill, McElroy, and Welsh, for example, incorporated a section on solecisms in the manner of Campbell, though these sections were usually a good deal longer and more detailed than Campbell's discussion. Wendell merely referred in passing to a few solecisms, but Genung in *Practical Elements* gave over thirty-five pages to such matters as syntax, collocation, reference, correlation, use of conjunctions, and negatives (pp. 110–146). This discussion did not amount to a systematic survey of grammar, but it was a considerably more elaborate treatment than had been found in preceding college rhetoric texts. Similar material was included by Kellogg in his *Text-Book on Rhetoric* and Clark in his *Practical Rhetoric*. At Harvard, where A. S. Hill's *Principles* was the text for the big required course in composition, a short grammatical handbook, E. A. Abbott's *How to Write Clearly,* [10] was used to supplement the treatment of solecisms in Hill's book. The Abbott manual was divided into two main sections, one consisting of about forty-five rules aimed at producing clearness and force, and the other containing thirteen rules to secure brevity. About half the book was exercises. The rules themselves were generally expressed negatively and with considerable assurance.

During the 1890s grammar for a time dropped out of college-level rhetoric texts almost entirely. The explanation lay in several things. For one, the middle and later nineties were the time when the paragraph enjoyed its greatest vogue; emphasis shifted temporarily from mechanical correctness of sentences to correctness of paragraphs and, to some extent, of the whole composition. Another factor was the widespread reaction against the formal grammar of earlier years, now identified with an outmoded theory of education. In 1897 Gertrude Buck spoke of the "all but universal disfavor into which the study of grammar has fallen,"[11] and in the same year O. F. Emerson referred to the same fact. Emerson added that a chief reason for the current unpopularity of grammar was that grammar teaching had too often been "little more than the presentation, in the least interesting form, of certain dogmatic statements laid down by various so-called grammarians."[12] Even more significant, perhaps, was the fact that rapidly swelling college enrollments, coupled with the unprecedented amount of writing that was being required of freshman students, had magnified the problem of ungrammatical English to overwhelming dimensions. The composition teachers' feeling of frustration was further heightened by the agitation over the Harvard Reports. Confronted with what seemed to be an impossible situation, college teachers renewed the old cry of "The high schools are to blame." They tried, in effect, to wash their hands of the whole affair: grammar was not a college subject anyway; the business of the college was higher instruction, and the rudiments of English grammar certainly did not fall within this category.

Reflecting this attitude, nearly all the college-level rhetoric texts temporarily abandoned grammar. In most books there was no vestige left, not even the usual lists of solecisms. But grammar was due for a revival in the next century, and it was not long before signs of it began to appear. It soon became obvious that college English teachers could not, after all, resign the job of grammar instruction exclusively to the lower schools. This solution, no matter how desirable it appeared from the college teachers' point of view, simply was not realistic. Enrollments continued to increase, daily themes were still the fashion, and the high school preparation of students seemed no better than ever—in fact, by the end of the century the trouble was rendered more acute by the appearance in college classes of second-generation Americans who had usually spoken a foreign language at home before they had learned English.

Thus grammar soon began to come back. Newcomer's *Elements* (1898), Genung's *Working Principles* (1900), Espenshade's *Essentials* (1904) all included discussions of grammar.

In 1902 A. S. Hill published a revision of *The Foundations of Rhetoric* under the title *Beginnings of Rhetoric and Composition*, in which there was a greatly expanded treatment of grammar. In the *Foundations*, published ten years before, there had been about 170 pages given to words and another hundred to sentences, but the discussion was more rhetorical than grammatical: principles to govern choice in diction and sentence structure, with much room given to good use. The later book had 300 pages on the parts of speech alone; principles of choice figured prominently, but there was a large admixture of purely grammatical material, all of it negative in tone.

Discussions of grammar and usage, whether in rhetoric texts or in grammatical handbooks, were still in the tradition of eighteenth century prescriptive grammar in spite of the great progress that philology and linguistics had made in the nineteenth century. There were a few critics of this state of affairs. O. F. Emerson, for example, wrote in 1897:

> The teaching of English grammar should take account of the fundamental principles of linguistic development. The teacher should know and emphasize the fact that grammar is the description of a more or less unstable and changing medium of expression; that language is not hedged about by any divinity, but is merely a human institution, subject to human infirmity and human caprice; that what is grammatically correct in one age may not be in the next; that changes in language proceed along certain lines and under certain influences, a full understanding of which could not fail to make the study of grammatical relations more interesting and more effective.[13]

Gertrude Buck in 1898 published an article on "The Psychological Significance of the Parts of Speech,"[14] in which she foresaw a revolution in grammar comparable to those that had refashioned logic, psychology, and the physical sciences. She urged that a concept of organic growth replace the prevailing static conception of grammar, which assumed that in the making of a sentence "the parts of speech are added one to another as ingredients in a cake" (p. 271). In another article Buck attacked the Reed and Kellogg sentence-diagram on the same grounds—that it was psychologically false to the real nature of a sentence.[15]

Textbooks embodying the new point of view were rare, though one, surprisingly enough, had been published as far back as 1877 by William Dwight Whitney, professor of Sanskrit at Yale, and America's outstanding linguistics scholar in the nineteenth century. Whitney's little book, *Essentials of English Grammar*,[16] being based on the scientific view of language, was highly unusual in this period. In the preface Whitney said that the object of grammar study is not to teach the correct use of English; instead, grammar is "the reflective study of language, for a variety of purposes, of which correctness of writing is only one, and a secondary or subordinate one—by no means unimportant, but best attained when sought indirectly," by practice and correction both in the school and the home. He added that "no one ever changed from a bad speaker to a good one by applying the rules of grammar to what he said," since "one must be a somewhat reflective user of language to amend even here and there a point by grammatical reasons." The reason he gave for teaching grammar (in his sense of the term) to persons who are already users of the language concerned was that it is the best way to turn the student's attention to the basic principles and relations of language as they are illustrated in his own speech and writing (pp. iii–iv).

His attitude toward grammar was, as one would expect, descriptive rather than prescriptive. The grammarian is one who records and arranges the facts of language use; he is in no way a lawgiver (p. v). Whitney said further that he had tried to avoid the use of hard and fast rules for fear they might be applied mechanically (p. vi). The text of the book itself was in keeping with the attitudes expressed in the preface. It was simply a description and organization of the facts of usage. Rules were very rare. It was, in short, totally unlike the other grammars of the period; about the only point of contact between his book and those of other men then writing on grammar was the fact that he concluded every chapter with parsing exercises.

Another unconventional grammar text was Scott and Buck's *A Brief English Grammar* (1905).[17] The fundamental ideas of the book were "the social function and the organic structure of language," though the authors admitted freely that the book did not answer finally the question of how these ideas could best be applied to actual language teaching. It was experimental. They had tried to treat the forms of language as they are conditioned by the functions of language; that is, inflections, words, sentence elements had been discussed in the light of what part each plays in the central act of communication of which the sentence is the means. A special order of topics was adopted in an effort to make these relations clear. The grammatical rules in the book were descriptive rather than prescriptive, and on the whole the book was quite close to the approach of much more recent texts.

Neither of these books seems to have had a wide sale, and neither exerted any influence on other grammar texts. They were ahead of their time. In the new century the preferences of teachers were fulfilled more satisfactorily by Woolley's *Handbook of Composition*, which soon set the tone for other texts and, in a sense, for composition instruction generally.

THE IDEAL OF CORRECTNESS

Beginning shortly after the appearance of the Harvard English entrance examination—and, perhaps, in no small measure because of it—there was an increased insistence on rhetorical and grammatical correctness as the most important qualities in student writing. The sort of correctness desired, however, was superficial and mechanical. For a brief time in the nineties, as mentioned above, this emphasis diminished as the paragraph and the whole composition took precedence over the sentence and smaller units; but when the Harvard Reports directed attention once more to such matters as elementary grammar, punctuation, spelling, and other mechanical details, the broader focus of the nineties rapidly narrowed once more. The new emphasis on correctness was, in fact, even narrower than that which had preceded it, for rhetorical doctrine by the end of the century had become little more than the forms of discourse and Unity-Coherence-Emphasis; thus grammar and mechanics usurped nearly the whole field.

The Harvard entrance examination in English, which was the first such requirement imposed by an American college, did much to encourage the ideal of correctness. The examination was influential in two ways: First, since Harvard was at this time a leader in educational reform—and since it enjoyed the prestige of being America's oldest and most noted institution of higher learning—many of its innovations were copied widely by other colleges. This was true of the English entrance requirement—so much so that already by 1886 the newly formed New England Commission of Colleges was given as one of its first tasks the standardizing of books on which entrance examinations were based.[18] Second, by exacting of entering students a certain standard of preparation in English, Harvard exerted strong pressure on preparatory schools and high schools to increase the quantity of work in English and to give it a certain direction. Other colleges, following Harvard's lead, increased the pressure and brought it to bear over a wider area.

An idea of how the entrance requirement in English abetted the ideal of correctness can be gained from A. S. Hill's remarks on the examination given in 1879. (Hill was in charge of the rhetoric work at Harvard and at that time had the responsibility for framing the examination.) The composition assignment for the 1879 examination read:

> Write a short composition upon one of the subjects given below.
>
> Before beginning to write, consider what you have to say on the subject selected, and arrange your thoughts in a logical order.
>
> Aim at quality rather than quantity of work.
>
> Carefully revise your composition, correcting all errors in punctuation, spelling, grammar, division by paragraphs, and expression, and making each sentence as clear and forcible as possible. If time permits, make a clean copy of the revised work.

    I. The Character of Sir Richard Steele.
   II. The Duke of Marlborough as portrayed by Thackeray.
  III. The Style of "Henry Esmond."
  IV. Thackeray's account of the Pretender's visit to England.
   V. Duelling in the Age of Queen Anne.[19]

Students presumably had prepared themselves on Shakespeare's Macbeth, Richard II, and Midsummer Night's Dream; Thackeray's Henry Esmond; Scott's Guy Mannering; Byron's Prisoner of Chillon; Macaulay's Essay on Addison; and the Sir Roger de Coverley essays in the Spectator.

Three hundred and sixteen students took the examination. Of this number, 157 (50 per cent) were failed.[20] Only a rather small minority of the failures—between an eighth and a tenth—were, said Hill, due to ignorance of the books. Others "showed such utter ignorance of punctuation as to put commas at the end of complete sentences, or between words that no rational being would separate from one another; and a few began sentences with small letters, or began every long word with a capital letter. Many, a larger number than usual, spelled as if starting a spelling reform, each for himself. . . . Many books were deformed by grossly ungrammatical or profoundly obscure sentences and some by absolute illiteracy."[21] Only fourteen candidates received grades high enough to pass "with credit," though Hill said that "If the examiner erred, it was in giving the candidate the benefit of too many doubts, in tempering justice with too much mercy."[22] "On the whole," concluded Hill, "the examination makes a poor showing for the schools that furnish the material whereof the university which professes to set up the highest standard in America, has to make educated men."[23] The implication was that Harvard had no responsibility at all in the matter; the lower schools were shirking a job that belonged to them alone.

The nature of the Harvard examination, as well as the standards by which it was graded, remained substantially unchanged till near the end of the century. In 1882, however, L. B. R. Briggs, a member then of Hill's staff, introduced a feature which pointed the examination even more directly toward correctness in mechanical details. This innovation was the practice of requiring candidates to correct specimens of "bad English." For the first years there were twenty sentences to be corrected, but toward 1890 the number was reduced to twelve or fifteen. The sentences were chosen, Briggs said, "from the examination books of earlier years, from student themes, from newspapers, and from contemporary literature."[24] Briggs' attitude toward this sort of examination was that it "is a valuable test of acuteness and accuracy. Preparation for it calls for early and intimate knowledge of the groundwork of English grammar; for continuous effort to apply that knowledge rationally; for long practice in writing, under faithful supervision . . . ."[25] Briggs' idea of bad English was chiefly English that is "ungrammatical." "What shall I print as 'Specimens of Bad English?'" he asked.

> It is idle to say, "Confine your choice to what every educated man knows to be bad." The obscure is prohibited; the illiterate insults both boy and teacher,—not to mention the University: but outside of the obscure and the illiterate there is nothing that every educated man knows to be bad.
>
> What is more vulgar than *you was?*—yet some teachers defend it; more illegitimate than *it don't?*—yet many teachers use it; more slip-shod than I *don't know as?*—yet most teachers never notice it; more inexact than dangling participles?—yet good authors employ them; more offensive to a trained eye or ear than *to thoroughly appreciate* or *to cordially thank?*—yet of such phrases professors (even professors of English) are guilty again and again.
>
> What is a surer sign of second-rate diction than the confusion of *shall* and *will?* Yet a teacher, writing to ask me why his best pupil failed at the English examination, ignores the commonest truths about *shall* and *will.*

. . . Indeed, I have heard a college professor declare that the distinction is "all purism."

It is just such errors as I have named that college examination-papers should take pains to condemn; for to just such errors half-educated young men are continually exposed.[26]

Writing on the results of the 1888 entrance examination, Briggs made nearly the same specific criticisms that Hill had made nine years before:

Spelling is bad, and probably always will be: *loose* for *lose* is so nearly universal that *lose* begins to look wrong; *sentance* prevails; *dissapointed* and *facinating* are not unusual; sporadic cases are *Sir Tobby* [Belch], *Sheassphere* [of Stratford], and *welthey aeris* [Portia of Belmont]. Punctuation is frequently inaccurate—that is to say, unintelligent and misleading. The apostrophe is nearly as often a sign of the plural as of the possessive; the semicolon, if used at all, is a spasmodic ornament rather than a help to the understanding; and—worst of all—the comma does duty for the period, so that even interesting writers run sentence into sentence without the formality of full stop or of capital. . . . As for paragraphing, I am aware that it is a delicate art: yet that is no reason why some whole essays should be single paragraphs—solid, unindented blocks of conglomerate; or why in others nearly every sentence should make a paragraph by itself, so that a page, except for its untidiness, might be taken from a primer.[27]

The Harvard influence continued to spread during the eighties and nineties, not only through the copying of its entrance requirement but also through the considerable personal and professional influence exerted by its English faculty. Hill's *Principles of Rhetoric*, for instance, which epitomized the ideal of correctness, was widely used throughout the country. In addition, Hill wrote articles setting forth his views and published them in popular magazines of national circulation.

Wendell and Briggs explained and defended the Harvard system at teachers' meetings and in professional journals. Still more important, the Harvard English faculty, which in the eighties and nineties was the largest and most distinguished in the country, trained a great many college English teachers, who then went forth to spread the Harvard gospel.

The ideal of superficial correctness was not, of course, something entirely new. It was, in a sense, an extension of existing tendencies—the dogmatic right-or-wrong approach to rhetorical and grammatical problems that had existed at least since the eighteenth century; and the mechanical, external view of the writing process that had characterized American rhetorical theory from the first. During the years before the Civil War, the emphasis on surface correctness did less harm than it did later: oral rhetoric, having been taken over by the elocutionists, then lay outside the field of rhetoric proper; and written rhetoric was more a set of abstract terms and precepts to be learned, than a discipline leading to the actual production of writing. After the Civil War, as literacy rose and as more and more writing was demanded in the colleges and high schools, the persistence of this narrow attitude caused serious disadvantages. Other subjects in the curriculum were modernizing their methods and examining critically their traditional assumptions so as to fit themselves into the new philosophy of education. Rhetoric ignored the fact that methods and assumptions suited to the abstract approach of earlier years would no longer be relevant in the new conditions. In spite of valuable new data being offered by psychology, linguistics, and philology, rhetorical theory continued to look on writing as a mechanical process, continued to see it from the outside. The assumption was that good writing automatically results from the mechanical application of fixed rules. Good writing meant, therefore, not effective writing, but writing that violated none of the rules. The barrenness of this attitude served to remove rhetorical theory ever farther from a realistic appreciation of the function of rhetoric, as well as insulating rhetorical instruction from a direct contact with the world around it.

The Shift from Theoretical
to Practical Rhetoric

CHAPTER ELEVEN

T HE MARKED CHANGE in emphasis that American rhetorical theory underwent in the last half of the nineteenth century, as educational philosophy moved away from the mental discipline theory and toward a more utilitarian approach, has been suggested earlier in connection with such specific items of theory as invention, style, and the concept of rhetoric as communication. It will be useful to look at this shift more closely, as a means of tying together the main trends of the period.

Rhetorical theory in the middle of the century was, as has been said before, predominantly abstract; mastery of it was an end in itself, more or less apart from any practical utility it might have as a guide to actual composition. Not long after 1850, signs of a break with this approach began to appear. Men like Day, Hope, Theremin, D. J. Hill, and Hervey set the tone of the earlier years by constructing elaborate systems of rhetorical theory, but at the same time a few other writers were already showing dissatisfaction with the complexity of these systems. Understandably enough, this movement appeared first in rhetoric texts designed for the lower schools—books such as Swinton's *School Composition* and Quackenbos' *First Lessons*. Both men said in the prefaces to their texts that existing books were much too difficult for younger students, and they announced as a chief aim of their own volumes the intention to bring the more useful aspects of rhetorical theory within the easy reach of such students. "It has seemed to the writer," said Swinton, "that there is room for a school manual of prose composition of medium size, arranged on a simple and natural plan, and designed, not to teach the theory of style and criticism, but to give school children between the ages of twelve and fifteen a fair mastery of the art of writing good English, for the ordinary purposes of life. Such he has endeavored to make the present book" (p. iv). The same desire was seen in Haven's *Rhetoric*, which was of college level. "Abstruse arguments about style and oratory, about the conflicting theories of taste and beauty, about conviction and persuasion, and the laws of mind, and the philosophy of language, are all good and valuable in their place; but a student may read and repeat them with but little more effect on his own habits of speaking or power to write well, than he would receive from an equal amount of study in mathematics, medicine, or law, or any other subject" (p. vii).

Nearly all the earlier books—even Day's *Art of Discourse* and Hill's *Science*—contained exercises of one sort or another, though most were analytical (a sort of rhetorical parsing) or were the counterpart of the exercises in correction of false syntax that were so prominent a feature of the grammar texts of the time. A few books, however, began to place more emphasis on actual writing; it is true that often enough the writing did not involve connected composition, but it was nevertheless symptomatic of a desire to make the study of rhetoric more practical. Haven, for instance, urged that students be required not only to produce examples of all kinds of figures of speech but also to write specimens of the various types of style which he had listed. Other writers, such as Quackenbos, John S. Hart, Swinton, and Boyd, included lists of composition subjects; and though many of the topics were poorly adapted to the knowledge and ability of the students, nonetheless the presence of these lists suggests that rhetoric for these men meant actual composition as well as the memorizing and reciting of rules.

Swinton, indeed, said in the preface to his *School Composition* that he would provide the pupil with an opportunity to "compose" from the opening pages of the book. "It is a matter of common experience," he wrote, "that children's power of producing, in an empirical way, is much in advance of their knowledge of the rationale of writing. . . ." Therefore, he thought, it was wrong to make them learn all the complex details of rhetorical theory before allowing them to write. "Pupils must first be taught *how to write at all*, before they can be shown how to write *well*. . ." (p. iii). It must be said, though, that Swinton's theory was better in its conception than in its execution. The composition that the pupil was asked to do in three-fifths of the book consisted of exercises involving words and sentences. Only the last section of the book required the pupil to write connected compositions of any length.

Punctuation and the use of capitals, which were at this time thought to belong to grammar rather than to rhetoric, did not at first appear in college-level rhetorical textbooks. But in those books designed for use in the lower schools—ones that usually included considerable material on grammar—punctuation and capitalization were regularly brought in. Boyd, Swinton, and Quackenbos all had sections on these matters in their books. In Quackenbos' *Advanced Course*, a text for use in both schools and colleges, there were about seventy-five pages on punctuation alone—an unusually full treatment. The explanation was that Quackenbos felt that punctuation was an unjustly neglected subject; therefore, he announced in the preface, he intended to present "a complete and thorough system, which should cover exceptions as well as rules, and provide for every possible case, however rare or intricate" (p. 6). D. J. Hill (*Elements*) and John S. Hart also discussed punctuation and capitals, though not so exhaustively as Quackenbos; both of these books were, like Quackenbos' *Advanced Course*, intended for precollegiate as well as collegiate instruction. The inclusion of this sort of material in rhetoric textbooks in these years was another sign of the movement away from a primarily abstract view of rhetoric. It was an effort to bring rhetoric down from metaphysical discussions of Taste and the Sublime to mundane details like the proper use of the semicolon. At the same time, it was clear evidence that more writing was being done in schools and colleges.

Another indication of the same tendency was the appearance of specific instructions in some of these early books for the writing of such things as letters (both business and personal), newspaper stories, editorials, and business documents such as promissory notes and receipts. Blair had mentioned "epistolary composition" in his *Lectures,* and some of the college texts in these years did also—those of Hepburn and Haven, for example. But the fullest treatments of these practical types of writing were found in the same books that included punctuation and the use of capitals: Swinton, Quackenbos (both *First Lessons* and *Advanced Course*), John S. Hart, and D. J. Hill (*Elements*). Since all these books were intended for use in the lower schools—some of them exclusively, and others in schools as well as colleges—there is some evidence here that the content of rhetorical instruction in the lower schools foreshadowed later developments in the colleges.

In the eighties and early nineties, as the break with the older theory of education became more pronounced, efforts increased to make rhetoric more practical, to simplify the complex doctrine of the older books and to give it more utilitarian applications. There were numerous complaints against the former approach to rhetoric that had demanded a student memorize great numbers of rules and principles but which had paid little attention to whether he could actually write well. Clark, for example, said in the preface to *Practical Rhetoric* that "In too many textbooks, the pupil is led through a labyrinth of abstractions bearing such names as 'Invention,' 'Taste,' 'Deduction,' 'Simplicity,' 'Partial Exposition,' 'Feeling,' 'Perfection,' 'The Sublime,' 'The Picturesque,' 'The Graceful,' 'The Novel,' 'The Wonderful,' and so on, until he becomes lost in a theoretical maze, while he goes on writing and speaking in the same obscure, clumsy forms that he used before he ever saw a Rhetoric" (pp. v–vi). In the preface to *Practical Elements* Genung attacked the old-fashioned discussions of figurative language: "The student can burden himself . . . with the names of some two hundred and fifty figures of speech; but when he gets beyond the name and inquires after the usage, he may safely omit two hundred and thirty-five of them as superfluous. . ." (p. xi). In his pamphlet *A Study of Rhetoric in the College Course* Genung con-demned the whole theory that had underlain earlier instruction in rhetoric and added that obviously "something was wrong in a course that so loaded the student with useless names and distinc-tions and yet left him helpless in the presence of a real literary task" (p. 6).

Opinions like these were widely held in the eighties. Books printed in the decade customarily avowed a "practical" aim, and in fact often included the word "practical" in their titles—Genung's *Practical Elements of Rhetoric,* Clark's *Practical Rhetoric,* Coppens' *Practical Introduction to English Rhetoric.* Clark declared in the preface to his book that the only reason why he had written a rhetoric text was "the desire to aid in giving to the rhetorical training in our schools a more practical character" (p. v). Kellogg said in his *Text-Book on Rhetoric* that he believed "the rhetoric needed is not that whose facts receive final lodgment in the pupil's memory, but that whose teachings are made to work their way down out of this into his tongue and fingers, enabling him to speak and to write the better for having studied it. . ." (p. 4). McElroy and Genung were reluctant to forego all instruction in formal principles, but they both insisted on practice to accompany the theory. "I have aimed," declared McElroy, "to strike the happy medium,—to make a book that shall teach composi-tion while it forces the student to think, and shall exhibit the principles of the art at the same time that it keeps uppermost the problem *How to Write.*"[1]

The importance of actual practice in writing as opposed to mere memorizing of rules was a prominent theme in the doc-trine of this time. Huffcut declared, "Throughout the entire course of a pupil's studies, from the time he can construct a simple sentence to the time he leaves the highest grade, there should be constant and rigorous drill in the writing of English. This part of the instruction is by far the most important, and is, at the same time, the part most frequently neglected."[2] Kellogg, Genung, Clark, and others stressed the same point. Often, how-ever, when practice was spoken of, it still meant exercises rather than connected writing. Nearly all the books contained exercises in expansion, contraction, and other modifications of sentences; exercises in correction of false syntax and inexact diction; exercises in figures of speech, stylistic qualities, and so on.

Perhaps the most interesting single development to come out of this emphasis on practice was the "daily theme," a device invented by Barrett Wendell in 1884. It immediately became popular at many other colleges and schools, and in fact still has its supporters today. At a conference of the New England Association of Colleges and Preparatory Schools in 1893, Wendell told how the idea came to him, how he managed the details of the plan, and what he expected it to accomplish. Because the "daily theme" was often misunderstood and misapplied later, it will be worth quoting Wendell at some length. "It was suggested to my mind," Wendell said,

> by talking with a friend who was connected with a Boston newspaper. He remarked the fact that whoever became a reporter, no matter how ignorant he began, learned by the very effort of reporting to express himself in a readable way, in a way that the public would like; and, at the same time, that reporting enormously stimulated observations of life, precisely the thing which I found my pupils in Harvard College to lack. Those two things,—a sort of facility of the pen, which makes their writing agreeable, as distinguished from correct, and a feeling that they are living in a real world as distinguished from a world of books—were secured to reporters by the simple fact of daily reporting. Acting on this suggestion, I introduced in my elective course the practice of requiring from every student a daily theme, which consists of a single page of probably fifty to a hundred words stating so far as possible, in the broadest sense, what that man has observed during the day. It may be something he has seen, it may be something he has thought about. The only requisites are that the subject shall be a matter of observation during the day when it is written, that the expression of it shall not exceed a hundred words or so, and that the style shall be fluent and agreeable.[3]

On each theme I make a brief note on the subject of the theme, and a brief note of the impression it makes upon me at the time. Then the themes are filed alphabetically, and ultimately I go over this work with the writers. When a student has written, perhaps, three or four weeks, he comes to my office, where we discuss both the substance and the style of his themes. And the curious part of it is that I find the two or three hours a day isn't anything like the tedious work you might think it would be. In certain aspects it is no more tedious than the reading of Pepys' Diary. You get these fragments of real life, which, if the class follows the work honestly, constantly improve both in accuracy and range of observation, and in facility and compactness of expression. They don't take much of a student's time either. I suppose a man ought to be able to write at the rate of ten words a minute, and there are not more than a hundred words in the theme; if a man can't do it in ten minutes, he can't do it properly. The amount of work is very small, and the amount of culture, in the broadest sense, is considerable. It is a source of training, for it brings the men into contact with the world; and its benefits seem to me to be so marked that I should feel very far from saying that it was not a good practice for a man even in the most advanced stages of learning (p. 660).

Wendell added that unless the teacher exercised some care, the writing of daily themes might do no more than strengthen bad habits already existing in the student. He also admitted that routine writing of this sort would not in itself lead to "polish and technical correctness"; he regarded daily themes as standing in the same relation to finished compositions as preliminary sketches stand to finished paintings (p. 667). His claims for the daily-theme method were, in other words, considerably more modest than those of some of the people who later advocated it. Wendell did require students in his course to write longer themes as well, since he regarded the shorter compositions as merely instrumental.

As rhetoric came in the eighties to be more and more concerned with the production of connected writing, discussions of
punctuation and capitals, which earlier had been found only in a
few books intended primarily for the lower schools, began to
appear in a majority of rhetoric texts regardless of level. The
reason for this was well expressed by Clark in a note that he
inserted before his section covering these mechanical aspects of
composition:

> On entering college, if not on entering the intermediate
> school, the student is supposed to be able to spell, capi-
> talize, and punctuate correctly and to put his manuscript
> generally in good form. Unfortunately, too many of our
> instructors proceed upon this hypothesis. Careful obser-
> vation shows, however, that a large proportion of Amer-
> ican under-classmen, to say nothing of graduates, have
> *not* this ability. To assume that they have, and to proceed
> upon this basis, is only to do irretrievable injury to all
> concerned.[4]

Clark then took up such things as manuscript spacing, under-
scoring, spelling, capitalization, punctuation, italics, and paragraphing, following the whole with nearly a hundred and fifty
sentences for practice in detecting errors (pp. 3–42). Similar
material was found in the books of Jameson, Kellogg, Coppens,
Welsh, and A. S. Hill (*Principles*), though usually only punctuation and the use of capitals were discussed.

Instructions for the writing of letters, usually both business
and social, were found in several of the books of the eighties—
Jameson, Kellogg, and Coppens, for instance—but the proportion was probably no greater than among the earlier texts. A new
item appeared, however, in the rule numbers and sets of correction symbols for themes that have since become so familiar in
composition handbooks. They were a sign of the growing size
of classes, and of more frequent composition assignments.
Jameson's *Rhetorical Method* seems to have been the earliest text
to include these features: all the "articles" (discussions of specific
items) were numbered throughout the book in a single serial; at
the end there was a code of numerals and abbreviations by which

"The correction of written work may be facilitated. . ." (p. 102). Huffcut, in his pamphlet *English in the Preparatory Schools*, gave a detailed list of abbreviations for use in theme correction. Many of the ones still in use today appeared there: "cap.," "l.c.," "p.," "red.," and "K." for "awkward" (pp. 25-26). Clark's article "The Art of English Composition" contained directions to teachers for making up a list of rule numbers to use in theme correction, even though the textbook being used did not number its rules.

In the middle and later nineties there was unanimous agreement that the main, and usually the only, purpose of rhetoric is to teach students to write. A few men, such as Genung, Cairns, and Carpenter, mentioned the critical purposes of rhetoric, saying it will open the way to appreciation of literature; but they regarded this as secondary. Rhetoric had to lead to actual composition. Under the old system of formal rhetoric the aim had been, as Espenshade said, to give the student "a maximum amount of theory and a minimum amount of practice." There had been no clear understanding of "how important it is that students should first of all learn how to write clear and vigorous English" (p. 12). Carpenter remarked in *Exercises* that the earlier rhetoric "was cumbersome both because it laid undue stress on much that has now become of subordinate importance and on matter that now lies as wholly outside the natural limits of the subject as surgery lies outside the province of the modern barber, and because the philosophic treatment of an art so soon becomes an object of knowledge in itself—a science—and tends to grow as a system at the expense of the art itself" (p. 7). The new rhetoric did not entirely forego instruction in rhetorical principles, but the principles were kept at a minimum. The ideal, in the words of Hale, was "a certain amount of principle and a great deal of practice" (p. 4).

This emphasis on practice in actual writing was apparent somewhere in all the books of the nineties, and in most it was pervasive. The titles of many of the books were one indication of the trend: *Talks on Writing English, Introduction to Theme-Writing, Constructive Rhetoric, Elements of Rhetoric: A Course in Plain Prose Composition, Freshman Composition*, etc. Most writers, as has been said earlier, did not bother with philosophical distinctions between rhetoric as an art and as a science; those few who did were unanimous in believing it is an art, or at least that this side of it is by far the more important. The others tacitly assumed they were dealing with applied or "constructive" rhetoric.

In the nineties the desire to simplify the complex rhetorical doctrine of earlier years was even more acute than it had been in the previous decade. Many of the books were short—two hundred pages or less—and theory was held to a minimum. Carpenter in *Exercises* remarked that he had said very little about style, since what the student needed first was the ability to write clearly, correctly, and with vigor. The finer points of style could be deferred (p. iii). Scott and Denney in *Paragraph-Writing* said pointedly that "Questions of word-usage are left to be answered by reference to the dictionary" (p. viii). Newcomer declared in *Elements of Rhetoric* that most of the material in rhetoric texts was traditional and of no use except for critical purposes. "Good writing depends chiefly on half a dozen things—on managing properly the few words that represent the germ ideas, on keeping sentences from being submerged by the weight of their own clauses, on attending to the articulation (the relation-words of all kinds, the pronouns), on logical arrangement and proportionate emphasis of ideas. These few things are emphasized here" (pp. iii-iv). Genung's *Outlines* contained condensed rules printed in the margins, and numbered consecutively throughout the book. "In this way," said Genung, "the attempt is made to bring the core of the rhetorical art into small and manageable compass. . ." (p. iii).

Exercises, providing chiefly for practice in connected writing, were an almost invariable feature of texts after 1893. Some, in fact, such as the Scott and Denney books and those by Carpenter, gave more space to exercises than to text. There were a few books that retained exercises in the correction of faulty sentences—Genung's *Outlines*, for example, or Newcomer's *Elements*. But Scott and Denney, Hale, Espenshade, and numerous others avoided them. Espenshade criticized particularly the earlier practice of quoting passages from standard authors and having the student "correct" the barbarisms, solecisms, etc., that were reputed to be in the selections. "The makers of our literature have fairly won their way to fame," said Espenshade, "and they have not committed any faults so serious that they deserve to be put in the pillory by every schoolmaster" (p. vi).

Appendixes on capitalization, punctuation, and sometimes spelling became more numerous than ever. Lists of theme-correction symbols and abbreviations were frequent, suggesting the greatly increased amount of student writing being done. Carpenter (*Elements*) gave instructions on how to prepare notebooks and examination papers. Newcomer (*Practical Course*) included discussions on the writing of news stories, editorials, and book reviews. Scott and Denney's *Elementary English Composition* took up "Conversation-English" and "Recitation-English." And besides all these indications of a complete reaction against the abstract rhetoric of former years, there were the alphabetical lists of disputed or faulty diction that were designed for quick and easy reference by the student as he wrote or revised.

In the 1890s, which marked the height of the daily-theme vogue, most teachers seem to have agreed with Arlo Bates that "The way to write is to write."[5] The ideal of constant practice flourished. It did not, however, go unchallenged. One of the major controversies at meetings of English teachers and in the teaching journals of the time was whether practice in writing, or the reading of literature, is the better way to teach composition. The most eloquent advocate of the literary point of view was Dr. Samuel Thurber, Principal of the Girls' High School, Boston. Literally dozens of his articles can be found in the educational periodicals of the 1890s, most of them on this theme. "Thoroughly pernicious," said Thurber in one article, "is the notion that pupils must be made to compose something every day, for the sake of practice in composing. If you undertake this daily composition enterprise you must rake together all the pettinesses of current life for your material; you must expect, at best, a wish-wash of trivialities; the stuff is too abundant to be read; it is too thin to interest anybody, even if it could be read. You do ill to set up the ideal of fluency as the goal of your composition teaching. The market is glutted with fluency. . . ."[6] Young children, said Thurber, cannot be taught English at all; they learn solely by observation and imitation. The youth can be taught only slightly more than the child. As for the adult, he learns far less from books on rhetoric than from observation and a love for literature.[7]

> Only he who can read with pleasure can possibly acquire the language in which books are written,—the literary form of English, command of which is the pre-eminent note and characteristic of culture. The rhetoric attempts to prune colloquial, faulty English into good literary English. The attempt is futile. The reading habit presents the literary English as an actual, existing, fully-formed entity, familiar association with which results in the acquirement of its forms. He who will not or cannot read pores in vain over manuals of rhetoric. He who can and will read acquires all that the rhetoric had to teach.[8]

Thurber wanted to abolish all rhetoric texts ("If you cannot make up your minds to do this, you are still in the bonds of iniquity")[9] and eliminate special teachers of composition. He wanted all the teachers of a school to serve as English teachers, to correct bad English whenever they came across it. "If the teachers of a school are gentlemen and ladies of culture, they know good English from bad, are competent to correct errors, and to appreciate the good qualities of writing. A single teacher laboring over the correction of great masses of composition effects nothing."[10]

Thurber had some support from other quarters. In 1896 the *Century Magazine* published an unsigned article called "Two Ways of Teaching English,"[11] in which the theory of frequent practice was attacked. The author did not go as far as Thurber in throwing out all practice in writing, but he insisted that "No amount of mere grammatical and rhetorical training, nor even of constant practice in the art of composition, can attain the result reached by the child who reads good books because he loves to read them." Speaking of the "drudgery" that composition work imposes on both pupil and teacher, the writer declared "there is no educational method at present that involves so enormous an outlay of time, energy, and money, with so correspondingly small a result" (pp. 793–794). Ten years later a committee of the New England Association of Teachers of English made a report on rhetoric and composition textbooks in which a similar emphasis was reflected. Clear expression comes from clear thinking, and clear thinking comes not from "the dry pages of a grammar" but from the reading of good literature.[12]

On the other hand, this preponderant emphasis on literature in the composition course was assailed. William E. Mead, in a 1901 report of the Modern Language Association on "The Undergraduate Study of English Composition," said that the argument for reading literature as a means of teaching composition had not yet been demonstrated. He recognized the value of reading and admitted that unless students had something to write about, their practice in composition would be futile. At the same time, he argued, "to rely wholly upon reading as a means of reaching the rhetorical goal is . . . about as satisfactory as trying to walk on one leg instead of two."[13] Joseph V. Denney, in his pamphlet *Two Problems in Composition-Teaching*, took a similar position. There are distinct benefits to be got from careful reading of the English classics, but reading is not a substitute for actual practice in writing. Denney subjected Thurber's argument to a close analysis, pointing out what skills may reasonably be expected to result from wide reading, and then observed that these skills are not the same ones that are required for writing. Reading is a receptive, writing a productive activity.

> The power to organize his own ideas, in written or oral speech, the power to deal with situations of which he is himself a vital part,—this is the power which composition-training seeks to develop in the pupil, and which practice in writing and speaking on subjects within the range of his own observation and experience can alone adequately call into activity. Those who would abolish direct attempts to teach composition, who believe that reading may profitably supplant practice in

writing, take no account of this, the most essential function of composition-work. To them, instruction in composition means merely sentence-tinkering, form dissociate from thought, writing for the sake of writing (p. 5).

If reading really were the sole cause of good writing, added Denney, then college seniors, after a dozen years of reading in the lower schools and four more in college, might be expected to write with considerable skill. The facts, however, were otherwise (p. 6).

The books of Scott and Denney showed that neither man wished to undervalue the importance of literature; all their texts were full of illustrative extracts, and one of them (*Composition-Literature*) was almost as much an anthology as a rhetoric. Scott, in a little article called "A Brief Catechism on Textbooks in English,"[14] said that one of the requirements of a good English textbook is that it must put before the student "choice specimens of prose and poetry adapted to his stage of development." These selections, thought Scott, will help the student to arrive at standards for his own use of language, as well as provide a stimulus for him to express his own ideas. But, he believed, there must also be a considerable amount of writing done; to rely exclusively on literature is not enough (p. 361). That most other rhetoricians of the nineties agreed with this position is plain from the textbooks. The combination of literary extracts with assignments in composition was a common one.

This dispute over the relative value of practice and reading was significant in a number of ways. First, the heavy increase in both school and college enrollments in the nineties meant large, unwieldy classes; there were frequent references in books and articles of the period to "overburdened teachers." It is not unlikely that some of the support Thurber got came from teachers looking for a plausible way out of correcting daily themes from several classes numbering fifty or sixty students each. Second, Thurber's argument was given force by the new study of educational psychology, which emphasized the importance of imitation in the learning process: expose the child to plenty of good literature, Thurber assumed, and he would unconsciously model his own use of language on what he read. Third, by the mid-1890s literature was no longer on the defensive in either schools or colleges; that it had already won a secure place for itself is suggested by the mere fact that its more ardent partisans could make such sweeping claims for it. Finally, the dispute was evidence of dissatisfaction with the results of composition training. Even though formal rhetoric had been abandoned and the ideal of frequent practice in writing set up, students still did not seem to write the way their teachers thought they should. The popular clamor over the Harvard Reports focused attention on the problem. It is not surprising that some critics urged giving up the whole thing. Do away with composition and composition textbooks, do away with special composition teachers. It is possible to look at Thurber's argument as a rationalization, a way around the problem rather than a direct solution of it.

The whole movement away from the abstract rhetoric of mid-century ran parallel to comparable changes in educational philosophy. When the old required curriculum gave way to the elective system, and when the disciplinary ideal was supplanted by a more utilitarian aim, rhetorical theory gradually fell into line. Beginning in the lower schools, where the new European theories of education were first felt, and extending gradually to the colleges, the aim of rhetorical instruction became that of teaching students to write acceptably, rather than loading them down with a mass of principles to be committed to memory. As more writing came to be required in rhetoric classes, it quickly became apparent that such elaborate systems of rhetorical theory as those of Day and Bascom did little to ensure acceptable compositions. As a result, rhetorical doctrine was simplified, with the aim of pruning it of unessentials and thus making it practical. Though such obvious aspects of the older theory as philosophical discussions of invention and lists of figures of speech and types of style were got rid of, what happened in general was simply that the new doctrine was made a more generalized version of the old. That is, instead of making a clean break with the complicated systematic rhetoric of the 1860s, later theorists devised or redefined abstract terms which, though fewer than before, included more under each of them. Wendell's Unity-Mass-Coherence is a case in point. Thus the simplification of theory was more apparent than actual.

The other efforts to make rhetoric "practical" were an outgrowth of the new emphasis on practice. Since the rhetorical instruction of mid-century had been chiefly theory without practice, the tendency at the end of the century was to urge mainly practice without theory, or at least with a bare minimum of theory. But, besides calling forth such reactions as Thurber's, this approach actually required the presence in rhetoric textbooks of a good deal of theoretical material that had not commonly been found in the earlier books—chiefly, material on grammar, punctuation, spelling, and the use of capitals. This was theory of a more mundane sort than the earlier disquisitions on the Sublime and the nature of the Nervous Style. It looked, it is true, toward the actual production of writing—something that the older theory had not—but it was intended to secure in that writing no more than a superficial correctness in mechanical details. As rhetorical theory narrowed and became rigid after 1900, centered as it was around a few sets of abstractions, this sort of material bulked ever larger in composition textbooks. It is not inaccurate to say that rhetorical instruction in the first part of the twentieth century, though requiring a considerable amount of writing, was almost as "impractical," almost as unrelated to the realities of communication as the instruction had been fifty years before.

Conclusion

CHAPTER TWELVE

T HE LAST HALF of the
nineteenth century was
a transitional period in
rhetorical theory. The
classical tradition of rhet-
oric had just about evaporated by the time of Blair and Campbell
in the eighteenth century, but these men, in spite of individual
differences, succeeded in formulating a systematic and fairly
homogeneous body of theory, grounded in eighteenth century
psychology and serving the cultural needs of the time. This
theory became itself the source of a new tradition lasting for
nearly a hundred years. Until about 1880, American rhetorical
texts were little more than revisions of Blair's *Lectures* and
Campbell's *Philosophy*. The elaborate theoretical structures of
the British books, with their enunciation of laws of rhetoric
based on laws of mind, fitted in well with the mental discipline
theory that underlay American higher education. When this
theory began to lose its hold because of attacks on its psychological basis and because of its remoteness from specific practical applications, the British rhetorical tradition was abandoned.
Systematic rhetoric was identified with a philosophy of education rapidly going out of fashion. There was then the question,
what sort of approach to rhetoric would accommodate itself to
the new attitude that regarded education as a practical fitting
for life in modern industrial society.

The answer to this question took many forms as rhetoricians groped to find a central attitude on which to found a new

rhetoric. The first solution proposed was simple surgery: cut away the catalogs of emotions, the long lists of figures of speech, the disquisitions on the Sublime and the Pathetic—features that now seemed anachronistic—and thus reduce rhetorical theory to its essentials without disturbing its basic character. This tendency culminated in Barrett Wendell's formula Unity-Coherence-Emphasis, which was designed to replace sets of injunctions that in earlier texts had covered scores of pages. Another solution was to make rhetoric "practical," to insist that rhetorical principles were valuable only as far as they led to actual skill in writing. In its ultimate form, this attitude resulted in the "daily theme," constant practice and little or no theory. Other men thought rhetoric could be rejuvenated by allying it more closely with the popular new study of English literature—either through rhetorical analysis of masterpieces or through wide reading in good literature apart from any rhetorical injunctions. Bain's "forms of discourse" were welcomed as a device around which rhetorical instruction could be centered. Scott and Denney proposed the paragraph as the central prose unit, mastery of which would lead to mastery of most other details of composition. For a brief time the conception of writing as communication filling social needs received some support. Running beneath all these theories, however, and stronger than any of them, was the doctrine of mechanical correctness.

A few of these devices and theories were fruitful, most were not. Each was advanced by its originator in full confidence that it was the right and only answer to the problem that rhetoric faced: how to become once more a vital discipline, in step with the age. The trouble was that these men lacked a perspective comprehensive enough to see rhetoric in all its ramifications. The solutions they proposed were partial, so that after 1880 American rhetorical theory splintered into many little separate emphases, each having its day of popularity and its enthusiastic supporters, but none being broad enough to furnish the basis for a significant new tradition. The solitary exception was Fred Newton Scott, who tried to create a new system of rhetorical theory drawing on the data of experimental psychology and linguistics. Scott's approach was fundamental, and, had it become popular, would have made the subsequent history of rhetorical theory far different from what it actually was. But Scott was ahead of his time. The new psychology, that offered so many opportunities for enriching rhetorical theory, was not widely enough understood for its bearing on rhetoric to be appreciated. The same may be said of linguistics. Therefore, when the clamor aroused by the Harvard Reports reached its height, Scott's ideas were smothered by the demand for correctness.

In the twentieth century, as the narrower tendencies of the nineties set the tone for composition instruction, rhetorical theory atrophied. The "four forms of discourse" became almost universal as the organizing principle of rhetoric textbooks, and discussions of the units of prose composition became merely the application of Unity-Coherence-Emphasis to each unit in turn. A survey of some twenty rhetoric texts published between 1900 and 1915 shows the "four forms" prominent in sixteen of them, and Unity-Coherence-Emphasis in fourteen. There was nothing really new added to rhetorical theory until the third decade of the century. New books were simply rearrangements of old books—a sort of parasitism.

At the same time, rhetorical instruction became routinized. The triumph of the "four forms" and of Wendell's "principles of composition" meant the end of any tendency there might have been to recognize the communicative function of language, and the office of rhetoric in ministering to social needs. These two items of theory encouraged writing by formula, writing as an academic exercise to illustrate certain abstract principles or fulfill certain specifications imposed neither by the needs of the student nor by the requirements of the subject or situation. It was writing in a social vacuum, with no motivation behind it except the necessity of handing in a theme.

The routine, mechanical nature of composition work was greatly accentuated by the renewed emphasis on surface details of writing. Already in the 1890s grammar, punctuation, and capitalization had begun to take up an increasing amount of space in rhetorics, and books like Genung's *Outlines of Rhetoric* and A. S. Hill's *Foundations of Rhetoric* had foreshadowed later developments. Grammar in the lower schools had been de-emphasized for a time in the late eighties and the nineties as a reaction against the way it had previously been taught. But the Harvard Reports, which made a national issue of "bad" (that is, incorrect) English, forced the schools to turn their attention back to grammar, since it was insisted that such instruction was no part of the duty of the college or university. Students presenting themselves for admission to college continued, however, to make mechanical errors in their English entrance examinations. Since the colleges could not bar everyone who misspelled words or joined sentences with commas, the college course in English composition soon gave less attention to rhetoric and more to grammar and mechanics.

Sections on grammar were found in about forty per cent of the rhetoric texts of the first fifteen years of the twentieth century, often accompanied by glossaries of faulty usage. Rules on punctuation appeared in more than half the books, and instructions on the use of capitals in nearly a third. But these treatments of grammar and mechanics apparently were not enough. In 1907, as what one writer called "the grammar craze" continued to mount, a book appeared that met perfectly the requirements of the prevailing attitude toward rhetorical instruction: Edwin C. Woolley's *Handbook of Composition*. The first edition consisted of 350 numbered rules covering grammar, usage, sentence structure, punctuation and capitals, spelling, manuscript form, etc. There was a glossary of faulty usage at the end composed of 319 items, as well as appendixes on grammatical terminology and pronunciation (really, mispronunciation). The tone throughout was negative and dogmatic. Woolley freely admitted that his rules were dogmatic, that no exceptions were allowed even when they were known to exist; but he defended this practice as a special virtue of his book. A person who is lost in a city, said Woolley, does not want to be further confused by being told of a number of alternate routes to get where he wants to go. If only a single route is told him, he will be more likely to arrive at his destination. In the same way, the "erring composer of anarchic discourse" can be set right only by hard and fast rules that admit of no exceptions (pp. iv-v).

Woolley's book was popular and in its various revisions has undoubtedly been one of the most successful English text-books published in this century. Its influence on composition instruction, however, has been to narrow the field. It has been a powerful force in perpetuating that distorted view of the true nature and function of grammar that the over-prescriptive approach necessarily brings with it. It has encouraged an unreal conception of the writing process by exalting to the highest place what is, after all, only a subordinate part of composition: correctness in details. And finally, it has helped to entrench the view of writing as something that is done well if only it is done by rule.

In the 1890s English composition had been an important matter, whether or not one agreed with the authors of the Harvard Reports that it did not belong in college. It belonged somewhere, and if, as finally proved to be the case, the secondary schools could not train students to a sufficient level of competence, then the colleges would after all have to make good the deficiency. In a curriculum largely elective, freshman composition by the end of the century had become one of the few courses that every student had to take. The pattern persisted in the next century, but the feeling that composition was in a real sense important soon evaporated. In the nineties men well up in the hierarchy of English departments did not feel it beneath them to write a textbook on composition, or debate methods and materials of composition instruction in the professional journals and at gatherings of teachers. After 1900, as rhetorical theory settled in its several ruts, and as the composition teacher was reduced almost to a proofreader, the field rapidly lost status. Barrett Wendell took up literature, regretting that he had spent so much of his life trying, as he said, to teach the unteachable. Scott became increasingly interested in journalism. Genung specialized in literature and biblical scholarship. Gertrude Buck turned to literature. The best of the new men also were attracted to literature. And so it went. In schools with graduate programs in English, composition teaching was assigned to untrained graduate students. In schools less fortunate, full-time teachers of the lowest academic ranks were given the chore; they looked on it at best as a probationary period which they must undergo before being promoted to literature courses. Composition teaching became, in a very real sense, drudgery of the worst sort, unenlivened by any genuine belief in its value, shackled by an unrealistic theory of writing, and so debased in esteem that men of ability were unwilling to identify themselves with it permanently. It had reached this condition by 1915 or before, and in spite of the efforts of a few men like Sterling Leonard the condition persisted for another two decades.

The years from 1850 to 1900 cannot in any sense be called a great period in the history of rhetoric; yet it was important. It was the time that saw the rise of modern courses in English, both literature and composition. It was the time in which nearly every development that was to appear in rhetorical theory and instruction up to the middle 1930s was formulated. Most composition teaching today, in fact, is still being done in the shadow of rhetorical theory that came into prominence between 1885 and 1900. The "four forms of discourse," for instance, and the Unity-Coherence-Emphasis formula have by no means been widely discredited even now; nor has there appeared anything new in paragraph doctrine since its presentation by Scott and Denney in 1893. The ideal of correctness in mechanical details, which came in the later nineties to dominate rhetorical instruction, has today perhaps more supporters than any other single aspect of the rhetorical process.

The tradition of rhetoric is now some 2,400 years old— one of the longest traditions still represented in the modern curriculum. Teachers of composition today fail to recognize that they and their work are a part of that tradition. If a teacher is to have any perspective on his subject, he must know the tradition that lies behind it, know the place of himself and his times in the tradition, and, through this knowledge, be able to put a proper value on new developments in his subject as they appear. This dissertation is an attempt to fill in one neglected period in the history of rhetoric—not a great period, but one that is nevertheless significant. In the first place, it shows with unusual clarity how specific items of rhetorical theory appear, are developed, and finally are accepted. It was in these years that such notions as paragraph doctrine and the forms of discourse were first advanced, somewhat tentatively, then rapidly and uncritically assimilated into rhetorical theory, so that by the end of the period they were regarded as immutable laws of discourse. In the second place, these fifty years supply the immediate background for our present courses in composition and thus make more clear the nature of the tradition in which we are now working. A knowledge of this period should make it possible to evaluate more justly the rhetorical doctrine now being taught, as well as to place in a more accurate perspective whatever new tendencies may develop.

Notes

CHAPTER ONE
Main Trends in Higher Education 1850-1900

1. For an account of the origins and rise of mental and moral philosophy, see Herbert W. Schneider, *A History of American Philosophy* (New York, 1946), pp. 225-250.

2. James Burrill Angell, *The Reminiscences of James Burrill Angell* (New York, 1912), pp. 245-246.

3. Ellwood P. Cubberley, *Public Education in the United States*, rev. and enl. ed. (Boston, 1934), p. 691.

4. *Psychological Review*, VIII (May, July, November, 1901), 247-261, 384-395, 553-564.

5. Donald G. Tewksbury, *The Founding of American Colleges and Universities Before the Civil War* (New York, 1932), pp. 71-72, 73.

6. Thomas LeDuc, *Piety and Intellect at Amherst College* (New York, 1946), p. 23.

7. "A National University," *The Addresses and Journals of Proceedings of the National Education Association for 1874*, p. 74.

8. LeDuc, p. 15.

9. LeDuc, p. 53.

10. P. cxlviii.

11. Arthur M. Schlesinger, *The Rise of the City, 1878-1898*, Vol. X in *A History of American Life*, ed. A. M. Schlesinger and Dixon Ryan Fox (New York, 1933), p. 203.

12. Arthur Charles Cole, *The Irrepressible Conflict, 1850-1865*, Vol. VII, in *A History of American Life*, ed. Arthur M. Schlesinger and Dixon Ryan Fox (New York, 1934), p. 211.

13. Allan Nevins, *The Emergence of Modern America, 1865–1878*, Vol. VIII, in *A History of American Life*, ed. Arthur M. Schlesinger and Dixon Ryan Fox (New York, 1927), p. 287.

14. Nevins, p. 289.

15. Nevins, p. 287.

16. New York, 1891, copyright 1860.

17. Cubberley, p. 469.

18. Edward H. Reisner, *Nationalism and Education Since 1789: A Social and Political History of Modern Education* (New York, 1922), p. 425.

19. C. F. Thwing, *The American and the German University* (New York, 1928), p. 41.

20. Ernest L. Harris, "American Students in German Universities," *Report of the Commissioner of Education, 1900–1901*, II, 1517.

21. Samuel Eliot Morison, *Three Centuries of Harvard, 1636–1936* (Cambridge, Mass., 1936), p. 299.

22. *German Universities* (New York, 1874), p. 303.

23. "University Reform. An Address to the Alumni of Harvard at Their Triennial Festival, July 19, 1866," *Atlantic Monthly*, XVIII (1866), 301.

24. LeDuc, p. 51.

25. LeDuc, p. 50.

26. Morison, p. 298.

27. Morison, p. 299.

28. Edward Delavan Perry, "The American University," *Monographs on Education in the United States*, ed. N. M. Butler, 2 vols. (Albany, N.Y., 1900), I, 284.

29. John A. Walz, *German Influence in American Education and Culture* (Philadelphia, 1936), pp. 53–54.

30. Perry, p. 286.

31. Perry, p. 287.

32. "Inaugural Address as President of Harvard College," *Educational Reform: Essays and Addresses* (New York, 1898), p. 1.

33. At Columbia, for example, President Barnard between about 1868 and 1882 repeatedly urged the Trustees of the College to allow the introduction of the elective system, though formerly he himself had been one of the most uncompromising supporters of the prescribed course of studies. Barnard met a good deal of opposition to this proposal, as well as to his recommendations that graduate study, coeducation, and more science courses be authorized. By 1882, however, several of these changes had been effected, and the elective

system was operating with some latitude in the junior and senior classes. *Memoirs of Frederick A. P. Barnard*, ed. John Fulton (New York, 1896), pp. 379-395.

34. Samuel Eliot Morison, ed., "Introduction," *The Development of Harvard University Since the Inauguration of President Eliot, 1869-1929* (Cambridge, Mass., 1930), pp. xlii-xliii.

35. *Memories of Yale Life and Men, 1845-1899* (New York, 1903), pp. 89-90.

36. *Autobiography* (New York, 1904-05), I, 26.

37. *Autobiography*, p. 28.

38. Abraham Flexner, *Daniel Coit Gilman* (New York, 1946), pp. 10-11.

39. *Autobiography*, I, 29.

40. *A History of Higher Education in America* (New York, 1906), pp. 441-442.

41. Dwight, p. 152.

42. Dwight, p. 347.

43. Perry, p. 284.

44. Dwight, p. 92.

45. Dwight, p. 347.

46. *Connecticut Yankee, an Autobiography* (New Haven, Conn., 1943), p. 67.

47. New York, 1878.

48. In an article on vocational education written in 1917, John Dewey made some pertinent remarks on this subject. He pointed out that the classical curriculum (to which Porter is referring here) was, ironically, designed in the first place as a very "practical" sort of vocational or professional education—for the clergy, lawyers, physicians, clerks, etc. "For," he added, "it will be found true as a general principle, that whenever any study which was originally utilitarian in purpose becomes useless because of a change in conditions, it is retained as a necessary educational ornament (as useless buttons are retained on the sleeves of men's coats) or else because it is so useless that it must be fine for mental discipline. . . . Those who object most bitterly to any form of vocational training will often be found to be those whose own monopoly of present vocational training is threatened." "Learning to Earn: The Place of Vocational Education in a Comprehensive Scheme of Public Education," *School and Society*, V (1917), 331.

49. Francis Parsons, *Six Men of Yale* (New Haven, Conn., 1939), p. 111.

50. "Yale in Its Relation to the Development of the Country," *Report of the Commissioner of Education for 1902*, I, 594.

51. See Hinsdale, pp. 16-17, and Walz, pp. 14-15.

52. Quoted in Schneider, p. 235, n.

53. Herbert B. Adams, *The Study of History in American Colleges and Universities*, Bureau of Education Circular of Information No. 2, 1887, p. 94.

54. The first bachelor of science degree conferred in the United States was granted by the Lawrence Scientific School at Cambridge in 1851. Professor N. S. Shaler, affiliated with the School from 1858, attributed the introduction of the degree to Louis Agassiz, who "hoped, through the education which should lead to the degree, to break up the old collegiate routine." This is a quotation from a letter written by Shaler to B. A. Hinsdale, found in Hinsdale's *History of the University of Michigan*, ed. Isaac N. Demmon (Ann Arbor, Mich., 1906), p. 48, n.

55. Hinsdale, pp. 43-44.

56. Cole, p. 210. For a fairly detailed account of early instruction in history at Michigan, see Adams, pp. 87-123. Harvard established the first chair of history in 1839; its occupant was Jared Sparks.

57. Hinsdale, p. 44.

58. Hinsdale, p. 71.

59. See White, *Autobiography*, I, 278-279; and Hinsdale, p. 86.

60. James Burrill Angell, *Selected Addresses* (New York, 1912), p. 88.

61. Ibid., pp. 166-167.

62. Ibid., p. 169.

63. Ibid., p. 14.

64. Hinsdale, p. 71.

65. Angell, *Reminiscences*, pp. 245-246.

66. Hinsdale, p. 81.

67. Hinsdale, p. 80.

68. "Angell, James Burrill," *DAB*, I, 308.

CHAPTER TWO
The Field of English

1. Warren Guthrie, "The Development of Rhetorical Theory in America, 1685-1850," Part III, *Speech Monographs*, XV (1948), 69.

2. Timothy Dwight, *Memories of Yale Life and Men, 1845-1899*,

p. 376. For a fuller picture of these societies as they existed in the 1850s, see Guy R. Lyle, "College Literary Societies in the Fifties," *Library Quarterly*, IV (1934), 487–493.

3. *Educational Reform*, p. 2.

4. *Educational Reform*, p. 100.

5. G. H. Grandgent writes regarding Child that "One bitter note in his sweet cheeriness was sometimes aroused by the remembrance of the great proportion of his life that had been spent on theme-correcting." "The Modern Languages," *The Development of Harvard University*, ed. Morison, pp. 66–67.

6. Grandgent, p. 66.

7. Appendix, *Twenty Years of School and College English* (Cambridge, Mass., 1896), p. 58.

8. Grandgent, p. 75.

9. Grandgent, p. 67.

10. Appendix, *Twenty Years of School and College English*, pp. 55–57.

11. "An Answer to the Cry for More English," *Twenty Years of School and College English*, p. 8. (This essay was first published in 1879.)

12. Ibid.

13. Ibid., pp. 8–9.

14. See F. A. March, "The Study of Anglo-Saxon," *Report of the Commissioner of Education for 1876–77*, p. 477; W. G. T. Shedd, "The Influence and Method of English Studies," *Literary Essays* (New York, 1878), pp. 65–66.

15. March, pp. 477–478.

16. "John S. Hart, Principal of the Philadelphia High School," *American Journal of Education*, V (1858), 104.

17. March, p. 478.

18. See D. S. Gregory, "Review of Philological Works by Prof. Francis A. March of Lafayette College," *The Presbyterian Quarterly and Princeton Review*, n.s., III (1874), 748–749.

19. March, p. 478.

20. March, p. 479.

21. "Courses of Study in Colleges and Universities," *Report of the Commissioner of Education for 1888–89*, II, 1224–93.

22. Ibid., p. 1237.

23. Ibid., p. 1265.

24. Ibid., pp. 1267, 1269.

25. New York, 1866, copyright 1852.

26. Ed., with notes and illustrations, William Smith (New York, 1867).

27. *Connecticut Yankee*, pp. 111-114.

28. *History of the English Language* (New York, 1879).

29. Fred N. Scott, "English at the University of Michigan," *English in American Universities, by Professors in the English Departments of Twenty Representative Institutions*, ed., with an introduction, William Morton Payne (Boston, 1895), p. 116.

30. Martin W. Sampson, "English at the University of Indiana," *English in American Universities*, pp. 92-95.

31. Appendix, *Twenty Years of School and College English*, pp. 62-63.

32. See Giles Wilkeson Gray, "Research in the History of Speech Education," *Quarterly Journal of Speech*, XXXV (1949), 159-161.

33. "A Chapter in the Organization of College Courses in Public Speaking," *Quarterly Journal of Speech*, XII (1926), 1-11.

34. "Rhetoric and Public Speaking in the American College," *Education*, XIII (1892), 137. Some idea of the rapid growth of Greek-letter fraternities in the last two decades of the century can be got from the following figures: already by 1879 there were 462 chapters with 63,000 members; by 1898 there were 781 chapters having a total membership of 130,000. Arthur M. Schlesinger, *The Rise of the City*, pp. 208-209.

35. *Report of the Commissioner of Education*, 1899-1900, I, xlviii.

36. Scott, "English at the University of Michigan," p. 116.

37. Barrett Wendell, "English at Harvard University," *English in American Universities*, pp. 44-45.

38. Report No. XXVIII, now bound in *Reports of the Visiting Committees of the Board of Overseers of Harvard College* (Cambridge, Mass., 1902), pp. 117-157.

39. "Report of the Committee on Composition and Rhetoric," Report No. XLIX, pp. 275-287; and "Report of the Committee on Composition and Rhetoric," Report No. LXXI, pp. 401-424, both in *Reports of the Visiting Committees of the Board of Overseers of Harvard College* (1902). In these two reports George R. Nutter replaced Josiah Quincy on the committee, but Adams and Godkin remained.

40. *English in American Universities*, ed. Payne.

41. *Twenty Years of School and College English*.

42. Robert Herrick, "Methods of Teaching Rhetoric in Schools," No. 3 in *Teaching English* (Chicago, n.d.), pp. 2-3, 6.

43. Quoted in E. L. Godkin, "The Growing Illiteracy of American Boys," *The Nation*, LXIII (1896), 284.

44. William F. Brewer, "English at College," *The Nation*, LXIII (1896), 327.

45. "College-Entrance Requirements in English," *School Review*, IX (1901), 366.

CHAPTER THREE

Rhetorics and Rhetoricians

1. Warren Guthrie, "The Development of Rhetorical Theory in America, 1685-1850," Part III, p. 61, n.

2. Loc. cit.

3. Guthrie, p. 62, n.

4. "Courses of Study in Colleges and Universities," *Report of the Commissioner of Education, 1888-89*, p. 1239.

5. London, 1839, edition used here.

6. New York, 1875.

7. Guthrie, Part III, p. 63.

8. Guthrie, p. 63, n.

9. Louisville, Kentucky, 1846, reprinted from the 7th (octavo) edition.

10. Part III, p. 65, n.

11. "Courses of Study in Colleges and Universities," pp. 1224-93. The institutions listing Whately are the University of Denver, the University of South Carolina, Washington and Lee University, and Smith, Marietta, and Middlebury Colleges.

12. *Elements of Logic*, 1826.

13. *Elements of Rhetoric*, p. 17.

14. He is indebted to Campbell for the substance of this section, treating energy under Campbell's headings of choice, number, and arrangement of words (pp. 192-226).

15. Woodward's 3rd ed. (Philadelphia, 1810).

16. 2 vols. (Cambridge, Mass.).

17. 7th ed. (Andover, Mass., 1839).

18. Newman ties rhetoric not only with logic and grammar but also with "intellectual philosophy" (psychology), though he believes this useful mainly in explaining to us the phenomena of taste (pp. 15-16).

19. *Lectures Read to the Seniors in Harvard College* (Boston, 1856).

20. *The Flowering of New England, 1815-1865*, new and rev. ed. (New York, 1940), pp. 44-45.

21. Andover, Mass.

22. Philadelphia.

23. P. 2. Actually p. 1; it is a misprint.

24. 8th ed. (New York, 1867, copyright 1844).

25. 20th ed. (New York, 1858). The text seems to be that of the 2nd ed., copyright 1845.

26. "An Answer to the Cry for More English," p. 11.

27. *To College Teachers of English Composition* (Boston, 1928), pp. 2–3.

28. *Dean Briggs* (New York, 1926), p. 51.

29. Hill, "An Answer," p. 12.

30. "The Scholar Whom We Knew," *Amherst Graduates' Quarterly*, IX (February 1920), 71.

31. John M. Tyler, "John Franklin Genung," *Amherst Graduates' Quarterly*, IX (February 1920), 67–68.

32. Francis L. Palmer, "Professor Genung's First Class at Amherst," *Amherst Graduates' Quarterly*, IX (February 1920), 82.

33. Erskine, p. 73.

34. Erskine, p. 72.

35. G. F. Whicher, "Genung's Rhetoric," *The Nation*, CIX (1919), 658. Actually, Whicher is speaking here of the 1900 revision of the *Practical Elements* entitled *The Working Principles of Rhetoric*, but the books are very similar.

36. Whicher, p. 658.

37. Tyler, p. 69.

38. "The Modern Languages," in *The Development of Harvard University*, p. 76.

39. *Dean Briggs*, pp. 60–61.

40. Included in an article on Wendell's retirement in *Harvard Crimson*, LXXI (March 30, 1917), p. 5.

41. Briggs, as quoted by M. A. DeWolfe Howe in *Barrett Wendell and His Letters* (Boston, 1924), p. 84.

42. Briggs, p. 84.

43. Clarence D. Thorpe, "The Department of Rhetoric," in *The University of Michigan, an Encyclopedic Survey in 9 Parts*, Part III (*The College of Literature, Science, and the Arts* (Ann Arbor, Mich., 1943)), p. 560.

44. Thorpe, p. 560.

45. Thorpe, p. 564.

46. John Lewis Brumm, "In Memoriam, Fred Newton Scott," *Michigan Alumnus* (June 27, 1931), p. 655.

47. Shirley W. Smith, "Fred Newton Scott as a Teacher," *Michigan Alumnus* (February 4, 1933), p. 279.

48. Thorpe, p. 562.
49. Smith, p. 279.
50. Smith, p. 280.

CHAPTER FOUR
Rhetoric, 1850-1900: Definitions, Relations, Scope

1. The books of A. S. Hill, Genung, Wendell, and Scott will of course figure more or less prominently in the rest of this study, for they usually epitomize certain tendencies and often initiate new ones. A good many other books by less influential writers will be mentioned, however, since it is by studying these that one is able to get some perspective on the period as a whole.
2. Cincinnati.
3. New York.
4. New York, 1878.
5. 2nd ed. (New York, 1868, copyright 1867).
6. Princeton, New Jersey.
7. New York.
8. New York.
9. New York.
10. Boston.
11. Chicago.
12. New York.
13. (St. Louis), pp. 15-16.
14. Boston.
15. "English in Secondary Education," in George R. Carpenter, Franklin T. Baker, and Fred N. Scott, *The Teaching of English in the Elementary and Secondary School* (New York, 1903), pp. 219-220. The same distinction may be found in other books as well; for example, A. Howry Espenshade, *Essentials of Composition and Rhetoric* (Boston, 1904, copyright 1904), p. 16; and Robert Herrick and Lindsay Todd Damon, *Composition and Rhetoric for Schools*, rev. ed. (Chicago, 1902), pp. 16-17.
16. Boston.
17. New York.
18. Boston.
19. Boston.
20. 4th ed. (New York, 1896, copyright 1893), p. 2.
21. Philadelphia, 1875, copyright 1870.
22. 2nd ed. (Andover, Mass., 1864, copyright 1859).

23. *The Principles of Written Discourse* (New York, 1884), pp. 12-14.

24. New York, 1895, copyright 1885.

25. Boston, 1891.

26. The italics are Day's.

27. New York, 1864, copyright 1854.

28. "Rhetoric and Public Speaking in the American College," *Education*, XIII (1892), 129.

29. New York.

30. New York.

31. *Second High School Course* (New York).

32. Boston.

33. O. F. Emerson, "English in Secondary Schools," *Academy*, IV (Syracuse, N.Y., 1899), 238.

34. "Cornell Course in Rhetoric and English Philology," *Academy*, VI (Syracuse, N.Y., 1891), 183.

35. *Academy*, IV (Syracuse, N.Y., 1889), 382-383.

36. New York.

37. Boston.

38. Boston.

39. New York.

40. Ann Arbor, Mich.

41. New York.

CHAPTER FIVE
Subject Matter and Logic

1. *The Presbyterian Quarterly and Princeton Review*, III (n.s.) (1874), 664.

2. Haven, p. 311; Hill, *Science*, p. 4.

3. New ed., rev. and enl. (New York, copyright 1878, 1895).

4. Boston.

5. Boston, 1901, copyright 1899.

6. Rev. ed. (Boston, copyright 1896, 1909).

7. New York.

8. New York (1863), copyright 1851.

9. New York.

10. New York (1869), copyright 1860.

11. *Our English* (New York, 1888), pp. 96-97.

12. "The Art of English Composition," p. 378.

13. *English in the Preparatory Schools* (Boston, 1887), p. 13.

14. "The Art of English Composition," pp. 379-380.

15. *A Study of Rhetoric in the College Course* (Boston, 1887), pp. 26-28.

16. "Cornell Course in Rhetoric and English Philology," p. 189.

17. Boston, 1894, copyright 1893.

18. 3rd ed., rev. (New York, 1904, copyright 1902).

19. *Two Problems in Composition-Teaching* printed as No. 3 in *Contributions to Rhetorical Theory*, ed. F. N. Scott (Ann Arbor, Mich., n.d.).

20. New York.

21. *The Art of Oratorical Composition* (New York, 1885).

22. Hill, *Principles*, 1878 ed., pp. 184-247; Genung, *Practical Elements*, pp. 407-446.

23. The edition used in this study is that of 1905, "revised and augmented," prepared in collaboration with Henry B. Huntington (Boston, copyright 1895, 1905).

24. New York.

25. *A Practical Rhetoric* (New York, 1889, copyright 1886), p. 28.

26. *Practical Elements*, pp. 176-185, 194-210.

27. *Exercises in Rhetoric and English Composition*, pp. 139-140, 156-160, 179-182.

28. *Talks, First Series*, p. 29.

29. New York, 1901, copyright 1897.

30. "Unity, Coherence, and Emphasis," *University of Wisconsin Studies in Language and Literature*, No. 2 (1918), pp. 77-98.

CHAPTER SIX
The Forms of Discourse

1. American ed., rev. (New York).

2. *Lectures on Metaphysics and Logic*, ed. H. L. Mansel and John Veitch, 4 vols. (Edinburgh, 1865), I, 189.

3. *Mental Science; a Compendium of Psychology, and the History of Philosophy* (New York, 1879, copyright 1868), pp. 371-385.

4. (London, 1904), p. 203.

5. *Elements of Criticism*, rev. and ed. James R. Boyd (New York, 1867, copyright 1855), pp. 404-421.

6. *Art of Discourse*, pp. 48-50, 70-82.

7. *The Elements of Logic, a Text-Book for Schools and Colleges; Being The Elementary Lessons in Logic. By W. Stanley Jevons, Recast by David J. Hill* (New York).

8. New York.

9. *Structure of English Prose*, p. 23.

10. Gilmore, pp. 43-55; McElroy, pp. 292-309.

11. *Principles*, 1878 ed., pp. 167-244.

12. *Practical Rhetoric*, p. 263.

13. *Practical Elements*, pp. 324-325.

14. New York, 1892, 1893.

15. Philadelphia.

16. *The New Composition-Rhetoric* (Boston).

17. New York.

18. New York.

19. *Contributions to Rhetorical Theory*, No. 6 (Ann Arbor, Mich., 1906).

CHAPTER SEVEN
The Communicative Function of Rhetoric

1. *Art of Discourse*, p. 6.

2. *Eloquence a Virtue*, pp. 156-176.

3. *Rhetorical Method*, pp. 91-95.

4. *Principles*, 1878 ed., pp. iii-iv.

5. *Principles*, rev. ed., p. v.

6. Boston.

7. Boston.

8. Sophie Chantal Hart, "English in the College," *School Review*, X (1902), 368.

9. *Two Problems in Composition-Teaching*, pp. 7-8.

10. *Educational Review*, XXII (1901), 371-382.

CHAPTER EIGHT
The Paragraph

1. Chicago.

2. (London.) There is no date given in the book itself, though the Library of Congress card gives 1861 as the year of publication.

3. (London, 1904), p. 279.

4. *Autobiography*, p. 279.

5. See Lewis, p. 20; and Fred Newton Scott and Joseph V. Denney, *Paragraph-Writing*, 3rd ed., rev. and enl. (Boston, 1893), p. 106, where the testimony of William Minto is cited.

6. Lewis, pp. 29-30.

7. *Principles*, 1878 ed., pp. 157-158.

8. *Paragraph-Writing*, p. 106.

9. A. T. Robinson, "The Question of Text-Books in Composition," *Science*, XXXVII (January 10, 1913), 61.

10. The book had apparently first been printed locally in Ann Arbor in 1891 for use in Scott's own classes. The 1893 edition was an expanded version published by Allyn and Bacon for national distribution.

11. Boston, 1893.

12. "Theory of the Paragraph," pp. 93-106.

13. New York.

14. New York.

15. New York.

CHAPTER NINE
Style

1. *The Philosophy of Style, Together with An Essay on Style by T. H. Wright*, ed. Fred N. Scott, 2nd ed. (Boston, 1892), p. 3.

2. An exception should perhaps be made for Scott and Denney's *Paragraph-Writing*, where "The General Laws of the Paragraph" were given as unity, selection, proportion, sequence, variety (pp. 4-17).

3. Blair, pp. 175-177; Cicero, *De Oratore*, trans. H. Rackham, 2 vols. (Cambridge, Mass., 1942), pp. 2, 121, 123.

4. Bain, *Mind and Body. The Theories of Their Relation* (New York, 1875), pp. 82-83.

5. *Elements*, p. 245; *Practical Course*, p. 82.

6. *Exercises*, pp. 199-200.

7. *Contributions to Rhetorical Theory*, No. 1 (n.p., n.d.).

8. *Contributions to Rhetorical Theory*, No. 5 (Ann Arbor, Mich., 1899).

9. *The Metaphor*, p. iii.

CHAPTER TEN
Diction, Usage, Grammar

1. "Pronunciation," *American College Dictionary*, ed. Clarence L. Barnhart (New York, 1948), p. xxii.

2. Hill, *Elements*, pp. 27-42; Quackenbos, *Advanced Course*, pp. 270-284; Hart, pp. 68-83.

3. Boston.

4. 3rd American ed. (New York, 1817).

5. Fredericktown, Maryland.

6. Albany, New York.

7. Philadelphia, 1869, copyright 1846.

8. Philadelphia, 1875, copyright 1874.

9. New York, 1909. Unfortunately, it was not possible to secure an earlier edition of this book than the one of 1909. According to the preface the 1909 edition is identical with the 1896 revision, except for correction of typographical errors.

10. Boston, 1879.

11. "The Psychology of the Diagram," *School Review*, V (1897), 470.

12. "The Teaching of English Grammar," *School Review*, V (1897), 129–130.

13. "The Teaching of English Grammar," p. 132.

14. *Education*, XVIII (1898), 269–277.

15. "The Sentence-Diagram," *Educational Review*, XIII (1897), 250–260.

16. Boston, 1898, copyright 1877.

17. Chicago.

18. G. R. Carpenter, "The Study of the Mother-Tongue," in Carpenter, Baker, and Scott, *The Teaching of English in the Elementary and the Secondary School*, pp. 49–50.

19. Hill, "An Answer to the Cry for More English," in *Twenty Years of School and College English*, p. 9.

20. Loc. cit.

21. "An Answer to the Cry for More English," p. 10.

22. Ibid., pp. 10–11.

23. Ibid., p. 11.

24. "The Harvard Admission Examination in English," in *Twenty Years of School and College English*, p. 17.

25. "The Correction of Bad English As a Requirement for Admission to Harvard College," *Academy*, V (Syracuse, N.Y., 1890), 312.

26. "The Correction of Bad English," pp. 304–305.

27. "Harvard Admission Examination," pp. 23–24.

CHAPTER ELEVEN
The Shift from Theoretical to Practical Rhetoric

1. *Structure of English Prose*, p. iii.

2. Huffcut, p. 10.

3. From Wendell's remarks during a discussion at the Conference of the New England Association of Colleges and Preparatory Schools,

December 1893. The discussion is reported in *School Review*, I (1893). The present quotation is on pp. 659-660.

4. *Practical Rhetoric*, p. 2.

5. *Talks, First Series*, p. 20.

6. "Five Axioms of Composition Teaching," *School Review*, V (1897), 14.

7. "An Address to Teachers of English," *Education*, XVIII (1898), 516.

8. "An Address to Teachers of English," p. 520.

9. "An Address to Teachers of English," p. 524.

10. "Five Axioms," pp. 14-15.

11. LXI (1896), 793-794.

12. Homer P. Lewis and others, "Textbooks in Rhetoric and in Composition," Report of the Standing Committee of the New England Association of Teachers of English on Aids in Teaching English, *School Review*, XIV (1906), 1.

13. *PMLA*, XVII (New Series 10) (1902), xxii.

14. *Educational Review*, XXXVII (1909), 359-361.

Bibliography

PRIMARY SOURCES

Books

Abbott, Edwin Abbott. *How to Write Clearly; Rules and Exercises on English Composition.* Boston: Roberts Brothers, 1879.

Adams, John Quincy. *Lectures on Rhetoric and Oratory, Delivered to the Classes of Senior and Junior Sophisters in Harvard University* (2 vols.). Cambridge, Mass.: Hilliard and Metcalf, 1810.

Angus, Joseph. *Handbook of the English Tongue. For the Use of Students and Others.* London: The Religious Tract Society, n.d.

Bain, Alexander. *Autobiography.* London: Longmans, Green and Co., 1904.

——— *English Composition and Rhetoric. A Manual* (American edition, revised). New York: D. Appleton and Co., 1866.

——— *On Teaching English.* New York: D. Appleton and Co., 1887.

Baker, George P. and Henry B. Huntington. *Principles of Argumentation* (revised and augmented). Boston: Ginn and Co., 1895, 1905.

Baldwin, Charles Sears. *Ancient Rhetoric and Poetic.* New York: The Macmillan Co., 1924.

——— *A College Manual of Rhetoric* (3rd edition, revised). New York: Longmans, Green and Co., 1904, copyright 1902.

——— *Composition, Oral and Written.* New York: Longmans, Green and Co., 1909.

245

———— *The Expository Paragraph and Sentence. An Elementary Manual of Composition.* New York: Longmans, Green and Co., 1901, copyright 1897.

———— *Writing and Speaking, a Text-Book of Rhetoric* (3rd edition). New York: Longmans, Green and Co., 1909.

Ball, Margaret. *The Principles of Outlining.* Boston: B. H. Sanborn and Co., 1910.

Bascom, John. *Philosophy of Rhetoric.* New York: Woolworth and Ainsworth and Co., 1872 (first printing: Boston: Crosby and Ainsworth, 1866).

Bates, Arlo. *Talks on Writing English, First Series.* Boston: Houghton Mifflin and Co., 1896.

———— *Talks on Writing English, Second Series.* Boston: Houghton Mifflin and Co., 1901.

Blair, Hugh. *Lectures on Rhetoric and Belles Lettres.* London: Charles Daly, 1839 (first edition: London, 1783).

Boyd, James R. *Elements of English Composition, Grammatical, Rhetorical, Logical, and Practical. Prepared for Academies and Schools.* New York and Chicago: A. S. Barnes and Co., 1869, copyright 1860.

———— *Elements of Rhetoric and Literary Criticism* (8th edition). New York: Harper and Brothers, 1867, copyright 1844.

Boynton, Percy H. *Principles of Composition.* Boston: Ginn and Co., 1915.

Brewster, William T. *English Composition and Style.* New York: The Century Co., 1912.

———— *Studies in Structure and Style (Based on Seven Modern English Essays)*, with an introduction by G. R. Carpenter. New York: The Macmillan Co., 1896.

———— *The Writing of English.* London: Williams and Norgate, n.d.

Brown, Rollo Walter and Nathaniel W. Barnes. *The Art of Writing English; A Book for College Classes.* New York: American Book Co., 1913.

Bryant, Frank Egbert. *On the Limits of Descriptive Writing Apropos of Lessing's Laocoon* (Contributions to Rhetorical Theory, No. 6, edited by Fred Newton Scott). Ann Arbor, Mich.: Ann Arbor Press, 1906.

Buck, Gertrude. *A Course in Argumentative Writing.* New York: H. Holt and Co., 1899.

———— *Figures of Rhetoric: A Psychological Study* (Contributions to Rhetorical Theory, No. 1, edited by Fred Newton Scott). N.p., n.d.

——— The Metaphor—A Study in the Psychology of Rhetoric (Contributions to Rhetorical Theory, No. 5, edited by Fred Newton Scott). Ann Arbor, Mich.: Inland Press, 1899.

——— The Social Criticism of Literature. New Haven, Conn.: Yale University Press, 1916.

Buck, Gertrude and Elisabeth Woodbridge. A Course in Expository Writing. New York: H. Holt and Co., 1899.

Buck, Gertrude and Elisabeth Woodbridge Morris. A Course in Narrative Writing. New York: H. Holt and Co., 1906.

Cairns, William B. The Forms of Discourse (revised edition). Boston: Ginn and Co., 1896, 1909.

——— Introduction to Rhetoric. Boston: Ginn and Co., 1901, copyright 1899.

Campbell, George. The Philosophy of Rhetoric. New York: Harper and Brothers, 1875 (first edition: Edinburgh, 1776).

Canby, Henry S. and J. B. Opdycke. Elements of Composition for Secondary Schools. New York: The Macmillan Co., 1913.

Canby, Henry S. and others. English Composition in Theory and Practice. New York: The Macmillan Co., 1909.

Carpenter, George R. Elements of Rhetoric and English Composition, Second High School Course. New York: The Macmillan Co., 1900.

——— Exercises in Rhetoric and English Composition (Advanced Course). New York: The Macmillan Co., 1896, copyright 1893.

——— Rhetoric and English Composition. New York: The Macmillan Co., 1906.

Carpenter, George R., Franklin T. Baker, and Fred N. Scott. The Teaching of English in the Elementary and the Secondary School. New York: Longmans, Green and Co., 1903.

Channing, Edward T. Lectures Read to the Seniors in Harvard College. Boston: Ticknor and Fields, 1856.

Cicero. De Oratore, translated by H. Rackham (2 vols.). Cambridge, Mass.: Harvard University Press; London: William Heinemann, Ltd., 1942.

Claggett, Rufus. Elocution Made Easy. New York: Paine and Burgess, 1845.

Clark, J. Scott. A Practical Rhetoric, for Instruction in English Composition and Revision in Colleges and Intermediate Schools. New York: Henry Holt and Co., 1889, copyright 1886.

Comstock, Andrew. Practical Elocution; or, The Art of Reading Simplified. Philadelphia: Uriah Hunt, 1830.

Cook, Albert S. *The Higher Study of English*. Boston: Houghton Mifflin Co., 1906.

Copeland, Charles Townsend and H. M. Rideout. *Freshman English and Theme-Correcting in Harvard College*. New York: Silver, Burdett and Co., 1901.

Coppens, Charles. *The Art of Oratorical Composition*. New York: Schwartz, Kirwin, and Fauss, 1885.

—— *A Practical Introduction to English Rhetoric* (4th edition). New York: Catholic Publication Society Co., 1886.

Corson, Hiram. *The Voice and Spiritual Education*. New York: The Macmillan Co., 1896.

Day, Henry N. *The Art of Discourse* (2nd edition). New York: Charles Scribner and Co., 1867 (first published 1850 under the title *Elements of the Art of Rhetoric*).

DeMille, James. *The Elements of Rhetoric*. New York: Harper and Brothers, 1878.

Denney, Joseph V. *Two Problems in Composition-Teaching* (Contributions to Rhetorical Theory, No. 3, edited by Fred Newton Scott). Ann Arbor, Mich.: Inland Press, n.d.

DeQuincey, Thomas. "Style," "Rhetoric," "Language," in *Works of Thomas DeQuincey* (vol. 2: *Literary Criticism*), pp. 172-313, 314-371, 373-393. Boston: Houghton Mifflin and Co., 1876.

Espenshade, A. Howry. *The Essentials of Composition and Rhetoric*. Boston: D. C. Heath and Co., 1906, copyright 1904.

Fletcher, J. B. and G. R. Carpenter. *Introduction to Theme-Writing*. Boston: Allyn and Bacon, 1893.

Fulton, Edward. *Rhetoric and Composition*. New York: H. Holt and Co., 1906.

Gardiner, John Hays. *The Forms of Prose Literature*. New York: Charles Scribner's Sons, 1900.

Gardiner, John Hays, G. L. Kittredge, and Sarah Louise Arnold. *Manual of Composition and Rhetoric*. Boston: Ginn and Co., 1907.

Genung, John Franklin. *Handbook of Rhetorical Analysis. Studies in Style and Invention*. Boston: Ginn and Co., 1888.

—— *Outlines of Rhetoric*. Boston: Ginn and Co., 1893.

—— *The Practical Elements of Rhetoric*. Boston: Ginn and Co., 1886.

—— *A Study of Rhetoric in the College Course*. Boston: D. C. Heath and Co., 1887.

—— *The Working Principles of Rhetoric*. Boston: Ginn and Co., 1900.

Genung, John Franklin and Charles L. Hanson. *Outlines of Composition and Rhetoric*. Boston: Ginn and Co., 1915.

Getty, John A. *Elements of Rhetoric*. Philadelphia: E. Littell, 1831.

Gilmore, J. H. *The Outlines of Rhetoric for Schools and Colleges*. Boston: Leach, Shewell, and Sanborn, 1891.

Goodrich, Chauncey Allen. *Select British Eloquence*. New York: Harper and Brothers, 1853.

Greene, Samuel S. *An Analysis of the English Language*. Philadelphia: Cowperthwait and Co., 1875, copyright 1874.

—— *A Treatise on the Structure of the English Language*. Philadelphia: Cowperthwait and Co., 1869, copyright 1846.

Hale, Edward Everett, Jr. *Constructive Rhetoric*. New York: Henry Holt and Co., 1896.

Harding, Harold F. "English Rhetorical Theory, 1750–1800." Unpublished Ph.D. dissertation, Department of Speech and Drama, Cornell University, 1928.

Hart, James Morgan. *A Handbook of English Composition*. Philadelphia: Eldredge and Brother, 1895.

Hart, John S. *A Manual of Composition and Rhetoric*. Philadelphia: Eldredge and Brother, 1870.

Haven, E. O. *Rhetoric*. New York: Harper and Brothers, 1869.

Hepburn, A. D. *Manual of English Rhetoric*. Cincinnati: Van Antwerp, Bragg and Co., 1875.

Herrick, Robert and Lindsay Todd Damon. *Composition and Rhetoric for Schools* (revised edition). Chicago: Scott, Foresman and Co., 1902.

—— *New Composition and Rhetoric for Schools* (a revision by Lindsay Todd Damon). Chicago: Scott, Foresman and Co., 1899, 1902, 1911.

Hervey, George W. *A System of Christian Rhetoric*. New York: Harper and Brothers, 1873.

Hill, Adams Sherman. *Beginnings of Rhetoric and Composition*. New York: American Book Co., 1902.

—— *The Foundations of Rhetoric*. New York: Harper and Brothers, 1897, copyright 1892, 1893.

—— *Our English*. New York: Harper and Brothers, 1888.

—— *The Principles of Rhetoric, and Their Application*. New York: Harper and Brothers, 1878.

—— *The Principles of Rhetoric* (new edition, revised and enlarged). New York: American Book Co., 1878, 1895.

Hill, Adams Sherman, L. B. R. Briggs, and B. S. Hurlbut. *Twenty Years of School and College English*. Cambridge, Mass.: Harvard University Press, 1896.

Hill, David J. *The Elements of Rhetoric and Composition*. New York: Sheldon and Co., 1878.

—— *The Science of Rhetoric*. New York: Sheldon and Co., 1883, copyright 1877.

Hinsdale, B. A. *Teaching the Language Arts*. New York: D. Appleton and Co., 1896.

Hope, M. B. *The Princeton Text-Book in Rhetoric*. Princeton, N.J.: John T. Robinson, 1859.

Hoshor, John P. "The Rhetorical Theory of Chauncey Allen Goodrich." Unpublished Ph.D. dissertation, State University of Iowa, 1947.

Huffcutt, E. W. *English in the Preparatory Schools*. Boston: D. C. Heath and Co., 1887.

Hunt, Theodore W. *The Principles of Written Discourse* (2nd edition). New York: A. C. Armstrong and Son, 1884.

—— *Studies in Literature and Style*. New York: A. C. Armstrong and Son, 1890.

Jameson, Henry W. *Rhetorical Method*. St. Louis: G. I. Jones and Co., 1879.

Jamieson, Alexander. *A Grammar of Rhetoric and Polite Literature* (22nd edition). New Haven, Conn.: A. H. Maltby, 1842.

Kames, Henry Home, Lord. *The Elements of Criticism* (revised and enlarged by James R. Boyd). New York: A. S. Barnes and Co., 1855 (first edition: London, 1762).

Kellogg, Brainerd. *A Text-Book on Rhetoric*. New York: Clark and Maynard, 1880.

Kimball, Lillian G. *The Structure of the English Sentence*. New York: American Book Co., 1900.

Kirkham, Samuel. *A Compendium of English Grammar*. Fredericktown, Maryland: J. P. Thomson, 1823.

—— *English Grammar in Familiar Lectures* (11th edition, revised and enlarged). Albany, N.Y.: O. Steele, 1829.

Lamont, Hammond. *English Composition*. New York: Charles Scribner's Sons, 1906.

Lewes, George Henry. *The Principles of Success in Literature*, edited with an introduction and notes by Fred N. Scott (3rd edition). Boston: Allyn and Bacon, 1891.

Lewis, Edwin H. *The History of the English Paragraph*. Chicago: University of Chicago Press, 1894.

Linn, James W. *The Essentials of English Composition*. New York: Charles Scribner's Sons, 1912.

Lomer, Gerhard R. and Margaret Ashmun. *The Study and Practice of Writing English*. Boston: Houghton Mifflin and Co., 1914.

Lounsbury, Thomas R. *History of the English Language*. New York: H. Holt and Co., 1879.

McElroy, John G. R. *The Structure of English Prose. A Manual of Composition and Rhetoric* (4th edition). New York: A. C. Armstrong and Son, 1895, copyright 1885.

Minto, William. *A Manual of English Prose Literature*. Boston: Ginn and Co., 1893.

———— *Plain Principles of Prose Composition*. Edinburgh: William Blackwood and Sons, 1893.

Murray, Lindley. *An English Grammar* (2 vols., 3rd American edition, corrected and much enlarged). New York: Collins and Co., 1817.

Newcomer, Alphonso G. *Elements of Rhetoric: A Course in Plain Prose Composition*. New York: Henry Holt and Co., 1898.

———— *A Practical Course in English Composition*. Boston: Ginn and Co., 1894, copyright 1893.

Newman, John Henry, Cardinal. "Literature," in *The Idea of a University*, pp. 268–294. London: Longmans, Green and Co., 1902.

Newman, Samuel P. *A Practical System of Rhetoric* (7th edition). Andover, Mass.: Gould and Newman, 1839 (first published Portland, Maine, 1827).

Parker, Richard Green. *Aids to English Composition, Prepared for Students of All Grades* (20th edition). New York: Harper and Brothers, 1858, copyright 1845.

Pater, Walter. "Style," in *Appreciations, with an Essay on Style*, pp. 1–36. New York: The Macmillan Co., 1906.

Paul, Wilson B. "John Witherspoon's Theory and Practice of Public Speaking." Unpublished Ph.D. dissertation, State University of Iowa, 1940.

Payne, William Morton, editor. *English in American Universities*. Boston: D. C. Heath and Co., 1895.

Pearson, Henry G. *Freshman Composition*, with an introduction by Arlo Bates. Boston: D. C. Heath and Co., 1897.

Pence, Raymond W. *College Composition*. New York: The Macmillan Co., 1929.

Porter, Ebenezer. *Analysis of the Principles of Rhetorical Delivery as Applied in Reading and Speaking*. New York: Leavitt, 1827.

———— *Lectures on Eloquence and Style*. Andover, Mass.: Gould and Newman, 1836.

Quackenbos, George Payn. *Advanced Course of Composition and Rhetoric*. New York: D. Appleton and Co., 1864, copyright 1854.

────── *First Lessons in Composition*. New York: D. Appleton and Co., 1863, copyright 1851.

Quackenbos, John Duncan. *Practical Rhetoric*. New York: American Book Co., 1896.

Quintilian. *Institutes of Oratory*, translated by John Selby Watson (2 vols.). London: George Bell and Sons, 1887.

Reed, Alonzo and Brainerd Kellogg. *Higher Lessons in English*. New York: Charles E. Merrill Co., 1909.

Rush, James. *The Philosophy of the Human Voice* (6th edition, revised). Philadelphia: The Library Company of Philadelphia, 1900.

Russell, William. *The American Elocutionist*. Boston: Jenks and Palmer, 1840.

Scott, Fred Newton. *The Principles of Style*. Ann Arbor, Mich.: Register Publishing Co., 1890.

────── *References on the Teaching of Rhetoric and Composition* (Contributions to Rhetorical Theory, No. 4, edited by Fred N. Scott). N.p., n.d.

────── *The Standard of American Speech and Other Papers*. Boston: Allyn and Bacon, 1926.

Scott, Fred Newton and Gertrude Buck. *A Brief English Grammar*. Chicago: Scott, Foresman and Co., 1905.

Scott, Fred Newton and Joseph Villiers Denney. *Composition-Literature*. Boston: Allyn and Bacon, 1902.

────── *Composition-Rhetoric, Designed for Use in Secondary Schools*. Boston: Allyn and Bacon, 1897.

────── *Elementary English Composition*. Boston: Allyn and Bacon, 1900.

────── *The New Composition-Rhetoric*. Boston: Allyn and Bacon, 1911.

────── *Paragraph-Writing* (3rd edition, revised and enlarged). Boston: Allyn and Bacon, 1893.

Shaw, Thomas Budd. *A Complete Manual of English Literature*, edited with notes and illustrations by William Smith. New York: Sheldon and Co., 1867.

────── *Outlines of English Literature, a New American Edition*. New York: Sheldon and Co., 1866, copyright 1852.

Shedd, William G. T. *Literary Essays*. New York: Charles Scribner's Sons, 1878.

Sherman, L. A. *Analytics of Literature: A Manual for the Objective Study of English Prose and Poetry.* Boston: Ginn and Co., 1893.
—— *Elements of Literature and Composition, a Manual for Schools.* Lincoln, Nebraska: University Publishing Co., 1908.
Slater, John R. *Freshman Rhetoric.* Boston: D. C. Heath and Co., 1913.
Spencer, Herbert. *The Philosophy of Style, Together with An Essay on Style by T. H. Wright,* edited with an introduction and notes by Fred N. Scott (2nd edition). Boston and Chicago: Allyn and Bacon, 1892.
Stevenson, Robert Louis. "On Some Technical Elements of Style in Literature," in *Essays and Criticisms.* Boston: Herbert B. Turner and Co., 1903.
Swinton, William. *School Composition: Advanced Language-Lessons for Grammar Schools.* New York: Harper and Brothers, 1874.
Theremin, Francis. *Eloquence a Virtue; or, Outlines of a Systematic Rhetoric,* translated from the German by William G. T. Shedd, with an introductory essay. Andover, Mass.: Warren F. Draper, 1864 (first published 1850).
Thomas, C. S. and W. D. Howe. *Composition and Rhetoric.* New York: Longmans, Green and Co., 1908.
Thomas, Helen. *A Study of the Paragraph.* New York: American Book Co., 1912.
Thorndike, A. H. *Elements of Rhetoric and Composition.* New York: The Century Co., 1905.
Webster, W. F. *English: Composition and Literature.* Boston: Houghton Mifflin Co., 1900.
Welsh, Alfred H. *Complete Rhetoric.* Chicago: S. C. Griggs and Co., 1885.
Wendell, Barrett. *English Composition.* New York: Charles Scribner's Sons, 1891.
Whately, Richard. *Elements of Rhetoric.* Louisville, Kentucky: John P. Morton and Co., n.d. (first published: Dublin, 1828).
Whitney, William Dwight. *Essentials of English Grammar.* Boston: Ginn and Co., 1898, copyright 1877.
—— *Language and the Study of Language.* New York: Charles Scribner and Co., 1867.
—— *The Life and Growth of Language.* New York: D. Appleton and Co., 1892, copyright 1875.
Winchester, C. T. *Some Principles of Literary Criticism.* New York: The Macmillan Co., 1904.

Witherspoon, John. *Lectures on Moral Philosophy and Eloquence* (Woodward's 3rd edition). Philadelphia: 1810.

Woolley, Edwin C. *Handbook of Composition*. Boston: D. C. Heath and Co., 1907.

Woolley, Edwin C. *The Mechanics of Writing*. Boston: D. C. Heath and Co., 1909.

—— *Notes on English Composition*. Chicago: Quadrangle Press, 1904.

—— *Written English*. Boston: D. C. Heath and Co., 1915.

Articles

Adams, Charles Francis, E. L. Godkin, and Josiah Quincy. "Report of the Committee on Composition and Rhetoric," Report No. XXVIII, in *Reports of the Visiting Committees of the Board of Overseers of Harvard College*, pp. 117-157. Cambridge, Mass.: Harvard University Press, 1902.

Adams, Charles Francis, E. L. Godkin, and George R. Nutter. "Report of the Committee on Composition and Rhetoric," Report No. XLIX, pp. 275-287, in *Reports of the Visiting Committees of the Board of Overseers of Harvard College*. Cambridge, Mass.: Harvard University Press, 1902.

—— "Report of the Committee on Composition and Rhetoric," Report No. LXXI, pp. 401-424, in *Reports of the Visiting Committees of the Board of Overseers of Harvard College*. Cambridge, Mass.: Harvard University Press, 1902.

Anderson, Dorothy I. "Edward T. Channing's Definition of Rhetoric," *Speech Monographs*, XIV (1947), 81-92.

Baldwin, Charles Sears. "The College Teaching of Rhetoric," *Educational Review*, XLVIII (1914), 1-20.

—— "Freshman English," *Educational Review*, XXXII (1906), 385-394, 485-499.

Barbour, F. A. "History of English Grammar Teaching," *Educational Review*, XII (1896), 487-507.

—— "The Psychology of the Diagram," *School Review*, V (1897), 240-242.

Beardsley, George. "English Literature at the Colleges and Universities," *Educational Review*, XVI (1898), 185-191.

Beers, Henry A. "Entrance Requirements in English at Yale," *Educational Review*, III (1892), 427-443.

Beyer, T. P. "Anent Compulsory Composition in Colleges," *Educational Review*, XLIV (1912), 77-86.

Bradley, C. B. "The Classification of Rhetorical Figures," *Modern Language Notes*, I (1886), 140–142.

Brewer, William F. "English at College," *Nation*, LXIII (1896), 327.

Briggs, LeBaron Russell. "The Correction of Bad English As a Requirement for Admission to Harvard College," *Academy*, V (Syracuse, N.Y., 1890), 302–312.

Bronson, Walter C. "English Literature in Secondary Schools," *Academy*, IV (Syracuse, N.Y., 1889), 384–395.

Buck, Gertrude. "Make-Believe Grammar," *School Review*, XVII (1909), 21–33.

——— "The Present Status of Rhetorical Theory," *Modern Language Notes*, XV (1900), 167–174.

——— "The Psychological Significance of the Parts of Speech," *Education*, XVIII (1898), 269–277.

——— "The Psychology of the Diagram," *School Review*, V (1897), 470–472.

——— "Recent Tendencies in the Teaching of English Composition," *Educational Review*, XXII (1901), 371–382.

——— "The Sentence-Diagram," *Educational Review*, XIII (1897), 250–260.

——— "What Does 'Rhetoric' Mean?" *Educational Review*, XXII (1901), 197–200.

Carnegie, Andrew. "College-Bred Men in the Business World," *Report of the Commissioner of Education*, 1890, Part 2, p. 1143.

Carpenter, George R. "English Composition in Colleges," *Educational Review*, IV (1892), 438–446.

Clark, J. Scott. "The Art of English Composition," *Academy*, IV (Syracuse, N.Y., 1889), 369–384.

Clews, Henry. "College-Bred Men in the Business World," *Report of the Commissioner of Education*, 1890, Part 2, p. 1143.

Cooper, Lane. "On the Teaching of Written Composition," *Education*, XXX (1910), 421–430.

Cross, Wilbur L. "English in the Schools," *Education*, XXVIII (1908), 537–551.

Denton, George B. "Herbert Spencer and the Rhetoricians," *Publications of the Modern Language Association*, XXXIV (1919), 89–111.

Emerson, Oliver F. "English in Secondary Schools," *Academy*, IV (Syracuse, N.Y., 1889), 233–244.

——— "The Teaching of English Grammar," *School Review*, V (1897), 129–138.

Examiners in the University of Chicago. "The Preparatory Course in English," *School Review*, V (1897), 445-455.

Frink, H. A. "Rhetoric and Public Speaking in the American College," *Education*, XIII (1892), 129-141.

Gardiner, John Hays. "Training in Illiteracy," *School Review*, XVII (1909), 623-630.

Garrison, W. P. "English at Harvard and Elsewhere," *The Nation*, LV (1892), 299-300.

Godkin, E. L. "'The Growing Illiteracy of American Boys,'" *The Nation*, LXIII (1896), 284-285.

Goodwin, W. W. "The Root of the Evil," *Harvard Graduates' Magazine*, I (1893), 189-193.

Gore, Willard C. "Scientific Work in Rhetoric," *The Dial*, XXIII (1897), 210-211.

Greenough, J. J. "The English Question," *Atlantic Monthly*, LXXI (1893), 656-662.

Gregory, D. S. "Review of philological works by Prof. Francis A. March of Lafayette College," *The Presbyterian Quarterly and Princeton Review*, III (N.s., 1874), 745-751.

Gummere, F. B. "Metaphor and Poetry," *Modern Language Notes*, I (1886), 83-84.

Guthrie, Warren. "The Development of Rhetorical Theory in America, 1635-1850," *Speech Monographs*, XIII (1946), 14-22; XIV (1947), 38-54; XV (1948), 61-71; XVI (1949), 98-113; XVIII (1951), 17-30.

Hart, James Morgan. "Cornell Course in Rhetoric and English Philology," *Academy*, VI (Syracuse, N.Y., 1891), 181-193.

——— "On the Approaches to the English Language," *The Presbyterian Quarterly and Princeton Review*, III (N.s., 1874), 434-456.

Hart, Sophie C. "English in the College," *School Review*, X (1902), 364-373.

Henneman, John B. "The Study of English in the South," *Sewanee Review*, II (1894), 180-197.

Hooker, Bessie R. "The Use of Literary Material in Teaching Composition," *School Review*, X (1902), 474-485.

Hosic, James F. "Co-operation of All Departments in the Teaching of English Composition," *School Review*, XXI (1913), 598-607.

Hunt, Theodore W. "Rhetorical Science," *The Presbyterian Quarterly and Princeton Review*, III (1874), 660-678.

——— "The Study of English in American Colleges," *Educational Review*, XII (1896), 140-150.

Hurlbut, Byron S. "The Preparatory Work in English As Seen by a Harvard Examiner," *Academy,* VI (Syracuse, N.Y., 1891), 351-353.

"John S. Hart, Principal of the Philadelphia High School," *American Journal of Education,* V (1858), 91-106.

Kellogg, Brainerd. "On Teaching English," *School Review,* I (1893), 96-105, 152-162.

Lathrop, H. B. "Unity, Coherence, and Emphasis," *University of Wisconsin Studies in Language and Literature,* No. 2 (1918), pp. 77-98.

Lewis, Homer P., and others. "Textbooks in Rhetoric and in Composition," Report of the Standing Committee of the New England Association of Teachers of English on Aids in Teaching English, *School Review,* XIV (1906), 1-33.

Lounsbury, Thomas R. "Compulsory Composition in Colleges," *Harper's Magazine,* CXXIII (1911), 866-880.

McElroy, John G. R. "English in Secondary Schools," *Academy,* IV (Syracuse, N.Y., 1889), 244-255.

Magee, Helene B. "Prescribed English in College," *Educational Review,* XLV (1913), 95-97.

Manchester, O. L. and H. H. Manchester. "What Modern Philology Offers Secondary Education," *Educational Review,* XVI (1898), 262-274.

March, F. A. "The Study of Anglo-Saxon," *Report of the Commissioner of Education,* 1876-77, pp. 475-479.

Mead, William E. "The Undergraduate Study of English Composition," *Publications of the Modern Language Association,* XVII, New Series 10 (1902), x-xxiv.

Rahskopf, Horace G. "John Quincy Adams: Speaker and Rhetorician," *Quarterly Journal of Speech,* XXXII (1946), 435-441.

"Report of the Eighth Annual Meeting of the New England Association of Colleges and Preparatory Schools," *School Review,* I (1893), 587-667.

Rice, J. M. "The Futility of the Spelling Grind," *The Forum,* XXIII (1897), 163-172, 409-419.

Ringwalt, Ralph Curtis. "Intercollegiate Debating," *The Forum,* XXII (1897), 633-640.

Robinson, A. T. "The Question of Text-Books in Composition," *Science,* XXXVII (1913), 60-62.

Scott, Fred Newton. "Brief Catechism on Textbooks in English," *Educational Review,* XXXVII (1909), 359-361.

———— "College-Entrance Requirements in English," *School Review,* IX (1901), 365-378.

————— "The Report on College-Entrance Requirements in English," *Educational Review*, XX (1900), 289-294.

————— "What the West Wants in Preparatory English," *School Review*, XVII (1909), 10-20.

Searing, Annie E. P. "Why College Graduates Are Deficient in English," *Educational Review*, XVI (1898), 244-253.

Slosson, Preston W. "Prescribed English in College," *Educational Review*, XLV (1913), 407-409.

Smyser, Seldon F. "The Lack of Scientific Work in Rhetoric," *The Dial*, XXIII (1897), 141.

Thurber, Samuel. "An Address to Teachers of English," *Education*, XVIII (1898), 515-526.

————— "English Work in the Secondary Schools," *School Review*, I (1893), 650-655.

————— "Five Axioms of Composition Teaching," *School Review*, V (1897), 7-17.

Trueblood, Thomas C. "A Chapter on the Organization of College Courses in Public Speaking," *Quarterly Journal of Speech*, XII (1926), 1-11.

"Two Ways of Teaching English," *Century Magazine*, LI (1896), 793-794.

Wendell, Barrett. "English Work in the Secondary Schools," *School Review*, I (1893), 638-650.

SECONDARY SOURCES

Books

Adams, Herbert B. *The Study of History in American Colleges and Universities*. Bureau of Education Circular of Information, No. 2., 1887.

Angell, James Burrill. *The Reminiscences of James Burrill Angell*. New York: Longmans, Green and Co., 1912, copyright 1911.

————— *Selected Addresses*. New York: Longmans, Green and Co., 1912.

Bain, Alexander. *Mental Science: A Compendium of Psychology, and the History of Philosophy*. New York: D. Appleton and Co., 1879, copyright 1868.

————— *Mind and Body. The Theories of Their Relation*. New York: D. Appleton and Co., 1875.

Briggs, LeBaron Russell. *To College Teachers of English Composition*. Boston: Houghton Mifflin Co., 1928.

Brooks, Van Wyck. *The Flowering of New England, 1815–1865* (new and revised edition). New York: E. P. Dutton and Co., 1940, copyright 1936.

Brown, Rollo Walter. *Dean Briggs*. New York: Harper and Brothers, 1926.

———— *Harvard Yard in the Golden Age*. New York: Current Books, Inc., 1948.

Burgess, John W. *Reminiscences of an American Scholar; The Beginnings of Columbia University*, with a foreword by Nicholas Murray Butler. New York: Columbia University Press, 1934.

Cole, Arthur Charles. *The Irrepressible Conflict, 1850–1865*, vol. 7 of *A History of American Life*, edited by A. M. Schlesinger and Dixon Ryan Fox. New York: The Macmillan Co., 1934.

Collins, V. L. *Princeton*. New York: Oxford University Press, 1914.

Cross, Wilbur L. *Connecticut Yankee, An Autobiography*. New Haven, Conn.: Yale University Press, 1943.

Cubberley, Ellwood P. *Public Education in the United States* (revised and enlarged edition). Boston: Houghton Mifflin Co., 1934.

Curti, Merle. *The Social Ideas of American Educators*. New York: Charles Scribner's Sons, 1935.

DeGarmo, Charles. *The Essentials of Method* (revised edition). Boston: D. C. Heath and Co., 1892.

Dwight, Timothy. *Memories of Yale Life and Men, 1845–1899*. New York: Dodd, Mead and Co., 1903.

Edwards, Newton and Herman G. Richey. *The School in the American Social Order*. Boston: Houghton Mifflin Co., 1947.

Eliot, Charles William. *Educational Reform: Essays and Addresses*. New York: Century Co., 1898.

Fifteenth Census. *Population*, vol. I.

Fish, Carl Russell. *The Rise of the Common Man, 1830–1850*, vol. 6 of *A History of American Life*, edited by A. M. Schlesinger and Dixon Ryan Fox. New York: The Macmillan Co., 1927.

Flexner, Abraham. *Daniel Coit Gilman, Creator of the American Type of University*. New York: Harcourt, Brace and Co., 1946.

Flugel, J. C. *A Hundred Years of Psychology, 1833–1933*. New York: Macmillan Co., n.d.

Fulton, John. *Memoirs of Frederick A. P. Barnard*. New York: The Macmillan Co., 1896.

Hall, G. Stanley. *Life and Confessions of a Psychologist*. New York: D. Appleton and Co., 1923.

Hamilton, Sir William. *Lectures on Metaphysics and Logic*, edited by H. L. Mansel and John Veitch (4 vols.). Edinburgh: William Blackwood and Sons, 1865.

Hart, James Morgan. *German Universities: A Narrative of Personal Experience*. New York: G. P. Putnam's Sons, 1874.

Hill, David J. *The Elements of Logic, a Text-Book for Schools and Colleges; Being The Elementary Lessons in Logic, by W. Stanley Jevons, Recast by David J. Hill*. New York: Sheldon and Co., 1883.

—— *The Elements of Psychology: A Text-Book*. New York: Sheldon and Co., 1888.

Hinsdale, B. A. *History of the University of Michigan*, edited by Isaac N. Demmon. Ann Arbor, Mich.: University of Michigan, 1906.

Howe, M. A. DeWolfe, editor. *Barrett Wendell and His Letters*. Boston: Atlantic Monthly Press, 1924.

James, Henry. *Charles W. Eliot* (2 vols.). Boston: Houghton Mifflin Co., 1930.

James, William. *Psychology: Briefer Course*. New York: Henry Holt and Co., 1892, 1920, 1930.

Johnson, Clifton. *Old-Time Schools and School-Books*. New York: The Macmillan Co., 1904.

LeDuc, Thomas. *Piety and Intellect at Amherst College*. New York: Columbia University Press, 1946.

Morison, Samuel Eliot, editor. *The Development of Harvard University Since the Inauguration of President Eliot, 1869–1929*. Cambridge, Mass.: Harvard University Press, 1930.

—— *Three Centuries of Harvard, 1636–1936*. Cambridge, Mass.: Harvard University Press, 1936.

Mott, Frank Luther. *American Journalism; A History of Newspapers in the United States Through 250 Years, 1690–1940*. New York: The Macmillan Co., 1941.

Murphy, Gardner. *An Historical Introduction to Modern Psychology* (2nd edition, revised). New York: Harcourt, Brace and Co., 1930.

Nevins, Allan. *The Emergence of Modern America, 1865–1878*, vol. 8 of *A History of American Life*, edited by A. M. Schlesinger and Dixon Ryan Fox. New York: The Macmillan Co., 1927.

Norris, E. M. *The Story of Princeton*. Boston: Little, Brown and Co., 1917.

Parsons, Francis. *Six Men of Yale*. New Haven, Conn.: Yale University Press, 1939.

Paulsen, Friedrich. *The German Universities. Their Character and Historical Development*, translated by Edward D. Perry, with an introduction by Nicholas Murray Butler. New York: The Macmillan Co., 1894.

Porter, Noah. *The American Colleges and the American Public*. New York: Charles Scribner's Sons, 1878.

Pyre, J. F. A. *Wisconsin*. New York: Oxford University Press, 1920.

Reisner, Edward H. *Nationalism and Education Since 1789; A Social and Political History of Modern Education*. New York: The Macmillan Co., 1922.

Schlesinger, Arthur M. *The Rise of the City, 1878–1898*, vol. 10 of *A History of American Life*, edited by A. M. Schlesinger and Dixon Ryan Fox. New York: The Macmillan Co., 1933.

Schneider, Herbert W. *A History of American Philosophy*. New York: Columbia University Press, 1946.

Spencer, Herbert. *Education: Intellectual, Moral, Physical*. New York: D. Appleton and Co., 1891, copyright 1860.

Tappan, Henry P. *University Education*. New York: G. P. Putnam, 1851.

Tewksbury, Donald G. *The Founding of American Colleges and Universities Before the Civil War: with Particular Reference to the Religious Influences Bearing upon the College Movement*. New York: Teachers College, Columbia University, 1932.

Thwing, C. F. *The American and the German University; One Hundred Years of History*. New York: The Macmillan Co., 1928.

―――― *A History of Higher Education in America*. New York: D. Appleton and Co., 1906.

Turner, William. *History of Philosophy*. Boston: Ginn and Co., 1903.

Walz, John A. *German Influence in American Education and Culture*. Philadelphia: Carl Schurz Memorial Foundation, Inc., 1936.

White, Andrew D. *Autobiography* (2 vols.). New York: The Century Co., 1904–05.

Wills, Elbert Vaughan. *The Growth of American Higher Education; Liberal, Professional, and Technical*. Philadelphia: Dorrance and Co., 1936.

Articles

"Angell, James Burrill," *Dictionary of American Biography*, I, 304–309.

Brumm, John Lewis. "In Memoriam, Fred Newton Scott," *Michigan Alumnus* (June 27, 1931), p. 655.

Bryan, George S. "Genung and Rhetoric," *Amherst Graduates' Quarterly*, IX (1920), 78–81.

Butler, James D. "A Defence of Classical Studies. How Dead Languages Make Live Men," National Education Association, *Addresses and Journal of Proceedings for 1874*, pp. 187-204.
"Courses of Study in Colleges and Universities," *Report of the Commissioner of Education*, 1888-89, II, 1224-1361.
Dewey, John. "Learning to Earn: The Place of Vocational Education in a Comprehensive Scheme of Public Education," *School and Society*, V (1917), 331-335.
Erskine, John. "The Scholar Whom We Knew," *Amherst Graduates' Quarterly*, IX (1920), 71-77.
Franklin, Fabian. "Daniel Coit Gilman," *The Nation*, LXXXVII (1908), 380-382.
Harris, Ernest L. "American Students in German Universities," *Report of the Commissioner of Education*, 1900-1901, II, 1513-18.
Harris, W. T. "The Commissioner's Introduction," *Report of the Commissioner of Education*, 1899-1900, I, ix-lix.
Harvard Crimson. Article on retirement of Barrett Wendell, LXXI (30 March 1917), 1, 5.
Hedge, F. H. "University Reform. An Address to the Alumni of Harvard at Their Triennial Festival, July 19, 1866," *Atlantic Monthly*, XVIII (1866), 296-307.
Lyle, Guy R. "College Literary Societies in the Fifties," *Library Quarterly*, IV (1934), 487-493.
Neal, Robert W. "In the Book the Man," *Amherst Graduates' Quarterly*, IX (1920), 81-82.
Northrup, Cyrus. "Yale in Its Relation to the Development of the Country," *Report of the Commissioner of Education*, 1902, I, 588-594.
Palmer, Francis L. "Professor Genung's First Class at Amherst," *Amherst Graduates' Quarterly*, IX (1920), 82.
Perry, Edward Delavan. "The American University," in *Education in the United States*, edited by N. M. Butler (2 vols.), I, 251-318. Albany, N.Y.: J. B. Lyon Co., 1900.
Report of the Commissioner of Education, 1880, pp. c, cxxxvi, cxlviii.
Report of the Commissioner of Education, 1883-84, p. cxix.
Report of the Commissioner of Education, 1884-85, p. clxxv.
Smith, Shirley W. "Fred Newton Scott as a Teacher," *Michigan Alumnus* (4 February 1933), pp. 279-280.
"Tappan, Henry Phillip," *Dictionary of American Biography*, XVIII, 302-303.
Thorndike, E. L. and R. S. Woodworth. "The Influence of Improvement in One Mental Function upon the Efficiency of Other

Functions," *Psychological Review,* VIII (1901), 247–261, 384–395, 553–564.

Thorpe, Clarence D. "The Department of Rhetoric," in *The University of Michigan, an Encyclopedic Survey in 9 Parts,* Part 3: *The College of Literature, Science, and the Arts,* pp. 558–569. Ann Arbor, Mich.: University of Michigan Press, 1943.

Tyler, John M. "John Franklin Genung," *Amherst Graduates' Quarterly,* IX (1920), 65–70.

Whicher, G. F. "Genung's Rhetoric," *The Nation,* CIX (1919), 658.

White, Andrew D. "A National University," National Education Association, *Addresses and Journal of Proceedings for 1874,* pp. 58–76.

Index

Abbott, E. A. Work: *How to Write Clearly,* 195
Active Powers of Man (Reid), 3
Adams, Charles Francis, 44
Adams, Charles Kendall, 29
Adams, John Quincy. Work: *Lectures on Rhetoric and Oratory,* 55
Addison, Joseph, 154
Advanced Course of Composition and Rhetoric (Quackenbos), 84, 104, 122, 170, 171, 177, 207, 208
Agassiz, Louis, 232n.54
Aids to English Composition (Parker), 58–59, 122, 192
Alfred (king of West Saxons), 37
The American College Dictionary, 188
The American Colleges, and the American Public (N. Porter), 24
American Journal of Education, 37
Amherst College, 15, 63, 64, 66, 85, 105; leadership of, 26; religious mission of, 7, 8;

speech instruction at, 42; study of philology at, 37
amplifying paragraph, 159
Analysis of the English Language (Greene), 193
Analytics of Literature (Sherman), 91
Andover Academy, 57
Angell, James B., 17; as progressive educator, 20, 29, 30; sponsorship of speech instruction by, 42
Anglo-Saxon language, historical study of, 37, 38
Angus, Joseph, 154–155, 156. Work: *Handbook of the English Tongue,* 154
apperception, theory of, 5
argumentation: as category of discourse, 54, 122, 123, 124, 125, 126, 127, 128, 130–131, 132, 133–134, 138; logical vs. rhetorical perspectives on, 109–110; and paragraph structure, 163; process of, 110–113; recognition of audience in, 145, 147

265

Aristotle, viii, 52, 53, 58, 95, 110, 121, 177. Work: *Rhetoric*, 95, 143
Arnold, Matthew, 92
arrangement: criteria governing, 113-117; of paragraph, 154-165; as subcategory of invention, 97, 102; of whole composition, 165-166
art, rhetoric as, 77-81, 214
The Art of Discourse (Day), 77, 83, 101, 206
"The Art of English Composition" (Clark), 90, 213
associationism, 3, 4, 120
Association of Teachers of English of the North Central States, 107
audience (reader): communication with, through metaphor, 181-182; effects of metaphor on, 183-184; perception of images by, 135-136; psychology of, 143-144; receptivity of, as function of style, 172, 176-177; recognition of, by rhetoric, 141-152; rhetorical training of, 90; and writer's use of language, 56
Autobiography (Bain), 120, 155
Autobiography (White), 22
The Autobiography of Lincoln Steffens, xviii

Bacon, Francis, 34, 58
Bain, Alexander, xii, 164, 222; classification of composition by, 119-121, 122, 123, 124, 125-126, 127; classification of figurative language by, 177-178; on criteria governing arrangement, 113-114; on paragraph development, 155-156, 157,

158, 162; physiological psychology of, 4. Works: *Autobiography*, 120, 155; *The Emotions and the Will*, 4; *English Composition and Rhetoric*, 119, 120, 155, 177; *Mental Science*, 120; *The Senses and the Intellect*, 4
Baker, George Pierce, 133, 134. Work: *The Principles of Argumentation*, 112, 133
Baldwin, Charles Sears: and assigned composition topics, 107; classification of composition by, 128-131, 132, 133, 138; on criteria governing arrangement, 116; discussion of logic by, 111-112. Works: *A College Manual of Rhetoric*, 107, 111, 116, 128, 161, 166, 173; *The Expository Paragraph and Sentence*, 116, 133, 161, 166
Bancroft, George, 15, 27
barbarisms, 189
Barnard, Frederick A. P., 230n.33
Barnard, Henry, 37
Bascom, John, 219; emphasis on oral discourse, 84; on relationship between rhetoric and literature, 87; on relationship between rhetoric and other disciplines, 81, 82. Work: *Philosophy of Rhetoric*, 77-78, 144
Bates, Arlo, xii, 174; on arrangement of whole composition, 166; classification of composition by, 132-133, 138; definition of composition, 80; emphasis on practice, 215; on functions of figurative language, 178; recognition of audience by, 148-149. Work: *Talks on*

Writing English, 80, 116, 132, 148, 161, 173, 178, 213
Beattie, James, 2
Beginnings of Rhetoric and Composition (A. Hill), 166, 197
Beloit College, 26
Beowulf, 37, 38, 92
Berkeley, George, 2
Berlin, James A. Work: *Writing Instruction in Nineteenth-Century American Colleges*, viii
Blair, Hugh, 53, 54, 55, 57, 58, 59, 62, 75, 83, 85, 87, 95, 96, 125, 153, 155, 187; classification of composition by, 122, 126; on criteria governing arrangement, 113; definition of style, 170; emphasis on style, 169; on origin of figurative language, 176; on qualities of style, 170, 171; rules of usage, 188, 189. Work: *Lectures on Rhetoric and Belles Lettres*, 49-52, 86, 169, 208, 221
Booth, Wayne, xi. Work: "The Rhetorical Stance," xv
Bopp, Franz, 36
Boyd, James R., 113; and assigned composition topics, 104; classification of composition by, 123; emphasis on practice, 206, 207. Works: *Elements of English Composition*, 104, 123, 192; *Elements of Rhetoric and Literary Criticism*, 58
Brewster, W. T., 94. Work: *Studies in Structure and Style*, 92-93
"A Brief Catechism on Textbooks in English" (F. Scott), 218
A Brief English Grammar (Scott and Buck), 199
Briggs, LeBaron R., 61, 62, 67-68, 202-203, 204

Brooks, Van Wyck, 57
Brown, Rollo Walter, 61, 68
Browning, Robert, 64
Brown University, 13
Bryant, Frank E., xiii, 135-137, 138-139. Work: *On the Limits of Descriptive Writing Apropos of Lessing's Laocoon*, 135
Buck, Gertrude, xii, 138, 225; classification of composition by, 133-135; on function of metaphor, 181-186; on motivation of student writing, 151, 152; on origin of metaphor, 180-181, 182-183, 185-186; on student's self-analysis of reasoning, 112; on study of grammar, 195-196, 197-198, 199. Works: *A Brief English Grammar*, 199; *A Course in Argumentative Writing*, 112, 133; *A Course in Expository Writing*, 133, 134; *A Course in Narrative Writing*, 133, 134; *Figures of Rhetoric: A Psychological Study*, 180; *The Metaphor—A Study in the Psychology of Rhetoric*, 180; "The Psychological Significance of the Parts of Speech," 197; "Recent Tendencies in Teaching English Composition," 150-151
Bureau of Education, 38
Burgess, John W., 8
Burke, Edmund, 154
Burke, Kenneth, xi, xix
business documents, student exercises in writing, 208
Byron, George Gordon, Lord. Work: *The Prisoner of Chillon*, 201

Cairns, William B., 213; on
adaptation of discourse to
audience, 148; classification of
composition by, 128. Works:
The Forms of Discourse, 103,
128, 161; *Introduction to
Rhetoric*, 103, 148, 161
Campbell, George, 54, 55, 57, 59,
62, 75, 81, 82, 83, 95, 96, 115,
125, 146, 147, 153, 155, 187;
classification of composition
by, 121-122; emphasis on
style, 169; rules of usage,
52-53, 188-189, 190, 195.
Work: *Philosophy of Rhetoric*,
52-53, 121, 221
capitalization: ideal of correctness
in, 224; student exercises in,
207, 212
Carlyle, Thomas, 154
Carpenter, George R., 128; on
analysis of style, 92-93;
on arrangement of whole
composition, 165; on criteria
governing arrangement, 114,
116; definition of rhetoric,
80; emphasis on practice, 213,
214, 215; on functions of
figurative language, 178.
Works: *Elements of Rhetoric
and English Composition*, 88,
111, 160-161, 173, 215;
*Exercises in Rhetoric and
English Composition (Ad-
vanced Course)*, 80, 127, 161,
165, 213, 214; *Introduction
to Theme-Writing*, 161, 173,
213
Central High School (Philadelphia), 37
Century Magazine, 216
*Chambers's Information for the
People*, 120
Channing, Edward Tyrell, 56-57
Charles II (king of England), 67

Chaucer, Geoffrey, 34, 38, 39
Child, Francis J., 15, 33, 34, 37,
39, 60
child psychology, 5, 218
Christensen, Francis. Work: "A
Generative Rhetoric of the
Sentence," xv
Christianity: declining influence
on higher education, 6-9;
philosophical basis for, 2, 3
Cicero, 58, 95, 122, 176
Ciceronian division of a speech,
55
Clark, J. Scott, 114, 145, 158; and
assigned composition topics,
105; classification of
composition by, 126-127;
emphasis on practice, 208, 209,
212, 213; on rhetorical analysis
of literature, 90. Works: "The
Art of English Composition,"
90, 213; *Practical Rhetoric*,
195, 208, 209
classical education: cultivation of
mental discipline by, 24-25;
displacement of, in college
curriculum, 17-18, 19-20;
encroachment of philology
upon, 37; rationalist critique
of, 11
"Classifying Discourse:
Limitations and Alternatives"
(Larson), xiv
Coe College, xvii
coherence. *See* Unity-Coherence-
Emphasis
College Composition (Pence), 164
College English (journal), xvii
A College Manual of Rhetoric
(Baldwin), 107, 111, 116, 128,
161, 166, 173
College of New Jersey, 38, 55. *See
also* Princeton University
Columbia University, 8, 13, 30, 66;
introduction of elective

system, 230n.33; leadership of, 26; study of philology at, 38
Commission on English Planning Institute for Composition, xvii
"Common-Sense" philosophy, 2–3
communication: as function of rhetoric, 56, 77, 141–152, 222, 223; through metaphor, 181–182
comparison, use of figurative language in, 178
A Compendium of English Grammar (Kirkham), 192
A Complete Manual of English Literature (Shaw), 39
completeness, 98
Complete Rhetoric (Welsh), 79, 88, 90, 100
composition: as category of rhetoric, 84–85; classification of ("forms of discourse"), 51, 54, 56, 119–139, 152, 222, 223, 226, 227; contrasted with rhetoric, 79–80; definitions of, 80. See also whole composition
Composition-Literature (Scott and Denney), 88–89, 111, 131–132, 149, 166, 218
composition pedagogy: assignment of topics in, 103–109; assignment to low-prestige faculty, 225–226; in classical curriculum, 22; controversies surrounding, ix–xiv; emphasis on practice, 205–220; in English studies curriculum, 34–36; focus on paragraphs, 162, 163, 164; motivation of students by, 151, 152; in literary societies, 32; reaction against, 215–217, 219; remedial, 43, 44; responsibility of secondary and elementary schools for, 43, 44, 45, 46, 47, 72; in

rhetoric curriculum, 31–32; system of theme correction, 212–213, 215; teaching students to recognize audience, 149; transitional periods in, ix. See also rhetoric
Composition-Rhetoric (Scott and Denney), 79, 89, 107, 128, 131, 132, 163, 173, 179, 185
Comte, Auguste, 9
Comus (Milton), 34
conceits, 184, 185
Conference on College Composition and Communication, xv, xvi
Connors, Robert, xiv. Work: "The Rise and Fall of the Modes of Discourse," viii
Constructive Rhetoric (Hale), 103, 131, 178, 213
Contributions to Rhetorical Theory (F. Scott), 72, 135, 180
conviction, contrasted with persuasion, 51
Cooke, Josiah Parsons, 15
Coppens, Charles, 158, 212; on adaptation of discourse to audience, 145; classification of composition by, 126; on invention as province of rhetoric, 100–101; omits discussion of logic, 111. Work: A Practical Introduction to English Rhetoric, 88, 100, 111, 209
Corbett, Edward P. J. Work: "The Usefulness of Classical Rhetoric," xv
Cornell University, 7, 9, 106; leadership of, 17, 26; standards of scholarship at, 15; study of philology at, 38
correctness, ideal of, 166–167, 188, 190, 199–204, 220, 222–226

Corson, Hiram, 38
Cotton Mather (Wendell), 66
A Course in Argumentative
    Writing (Buck), 112, 133
A Course in Expository Writing
    (Buck and Woodbridge
    [Morris]), 133, 134
A Course in Narrative Writing
    (Buck and Woodbridge
    [Morris]), 133, 134
Cousin, Victor, 26
Coverley, Roger de, 201
Crary, Isaac Edwin, 26
criticism. See literary criticism
Cross, Wilbur L., 24, 39-40
Curriculum Study Centers,
    xvi-xvii

daily theme method, 86, 89, 103,
    163, 196, 210-211, 215-217,
    218, 222
Dana, R. H., Jr., 56
Dartmouth College, 26
Dartmouth College International
    Seminar on the Teaching of
    English, xvii
Darwin, Charles. Work: Origin of
    Species, 9
Darwinism, 4, 9-10
Day, Henry N., xii, 87, 146, 178,
    205, 219; on adaptation of
    discourse to audience, 142,
    144; classification of
    composition by, 122, 126;
    definition of rhetoric, 77;
    emphasis on oral discourse,
    84; on invention as province
    of rhetoric, 97-98, 99, 101;
    on relationship between
    rhetoric and other disciplines,
    81, 110; rules of usage, 188.
    Work: The Art of Discourse,
    77, 83, 101, 206
"Death—or Transfiguration?"
    (Kitzhaber), xvi

de Coverley, Roger, 201
DeMille, James, 84, 145, 178;
    on audience psychology,
    143-144; classification of
    figurative language by, 177;
    on construction of argument,
    110; definition of rhetoric,
    78; on invention as province
    of rhetoric, 97, 98-99; on
    logical vs. rhetorical
    perspectives on argument,
    110. Work: The Elements of
    Rhetoric, 78, 143-144
Denney, Joseph V., xii, 71, 158; and
    assigned composition topics,
    107-108; classification of
    composition by, 128, 131-132;
    definition of rhetoric, 79;
    discussion of logic by, 111; on
    functions of figurative
    language, 179, 185; on literary
    models for student
    compositions, 217-218; on
    paragraph development,
    161-164, 222, 226; recognition
    of audience by, 149-150; on
    relationship between rhetoric
    and literature, 88, 89. Works:
    Composition-Literature, 88-89,
    111, 131-132, 149, 166, 218;
    Composition-Rhetoric, 79, 89,
    107, 128, 131, 163, 173, 179,
    185; Elementary English
    Composition, 80, 86, 131, 150,
    190, 215; Paragraph-Writing,
    131, 160, 161-163, 164, 214;
    Two Problems in Composition-
    Teaching, 217
Department of Education, U.S.,
    xvi
De Quincey, Thomas, 129
description: as category of
    discourse, 120-121, 122, 123,
    124, 126, 127, 128, 129, 131,
    132, 135, 138-139; as method

of exposition, 134–135; and paragraph structure, 159, 163, 164; and perceptions of reader, 135–136; reliance on symbols, 136–137; suitability for student assignments, 105

The Development of Harvard University (Grandgent), 33

Dewey, John, 5, 231n.48. Work: *Psychology*, 5

Dial (magazine), 46

dialogs, as category of discourse, 126

Diary (Pepys), 211

Dickinson, Emily. Work: "The Snake," 182–183

diction: and communication with audience, 145, 146–147; importance to rhetorical theory, 187; qualities of style affecting, 171; rules of, 188–189, 190, 191; simplification of doctrine concerning, 215

Dictionary of American Biography, 60

didactic, the, as category of discourse, 122, 123

discourse, forms of, as rhetorical categories, 119–139

dissertations, as category of discourse, 123

The Diversions of Purley (Tooke), 37

division, 98

drill, development of mental faculties by, 2

Dryden, John, 34

Dudley, Fred, xviii

Dunster, Henry, 7

Dwight, Timothy, 20–21, 23, 24, 25

economy, theory of, 171–172, 173

Ede, Lisa S., xiv

Education: Intellectual, Moral, and Physical (Spencer), 11

education, university departments of, 5

Edwards, Jonathan, 2

elective system, 15, 16, 18–20, 24, 28, 30, 41, 76, 79, 82, 112–113, 230n.33

"Elegy" (Gray), 193

Elementary English Composition (Scott and Denney), 80, 86, 131, 150, 190, 215

Elements of English Composition (Boyd), 104, 123, 192

The Elements of Intellectual Science (N. Porter), 23

Elements of Logic (D. Hill), 125

The Elements of Moral Science (N. Porter), 23

Elements of Psychology (D. Hill), 125

The Elements of Rhetoric (DeMille), 78, 143–144

Elements of Rhetoric (Getty), 57–58

Elements of Rhetoric (Newcomer), 80, 116, 127, 161, 166, 189, 190, 196, 213, 214

Elements of Rhetoric (Whately), 53–55, 169

The Elements of Rhetoric and Composition (D. Hill), 77, 84, 87, 104, 125, 145, 157, 207, 208

Elements of Rhetoric and English Composition (Carpenter), 88, 111, 160–161, 173, 215

Elements of Rhetoric and Literary Criticism (Boyd), 58

Eliot, Charles W., 10, 23, 34; curricular reforms of, 17–18, 24; sponsorship of English studies by, 32–33, 60

Eliot, T. S., vii

elocution: displacement by speech instruction, 42, 86; emergence as academic discipline, 31; relationship of rhetoric to, 81, 82, 83; status as academic requirement, 33–34

Eloquence a Virtue (Theremin), 81
Emerson, O. F., 196, 197
Emerson, Ralph Waldo, 57
The Emotions and the Will (Bain), 4
English Composition (Wendell), 111,
  114, 128, 145, 159, 165, 176
English Composition and Rhetoric
  (Bain), 119, 120, 155, 177
English Grammar (Murray), 192
*English Grammar in Familiar
  Lectures* (Kirkham), 192
English in the Preparatory Schools
  (Huffcut), 213
English studies: competence of
  incoming freshmen, 34, 41,
  43–47; emergence as academic
  discipline, 60–61; emergence
  of speech instruction as
  separate discipline, 41–43;
  emphasis on history of
  language, 36–38; incorporation
  into academic structure, 31,
  32–33, 34, 40; in literary
  societies, 32; marginality to
  conservative curriculum, 22;
  shifting emphasis of, 63; topics
  encompassed by, 31–32, 33–36,
  38–41. *See also* composition
  pedagogy; rhetoric
entrance examinations/require-
  ments, 34, 41, 43, 45–46,
  166–167, 195, 199, 200–204,
  224
epic, as category of discourse, 121
epistemology, xiii
Erskine, John, 64–65
Espenshade, A. Howry, 161, 174,
  178; and assigned composition
  topics, 106–107; on criteria
  governing arrangement, 116;
  emphasis on practice, 213; on
  student exercises, 213–214.
  Work: *The Essentials of
  Composition and Rhetoric*,
  106, 128, 166, 190, 196

"Essay on Addison" (Macaulay), 201
essays, as category of discourse, 126
*Essays on Classical Rhetoric and
  Modern Discourse* (Connors,
  Ede, and Lunsford, eds.), xiv
*The Essentials of Composition and
  Rhetoric* (Espenshade), 106,
  128, 166, 190, 196
Essentials of English Grammar
  (Whitney), 198
esthetics, relationship of rhetoric
  to, 81, 82, 83
ethics, relationship of rhetoric to,
  81–82, 83
etymology, 192
evolution, theory of, 4, 9–10,
  36–37
excitation: as category of
  discourse, 122, 126; figurative
  language as expression of, 179
*Exercises in Rhetoric and English
  Composition (Advanced
  Course)* (Carpenter), 80, 127,
  161, 165, 213, 214
experimental psychology, 4–6,
  222–223
explanation: as category of
  discourse, 122, 126; processes
  of, 98
exposition: as category of discourse,
  120, 121, 122, 123, 124, 126,
  127, 128, 129, 131, 132, 133,
  138; description as method of,
  134–135; paragraph structure
  in, 156, 163
*The Expository Paragraph and
  Sentence* (Baldwin), 116, 133,
  161, 166

faculty psychology, 3–5, 24, 75,
  120, 132
figurative language, 51;
  classification of, 175,
  177–178, 179; effects on
  audience, 147; functions of,

175, 178–186; literary use of, 176–177; origin of, 175, 176, 180–181, 182–183, 185–186; student exercises in, 206; theoretical treatment of, 208

Figures of Rhetoric: A Psychological Study (Buck), 180

First Lessons in Composition (Quackenbos), 104, 192, 205, 208

Fiske, John, 10

Flemming, Arthur, xvi

Fletcher, J. B. Work: *Introduction to Theme-Writing*, 161, 173, 213

forms of discourse, as rhetorical categories, 119–139

The Forms of Discourse (Cairns), 103, 128, 161

Foucault, Michel, xiii

Foundations of Rhetoric (A. Hill), 127, 190, 197, 223

"4C, Freshman English, and the Future" (Kitzhaber), xv, xvi

Fowler, William C., 37

fraternities, Greek, 32, 42

Freshman Composition (Pearson), 80, 116, 127, 165, 213

Frieze, Henry S., 28–29

Frink, H. A., 42, 63, 85–86

Fulton, Robert I., 41–42

Gayley, C. M. Work: *An Introduction to the Methods and Materials of Literary Criticism*, 71

gender, influence on composition, xii

"A Generative Rhetoric of the Sentence" (Christensen), xv

Genung, John Franklin, xiv, 59, 68, 69, 71, 94, 161, 171, 174, 213, 225; academic career of, 63–65, 66; on adaptation of discourse to audience, 146–148; on arrangement of whole composition, 165; and assigned composition topics, 105–106; classification of composition by, 127, 128; on criteria governing arrangement, 114; definition of rhetoric, 65, 79; definition of style, 170; discussion of logic by, 111; emphasis on practice, 208–209, 214; on functions of figurative language, 178–179; on invention as province of rhetoric, 102, 103; on paragraph development, 158–159, 162, 163; rules of diction, 189, 190; rules of grammar, 195. Works: *Handbook of Rhetorical Analysis*, 90–91, 92; *The Outlines of Rhetoric*, 148, 165, 178, 190, 214, 223; *Practice Elements of Rhetoric*, 64, 65, 79, 90, 102, 128, 146–147, 158, 163, 165, 170, 189, 195, 208, 209; *A Study of Rhetoric in the College Course*, 209; *The Working Principles of Rhetoric*, 103, 128, 148, 196

Germany: experimental psychology in, 4–5; Scriptural interpretation from, 7; system of higher education, 8, 12–17, 20, 25, 26, 27, 28, 29

Getty, John A. Work: *Elements of Rhetoric*, 57–58

Gilman, Daniel Coit, 17, 26

Gilmore, J. H., xiv; on adaptation of discourse to audience, 146, 147, 148; classification of composition by, 126; on invention as province of rhetoric, 100; neglect of paragraphs by, 158; on relationship between rhetoric

Gilmore, J. H. *(Continued)*
and other disciplines, 83.
Work: *The Outlines of
Rhetoric*, 83, 146.
Gleason, H. A., xv
Godkin, E. L., 44
Goldsmith, Oliver. Work: *The
Vicar of Wakefield*, 35
Goodrich, Chauncey Allen, 22.
Work: *Select British
Eloquence*, 22
"good use," 52-53, 115-116,
188-190
Goodwin, William Watson, 15
grammar: competence of students
in, 201; descriptive studies of,
198-199; ideal of correctness
in, 202-203, 204, 224-225;
importance to rhetorical
theory, 187-188, 191,
194-197; relationship of
rhetoric to, 81, 82, 83;
relevance to composition, x;
rules of, 52-53, 192-195,
197-199; student exercises in,
206, 207, 212
Grandgent, C. H., 33-34, 66.
Work: *The Development of
Harvard University*, 33
Gray, Thomas. Work: "Elegy," 193
Great Britain, rhetorical theories
of, 49-55, 169-170, 221
Greece, 57, 141
Greeley, Horace, 60
Greene, Samuel S., 193. Works:
*Analysis of the English
Language*, 193; *Treatise on
the Structure of the English
Language*, 192, 193
Greet, W. Cabell, 188
Gregory the Great, 144
Grimm, Jakob, 36
Grimm, Wilhelm, 36
Guthrie, Warren, 50, 52, 53
Guy Mannering (W. Scott), 201

Hadley, James, 22
Hale, E. E., Jr., 214; and assigned
composition topics, 107; on
classification of figurative
language, 178; emphasis on
practice, 213; on invention
as province of rhetoric, 103.
Work: *Constructive Rhetoric*,
103, 131, 178, 213
Hall, G. Stanley, 5
Hamilton, Sir William, 3, 4, 82,
120, 126, 143, 172, 177
Hamilton College, 26
Handbook of Composition
(Woolley), 191, 199, 224-225
Handbook of English Composition
(J. M. Hart), 131
Handbook of Rhetorical Analysis
(Genung), 90-91, 92
Handbook of the English Tongue
(Angus), 154
Harrison, James Albert, 38
Hart, James Morgan, 13-14; and
assigned composition topics,
106; on rhetorical analysis
of literature, 89-90. Work:
*Handbook of English
Composition*, 131
Hart, John S., 37, 87, 145, 178,
188; on criteria governing
arrangement, 113; emphasis
on practice, 206, 207, 208;
emphasis on written
discourse, 84, 85; on
invention as province of
rhetoric, 96, 97; on qualities
of style, 171; on relationship
between rhetoric and other
disciplines, 81. Work: *A
Manual of Composition and
Rhetoric*, 81, 104
Hartley, David, 2
Harvard College, 50, 55, 56-57,
66, 67, 70, 71, 72, 73, 107,
210; admissions policy, 29;

curricular reform at, 17–20; emergence of English studies at, 32–36, 39, 40–41, 60–61; emergence of science at, 10, 11–12; entrance requirements and examinations, 34, 41, 43, 45–46, 166–167, 195, 199, 200–204; graduate program of, 13, 16; leadership of, 17; religious mission of, 6, 7; remedial English at, 44; speech instruction at, 42; standards of scholarship at, 14, 15, 30; study of philology at, 37; survey of literacy of incoming freshmen, 44–47; textbooks in use at, 62, 195

Harvard Reports, 44–47, 86, 88, 138, 163, 167, 196, 199, 219, 223, 224, 225

Harvard University Press, 46

Haven, E. O., 28, 145; emphasis on practice, 206, 208; on invention as province of rhetoric, 96. Work: *Rhetoric*, 87, 206

Hedge, F. H., 14

Henry Esmond (Thackeray), 201

Hepburn, A. D., 208; on adaptation of discourse to audience, 144–145; classification of composition by, 123–125, 126; definition of rhetoric, 76–77; on functions of figurative language, 179; on invention as province of rhetoric, 97, 99; on paragraph development, 156–157, 158, 159, 162; on qualities of style, 172; on relationship between rhetoric and literature, 87–88; on relationship between rhetoric and psychology, 82. Work: *Manual of English Rhetoric*, 76, 123–124, 144, 156, 172

Herbart, Johann Friedrich, 5, 105, 106

Hervey, George W., 205; on adaptation of discourse to audience, 144; classification of figurative language by, 179; on invention as province of rhetoric, 99. Work: *A System of Christian Rhetoric*, 99, 144, 179

Heyne, Moriz, 36

"Higher Criticism" of the Scriptures, 7

higher education: conservative model of, 20–26; curricular reforms in, 17–20; decline of religious influence on, 6–9; emergence of science in, 9–12, 17–18, 27–28; in English (*see* English studies); influence of German universities, 8, 12–17, 20, 25, 26, 27, 28, 29; progressive model of, 20, 26–30; in rhetoric (*see* composition pedagogy; rhetoric); theoretical changes in, 1–6

Higher Lessons in English (Reed and Kellogg), 193–194

higher rhetoric, 93–94

Hill, Adams Sherman, 59, 68, 69, 70–71, 148, 174, 178; academic career, 60–62; and assigned composition topics, 104–105; classification of composition by, 126, 127; on composition requirement, 35–36; on criteria governing arrangement, 114; definition of rhetoric, 78–79; directorship of Harvard's English studies program, 33; discussion of logic by, 111;

Hill, Adams Sherman *(Continued)*
exclusion of invention from
rhetoric, 99, 100, 103; on
Harvard entrance
examination, 200, 201, 203;
on paragraph development,
158, 159, 161; on qualities
of style, 171; recognition of
audience by, 145-146, 147;
rules of diction, 188-189,
190; rules of grammar, 197.
Works: *Beginnings of Rhetoric
and Composition,* 166, 197;
Foundations of Rhetoric, 127,
190, 197, 223; *The Principles
of Rhetoric, and Their
Application,* 62-63, 78, 100,
103, 161, 188, 195, 203, 212
Hill, David J., 188, 205; on
adaptation of discourse to
audience, 145; classification
of composition by, 125-126;
classification of figurative
language by, 177, 178;
definition of rhetoric, 77;
emphasis on written
discourse, 84, 85; exclusion
of invention from rhetoric,
96; on influence of rhetoric
on audience, 143, 144; on
logical vs. rhetorical
perspectives on argument,
109, 110; on paragraph
development, 157; on
qualities of style, 172-173; on
relationship between rhetoric
and literature, 87; on
relationship between rhetoric
and psychology, 82. Works:
Elements of Logic, 125;
Elements of Psychology, 125;
*The Elements of Rhetoric and
Composition,* 77, 84, 87, 104,
125, 145, 157, 207, 208; *The
Science of Rhetoric,* 77, 82, 85,

87, 96, 109, 125, 143, 157,
172, 177, 206
Hinsdale, B. A., 30
history, as category of discourse,
121, 126
History of the English Language
(Lounsbury), 38
History of the English Paragraph
(Lewis), 153
Holmes, Oliver Wendell (literatus
and physician), 57
Hope, M. B., 82, 96, 205; on
adaptation of discourse to
audience, 142-143, 144;
emphasis on oral discourse,
84; on relationship between
rhetoric and literature, 87, 88;
on relationship of logic to
invention, 109-110. Work:
*The Princeton Text-Book in
Rhetoric,* 77-78
Horner, Winifred, viii
How to Write Clearly (Abbott), 195
Huffcut, Ernest W.: and assigned
composition topics, 105;
emphasis on practice, 209;
system of theme correction,
213. Work: *English in the
Preparatory Schools,* 213
Hunt, Theodore W., 145;
classification of composition
by, 126: exclusion of invention
from rhetoric, 96, 99-100; on
relationship between rhetoric
and other disciplines, 83; on
vitality of style, 174-175.
Works: *The Principles of
Written Discourse,* 100, 126;
"Rhetorical Science," 96,
99-100; *Studies in Literature
and Style,* 90, 174-175
Huxley, Thomas Henry, 9

Idylls of the King (Tennyson), 64
An Index to English (Perrin), xviii

"The Influence of Improvement in
One Mental Function upon
the Efficiency of Other
Functions" (Thorndike and
Woodworth), 5-6
In Memoriam (Tennyson), 63
Intellectual Powers of Man (Reid),
3
Introduction to Rhetoric (Cairns),
103, 148, 161
*An Introduction to the Methods and
Materials of Literary Criticism*
(Scott and Gayley), 71
Introduction to Theme-Writing
(Carpenter and Fletcher), 161,
173, 213
invention: and assigned
composition topics, 103-109;
as function of rhetoric, 51-52,
53-54, 95-103; relationship of
logic to, 109-113; supremacy
of style over, 95, 169-170. *See
also* subject matter
Iowa State College, xviii, xx
isolated paragraph, 162
Ivanhoe (W. Scott), 35

James, William, xiii, 136. Work:
Principles of Psychology, 5
Jameson, Henry W., 126; and
assigned composition topics,
104, 107; neglect of audience
by, 145; system of theme
correction, 212-213. Work:
Rhetorical Method, 79, 104,
212
Jefferson, Thomas, 37
Jevons, William Stanley. Work:
Logic, 125
Johns Hopkins University, 5, 9;
leadership of, 17, 26;
standards of scholarship at,
15-16, 30
journalism, 70-71; qualities of style
affecting, 171; sharpening of

writing skills by, 210; student
exercises in, 208
Julius Caesar (Shakespeare), 34, 35

Kames, Lord, 121
Kansas, 41
Kansas City, Missouri, 41
Kant, Immanuel, 2
Kellogg, Brainerd, 126, 145, 158;
definition of rhetoric, 79;
emphasis on practice, 209, 212;
on invention as province of
rhetoric, 101-102; omits
discussion of logic, 111; rules
of grammar, 194, 198. Works:
Higher Lessons in English,
193-194; *A Text-Book on
Rhetoric,* 79, 101, 111, 195, 209
Kies, Paul, xviii
Kirkham, Samuel, 193. Works:
*A Compendium of English
Grammar,* 192; *English
Grammar in Familiar
Lectures,* 192
Kitzhaber, Albert R.: career of,
xvii-xxii; debate with Rice,
xv-xvi; directorship of
Curriculum Study Centers,
xvi-xvii. Works: "Death—or
Transfiguration?" xvi; "4C,
Freshman English, and the
Future," xv, xvi; *Themes,
Theories, and Therapy: The
Teaching of Writing in
College,* xv
Kuhn, Thomas, xiii

Lafayette College, 37
Lake Forest University, 38
land-grant colleges, 9, 12
Lane, George Martin, 15
Langer, Susanne, xiii
language, skillful use of, 56. *See
also* figurative language;
linguistics; words

Laokoön (Lessing), 136
Larned, William A., 22
Larson, Richard. Work:
"Classifying Discourse:
Limitations and Alternatives,"
xiv
Lathrop, H. B., xx, 117
Lawrence Scientific School, 12,
232n.54
"The Lay of the Last Minstrel"
(W. Scott), 35
Lectures on Eloquence and Style
(E. Porter), 57
*Lectures on Moral Philosophy and
Eloquence* (Witherspoon), 55
*Lectures on Rhetoric and Belles
Lettres* (Blair), 49-52, 86, 169,
208, 221
Lectures on Rhetoric and Oratory
(J. Adams), 55
LeDuc, Thomas, 8, 14-15
Leonard, Sterling A., 73, 226
Lessing, Gotthold Ephraim, 139.
Work: *Laokoön*, 136
letters (epistolary composition): as
category of discourse, 123,
126; student exercises in
writing, 208, 212
Lewes, George Henry. Work:
*The Principles of Success in
Literature*, 71
Lewis, E. H., 156. Work: *History of
the English Paragraph*, 153
linguistics: emergence as academic
discipline, 36, 37-38;
enrichment of rhetorical
theory by, 223; and instability
of grammar, 197
Linonian Society, 32
literary composition, as category
of discourse, 128-129
literary criticism: concern with
style, 174-175; relationship of
rhetoric to, 94, 174-175
literary societies, 32, 42

literature: attraction of academic
talent to, 225-226; as category
of rhetoric, 86-89;
"correction" by composition
students, 214-215; in English
studies curriculum, 34, 39-41;
historical study of, 38-39;
incompatibility with rules of
rhetoric, 85-86; informal
study of, 32; rhetorical
analysis of, 89-94; in rhetoric
curriculum, 31; study by
composition students, xi,
xvi-xvii, 64, 215, 216,
217-219, 222; as subject for
student compositions, 35, 64,
106, 107; symbolic language
in, 137; use of figurative
language in, 176-177
logic: guidance of invention by,
53-54; involvement of
invention with, 95; and
paragraph structure, 156;
psychological roots of, 112;
relationship of invention
to, 109-113; relationship
of rhetoric to, 81, 82, 83;
relevance to composing
process, x; as tool of
rhetoric, 52
Logic (Jevons), 125
Logic (Mill), 110
logical composition, as category of
discourse, 128, 129
Lounsbury, Thomas R., 39. Work:
*History of the English
Language*, 38
Love, Glen, xvii
Lowell, James Russell, 34
Lowell Institute, 68, 116
lower rhetoric, 93
Lunsford, Andrea, viii, xiv

Macaulay, Thomas, 154. Work:
"Essay on Addison," 201

Macbeth (Shakespeare), 64, 201
McCosh, James, 17
McElroy, John G. R., 145, 195;
classification of composition
by, 126; emphasis on practice,
209; on invention as province
of rhetoric, 101; on para-
graph development, 158.
Work: The Structure of
English Prose, 83, 101
MacIntyre, Alasdair C., xiii
McKeon, Joseph, 56
McMurrin, Sterling, xvi
The Making of Knowledge in
Composition: Portrait of an
Emerging Field (North), viii, xv
Malory, Sir Thomas. Work: Morte
d'Arthur, 64
A Manual of Composition and
Rhetoric (J. S. Hart), 81, 104
Manual of English Rhetoric
(Hepburn), 76, 123–124, 144,
156, 172
March, Francis A., 37, 38. Work:
Origin and History of the
English Language, 38
mass, principle of, 114, 115,
159–160. See also Unity-
Coherence-Emphasis
Massachusetts Institute of
Technology, 12, 160, 165–166
Masson, Prof., 120–121
Mather, Cotton, 7
Mätzner, Eduard, 36
Maudsley, Henry, 125
Mead, William E., 217
memory, development of, 2
mental and moral philosophy/
science, 2–6, 23–24; and
concepts of style, 171; on
influence of rhetoric over
audience, 143, 144; rhetoric as
category of, 80, 81, 82, 83
mental discipline, ideal of, 1–6,
24–25, 75, 76

Mental Science (Bain), 120
The Merchant of Venice (Shake-
speare), 35
metaphor: functions of, 181–186;
origin of, 180–181, 182–183,
185–186
The Metaphor —A Study in the
Psychology of Rhetoric (Buck),
180
method, 98–99
Michigan, pyramidal educational
structure of, 26, 72
Michigan Schoolmasters' Club, 107
A Midsummer Night's Dream
(Shakespeare), 201
Mill, John Stuart, 9, 96–97, 111.
Work: Logic, 110
Milton, John, 34. Work: Comus, 34
Missouri, 41
mixed metaphor, 184–185
Modern Language Association
(MLA), xvii, 217
moral philosophy. See mental and
moral philosophy/science
More, Sir Thomas. Work:
Utopia, 64
Morrill Act, 9, 12, 17
Morris, Elisabeth Woodbridge.
See Woodbridge [Morris],
Elisabeth
Morte d'Arthur (Malory), 64
Motley, John Lathrop, 57
Murray, Lindley, 192–193. Work:
English Grammar, 192

narration: as category of discourse,
120, 121, 122, 123, 124, 126,
127, 128, 129, 131, 132, 134,
135, 138; and paragraph
structure, 159, 163, 164;
suitability for student
assignments, 105
Nation (magazine), 47
National Council of Education, 46
National Education Association, 7

INDEX

Newcomer, A. G., 174; and
assigned composition topics,
106; on criteria governing
arrangement, 116; emphasis
on practice, 214, 215; on
functions of figurative
language, 178; rules of usage,
189-190. Works: *Elements of
Rhetoric*, 80, 116, 127, 161,
166, 189, 190, 196, 213, 214;
*A Practical Course in English
Composition*, 106, 111, 149,
161, 215
New England Association of
Colleges and Preparatory
Schools, 210
New England Association of
Teachers of English, 217
New England Commission of
Colleges, 200
"New Light" theology, 2
Newman, John Henry, Cardinal,
92, 154
Newman, Samuel P., 122, 123.
Work: *A Practical System of
Rhetoric*, 55-56, 122
New York *Tribune*, 9, 60
North, Stephen. Work: *The
Making of Knowledge in
Composition: Portrait of an
Emerging Field*, viii, xv
Northrup, Cyrus, 25, 26
Notre Dame University, 50
novels, as category of discourse, 126

obsolete words, 189
Office of Education, U.S., xvii
Ohio State University, 42
Ohio Wesleyan University, 41, 42
*On the Limits of Descriptive
Writing Apropos of Lessing's
Laocoon* (Bryant), 135
oratory: as category of discourse,
83-86, 123, 126, 128, 133;
qualities of style affecting,

171; recognition of audience
by, 142-143, 144, 145, 150
*Origin and History of the English
Language* (March), 38
Origin of Species (Darwin), 9
Outlines of English Literature
(Shaw), 39
The Outlines of Rhetoric (Genung),
148, 165, 178, 190, 214, 223
The Outlines of Rhetoric (Gilmore),
83, 146

paragraphing, competence of
students at, 203
paragraph(s): arrangement of,
113-114, 115, 116, 154-165;
in arrangement of whole
composition, 165, 166;
definitions of, 154, 155,
157, 162; as focus of
composition instruction,
162, 163, 164; importance in
rhetorical theory, 153-154,
155, 158, 160-161; theory of,
222, 226, 227
Paragraph-Writing (Scott and
Denney), 131, 160, 161-163,
164, 214
Park College, 41
Parker, Richard Green, 113, 122.
Work: *Aids to English
Composition*, 58-59, 122, 192
Parkman, Francis, 57
parsing, 192-193, 198
parts-to-whole approach to
composition, x, 165-166
pathetic, the, as category of
discourse, 122
Pearson, Henry G., 128, 161;
on arrangement of whole
composition, 165-166;
on criteria governing
arrangement, 116-117. Work:
Freshman Composition, 80,
116, 127, 165, 213

280

Peirce, Charles Sanders, xiii
Pence, R. W. Work: *College Composition*, 164
Pepys, Samuel. Work: *Diary*, 211
Perrin, Porter, xviii–xix, xx, xxi. Work: *An Index to English*, xviii
persuasion: as category of discourse, 54, 120, 121, 122, 123, 125, 126, 127, 128, 129, 130–131, 132–133, 138; contrasted with conviction, 51; as quality of style, 132; recognition of audience in, 145, 147; stylistic qualities of, 54–55
Pestalozzi, Johann Heinrich, 100, 105, 106
philology: emergence as academic discipline, 36–38; and instability of grammar, 197
Philosophy of Rhetoric (Bascom), 77–78, 144
Philosophy of Rhetoric (Campbell), 52–53, 121, 221
Philosophy of Style (Spencer), 71, 172
physiology, implications for psychology, 4
Pierce, John Davis, 26
Plato, viii
poetic metaphor, 181, 182–183
poetry: aim of, 84; as category of rhetoric, 87–88, 89, 120, 121, 123, 126; classification of, 51
Porter, Ebenezer. Work: *Lectures on Eloquence and Style*, 57
Porter, Noah, 17, 20, 23–25, 231n.48. Works: *The American Colleges, and the American Public*, 24; *The Elements of Intellectual Science*, 23; *The Elements of Moral Science*, 23
Positivism, 10

A Practical Course in English Composition (Newcomer), 106, 111, 149, 161, 215
Practical Elements of Rhetoric (Genung), 64, 65, 79, 90, 102, 128, 146–147, 158, 163, 165, 170, 189, 195, 208, 209
A Practical Introduction to English Rhetoric (Coppens), 88, 100, 111, 209
Practical Rhetoric (Clark), 195, 208, 209
A Practical System of Rhetoric (Newman), 55–56, 122
preliminary paragraph, 159
The Present State of Scholarship in Historical and Contemporary Rhetoric (Horner, ed.), viii
The Princeton Text-Book in Rhetoric (Hope), 77–78
Princeton University, 13, 17, 26. *See also* College of New Jersey
Principles of Argumentation (Baker), 112, 133
Principles of Physiological Psychology (Wundt), 4
Principles of Psychology (James), 5
The Principles of Rhetoric, and Their Application (A. Hill), 62–63, 78, 100, 103, 161, 188, 195, 203, 212
The Principles of Style (F. Scott), 93
The Principles of Success in Literature (Lewes), 71
The Principles of Written Discourse (Hunt), 100, 126
The Prisoner of Chillon (Byron), 201
Project English, xvi–xvii
propositional paragraph, 158
prose: aim of, 84; classification of, 51, 54, 56; statistical analysis of, 91–92
provincialisms, 189
Prussia, 13, 26

"The Psychological Significance of the Parts of Speech" (Buck), 197

psychology: audience, 143–144; challenge to mental and moral philosophy by, 4–6; and definition of argumentation, 133–134; and definition of exposition, 134–135; enrichment of rhetorical theory by, 222–223; on reader's perception of imagery, 135–136; relationship of rhetoric to, 81, 82, 83; relevance to composing process, ix–x; on role of imitation in learning, 218; roots of logic in, 112; behind theory of elective system, 19; behind theory of mental and moral philosophy, 3–4; on use of metaphorical language, 180–181

Psychology (Dewey), 5

punctuation: competence of students in, 201, 203; ideal of correctness in, 224; student exercises in, 207, 212

Quackenbos, George Payn, 87, 96, 113, 145, 188; and assigned composition topics, 104, 105, 107; classification of composition by, 122–123; classification of figurative language by, 177; emphasis on practice, 205–206, 207, 208; on qualities of style, 170, 171. Works: Advanced Course of Composition and Rhetoric, 84, 104, 122, 170, 171, 177, 207, 208; First Lessons in Composition, 104, 192, 205, 208

Quincy, Josiah, 44

Quintilian, 58, 95, 122

radical metaphor, 180–181, 182, 185–186

reader. See audience (reader)

"Recent Tendencies in Teaching English Composition" (Buck), 150–151

recitation (method of instruction): break with, 15; development of memory through, 2; entrenchment of, 14, 15, 21–22; of rhetorical principles, 32; and Socratic method, 25

Reed, Alonzo, 194, 198. Work: Higher Lessons in English, 193–194

Reid, Thomas, 2, 3, 4. Works: Active Powers of Man, 3; Intellectual Powers of Man, 3

related paragraph, 162

Report for 1880 (Commissioner of Education), 8–9

Report for 1888–89 (Commissioner of Education), 38

"Reports of the Committee on Composition and Rhetoric" (Harvard College), 44–47, 86, 88, 138, 163, 167, 196, 199, 219, 223, 224, 225

representative discourse, 126, 142

"reputable, national, present" (usage criteria), 52, 188

Research Planning Conferences, xvi

rhetoric: American theories of, 55–73, 221; arrangement of subject matter, 113–117; British theories of, 49–55, 169–170, 221; classification of composition by, 119–139; contrasted with composition, 79–80; definitions of, 57–58, 65, 75–81; discovery of subject matter in, 95–103; in English studies curriculum,

34; ideal of correctness in, 166-167, 188, 190, 199-204, 220, 222-226; importance of style in, 169-170; informal study of, 32; paragraph theory, 153-166; practical, 78-81, 205-220, 222; process of argument in, 109-113; reaction against practical emphasis, 215-217, 219; recognition of audience by, 141-152; relationship to other disciplines, 81-83; relevance to composition, xi-xii; style theory, 170-186, 188-199; topics encompassed by, 31-32, 83-94; transition from British to American textbooks, 49, 75; transition periods in, 221-222, 226-227. *See also* composition pedagogy

Rhetoric (Aristotle), 95, 143
Rhetoric (Haven), 87, 206
Rhetorical Method (Jameson), 79, 104, 212
"Rhetorical Science" (Hunt), 96, 99-100
"The Rhetorical Stance" (Booth), xv
Rice, Warner, xv-xvi
Richard II (Shakespeare), 201
"The Rise and Fall of the Modes of Discourse" (Connors), viii
Rochester Theological Seminary, 63
romance, as category of discourse, 126
Romantic movement, 92
Rome, 57, 58, 95, 141
Ruskin, John, 92
Rutgers University, 26
Ryle, Gilbert, xiii

St. John's College, 38
Salisbury, Edward Elbridge, 23

"Scale of Merit" grading, 15
School Composition (Swinton), 104, 156, 205, 206-207
School Review, 149
science: emerging importance to higher education, 9-12, 17-18, 27-28; influence on language study, 36-37; rhetoric as, 76-77, 78, 79, 80, 81, 82
The Science of Rhetoric (D. Hill), 77, 82, 85, 87, 96, 109, 125, 143, 157, 172, 177, 206
Scott, Fred Newton, xi, xii, 47, 59, 138, 151, 158, 225; academic career of, 70-73; on analysis of style, 93-94; and assigned composition topics, 107; classification of composition by, 128, 131-132; definition of rhetoric, 79; descriptive study of grammar, 199; discussion of logic by, 111; on functions of figurative language, 179, 185; on literary models for student composition, 218; as original thinker, 69-70, 71, 222-223; on paragraph development, 161-164, 222, 226; recognition of audience by, 149, 150; on relationship between rhetoric and literature, 88, 89. Works: "A Brief Catechism on Textbooks in English," 218; *A Brief English Grammar*, 199; *Composition-Literature*, 88-89, 111, 131-132, 149, 166, 218; *Composition-Rhetoric*, 79, 89, 107, 128, 131, 132, 163, 173, 179, 185; *Contributions to Rhetorical Theory*, 72, 135, 180; *Elementary English Composition*, 80, 86, 131, 150, 190, 215; *An Introduction to the Methods and Materials of Literary Criticism*, 71;

Scott, Fred Newton (*Continued*)
  Paragraph-Writing, 131, 160,
  161–163, 164, 214; *The*
  Principles of Style, 93
Scott, Patrick, viii
Scott, Sir Walter. Works: *Guy*
  Mannering, 201; *Ivanhoe*, 35;
  "The Lay of the Last
  Minstrel," 35
secondary schools: reform of
  composition instruction
  by, 46; responsibility for
  composition instruction, 43,
  44, 45, 46, 47, 72; responsibility for grammar instruction, 187, 191, 195, 196, 201
Second Sophistic period, 95, 141
Seelye, Julius H., 7, 63
Select British Eloquence
  (Goodrich), 22
selection, 98
The Senses and the Intellect (Bain), 4
sentence(s): analysis and diagrams,
  193–194, 198; arrangement
  of, 113–114, 115, 116; in
  arrangement of whole
  composition, 165, 166;
  qualities of style affecting,
  171; and structuring of
  paragraphs, 155; as unit
  of thought, 101–102
Shakespeare, William, xix, 34.
  Works: *Julius Caesar*, 34, 35;
  Macbeth, 64, 201; *The*
  Merchant of Venice, 35; *A*
  Midsummer Night's Dream,
  201; *Richard II*, 201; *The*
  Tempest, 35
Shaler, N. S., 232n.54
Shaw, Thomas B. Works: *A*
  Complete Manual of English
  Literature, 39; *Outlines of*
  English Literature, 39
Shedd, W. G. T., 81

Sheffield Scientific School, 12,
  39–40
Sherman, L. A., 91–92. Work:
  Analytics of Literature, 91
simile, 183
"The Snake" (Dickinson),
  182–183
Socratic method, 25, 72–73
solecisms, 195
Some Principles of Literary
  Criticism (Winchester), 94,
  174, 175
Sorbonne, the, 66
speaking societies, 42
speculation, as category of
  discourse, 122, 123
speech instruction, organization
  on credit basis, 41–43
spelling: competence of students in,
  201, 203; student exercises
  in, 212
Spencer, Herbert, 9, 125; on
  scientific curriculum, 10–11;
  theory of economy, 171–172,
  173. Works: *Education:*
  Intellectual, Moral, and
  Physical, 11; *Philosophy of*
  Style, 71, 172; "What
  Knowledge Is of Most
  Worth," 11
Spenser, Edmund, xix
"status," systems of, 95, 97, 99
Steffens, Lincoln, 14. Work:
  Autobiography, xviii
Stevenson, Robert Louis, 92
Stewart, Donald, viii. Work:
  "What Is an English Major,
  and What Should It Be?" viii
The Structure of English Prose
  (McElroy), 83, 101
Studies in Literature and Style
  (Hunt), 90, 174–175
Studies in Structure and Style
  (Brewster), 92–93

A Study of Rhetoric in the College Course (Genung), 209

A Study of the Paragraph (Thomas), 164

style: analysis of, 91–94; definitions of, 170; determination by audience, 142, 146, 147, 148; devaluation in rhetorical theory, 173–175; importance of, 95, 169–170; qualities of, 50, 53, 54–55, 56, 57, 170–173; role of figurative language, 175–186; rules of diction and usage, 188–191; rules of grammar, 192–199; simplification of doctrine of, 214; student exercises in, 206, 210, 211; variability of, 56

subject matter, 59, 206; assignment of, 103–109; criteria governing arrangement of, 113–117; of daily themes, 210–211; discovery of, 95–103; familiarity of students with, 54, 104–105, 106, 108, 109, 149, 150, 151, 152; literature as, 35, 64, 106, 107. *See also* invention

Sully, James, 125, 180

Summer Institutes, xvi

Sweet, Henry, 38

Swift, Jonathan, 154

Swinton, William: and assigned composition topics, 104; on criteria governing arrangement, 114; emphasis on practice, 205–206, 206–207, 208. Work: *School Composition*, 104, 156, 205, 206–207

symbolism, reliance of description on, 136–137

syntax, 192, 193, 206

A System of Christian Rhetoric (Hervey), 99, 144, 179

Taine, Hippolyte Adolphe, 90

Talks on Writing English (Bates), 80, 116, 132, 148, 161, 173, 178, 213

Tappan, Henry P., 15, 20, 26–29. Work: *University Education*, 27

Tate, Gary, xxi

teaching. *See* composition pedagogy

The Temper of the Seventeenth Century in English Literature (Wendell), 67

The Tempest (Shakespeare), 35

Temple, Sir William, 153

Tennyson, Alfred, Lord, 64. Works: *Idylls of the King*, 64; *In Memoriam*, 63

A Text-Book on Rhetoric (Kellogg), 79, 101, 111, 195, 209

Thackeray, William Makepeace. Work: *Henry Esmond*, 201

Themes, Theories, and Therapy: The Teaching of Writing in College (Kitzhaber), xv

Theremin, Francis, 205; on adaptation of discourse to audience, 142, 143; emphasis on oral discourse, 84; on relationship between rhetoric and ethics, 81–82. Work: *Eloquence a Virtue*, 81

Thomas, Helen, 164. Work: *A Study of the Paragraph*, 164

Thoreau, Henry David, 57

Thorndike, E. L. Work: "The Influence of Improvement in One Mental Function upon the Efficiency of Other Functions," 5–6

Thorpe, Clarence D., 70
Thurber, Samuel, xii, 215–216,
    217, 218–219, 220
Thwing, C. F., 22
Ticknor, George, 15, 18
Time magazine, xviii
Tooke, Horne. Work: *The
    Diversions of Purley,* 37
topics. *See* subject matter
topic sentence, 154–155, 156, 157,
    158, 161, 162
Transcendentalism, 3
transitional paragraph, 159
*Treatise on the Structure of the
    English Language* (Greene),
    192, 193
Trinity College, 26, 66
Trueblood, Thomas C., 41–42
truth, discernment of, 8, 13
*Two Problems in Composition-
    Teaching* (Denney), 217
"Two Ways of Teaching English"
    (anon.), 216–217
Tyler, Moses Coit, 29
Tyndale, William, 153
Tyndall, John, 9

"The Undergraduate Study of
    English Composition"
    (Modern Language
    Association), 217
Union College, 63
unity, 98; of paragraph, 154, 155,
    156, 157, 158
Unity-Coherence-Emphasis
    (Unity-Mass-Coherence), xx,
    113–117, 128, 138, 139, 152,
    159, 161, 164, 165, 189, 200,
    220, 222, 223, 226
University Education (Tappan), 27
University of Berlin, 66
University of California, 26
University of Chicago, xix, 9,
    26, 30

University of Illinois, 26
University of Indiana, 40
University of Iowa, xviii, 26
University of Kansas, xx–xxi, 41
University of Kentucky, 41
University of Leipzig, 63
University of Michigan, 5, 70, 93,
    94, 135, 138; English studies
    curriculum at, 40; graduate
    program of, xix, 72; intro-
    duction of curricular reform,
    15, 16; leadership of, 17; as
    model of progressive educa-
    tion, 20, 26–30; remedial
    English at, 44; speech
    instruction at, 42
University of Minnesota, 26
University of Missouri, 41
University of Notre Dame, 50
University of Oregon, xvi–xvii
University of Pennsylvania, 13, 26
University of Rochester, 83
University of Virginia, 37
University of Washington,
    xviii–xx
University of Wisconsin, 26
usage: importance of rhetorical
    theory, 187; rules of, 52–53,
    115–116, 188–191
"The Usefulness of Classical
    Rhetoric" (Corbett), xv
Utah State College, xx
Utopia (More), 64

The Vicar of Wakefield
    (Goldsmith), 35
vocational education, 231n.48
Vossius, Gerhard Johannes, 58
Vygotsky, Lev, xiii

Walker, Albert, xviii
Washburn College, 41
Washington State College,
    xvii–xviii

Wayland, Francis, 29
Weeks, Ruth M., 73
Welsh, Alfred H., 145, 171, 195, 212; classification of composition by, 127; definition of rhetoric, 79; on invention as province of rhetoric, 100; on rhetorical training of readers, 90. Work: *Complete Rhetoric*, 79, 88, 90, 100
Wendell, Barrett, 59, 61, 62, 71, 126, 128, 147, 171, 178, 220, 222, 223, 225; academic career of, 66–68; on arrangement of whole composition, 165; on criteria governing arrangement, 114–116, 117; on daily theme method, 210–211; as defender of Harvard entrance examination, 204; on effects of composition on reader, 145; on literary use of figurative language, 176–177; omits discussion of logic, 111; on origin of figurative language, 176; on paragraph development, 158, 159–160, 161; rules of usage, 189, 195. Works: *Cotton Mather*, 66; *English Composition*, 66, 68–69, 111, 114, 128, 145, 159, 165, 176; *The Temper of the Seventeenth Century in English Literature*, 67
The Westminster Review, 172
Whately, Richard, 59, 62, 75, 83, 95, 96, 110, 111, 143, 153; emphasis on invention, 169–170; on qualities of style, 171. Work: *Elements of Rhetoric*, 53–55, 169
"What Is an English Major, and What Should It Be?" (Stewart), viii

"What Knowledge Is of Most Worth" (Spencer), 11
White, Andrew D., 7–8, 15, 17, 21–22, 26, 28. Work: *Autobiography*, 22
White House Conference on Education, xvii
Whitney, William Dwight, 23, 37–38, 198. Work: *Essentials of English Grammar*, 198
whole composition, arrangement of, 165–166
whole-to-parts approach to composition, x, 165–166
Who Was Who, 60
Wilbur, Richard, xi
William Jewel College, 41
Williams College, 50
Winchester, C. T. Work: *Some Principles of Literary Criticism*, 94, 174, 175
Witherspoon, John, 31. Work: *Lectures on Moral Philosophy and Eloquence*, 55
Wittgenstein, Ludwig, xiii
Woodbridge [Morris], Elisabeth. Works: *A Course in Expository Writing*, 133, 134; *A Course in Narrative Writing*, 133, 134
Woodworth, R. S. Work: "The Influence of Improvement in One Mental Function upon the Efficiency of Other Functions," 5–6
Woolley, Edwin C. Work: *Handbook of Composition*, 191, 199, 224–225
Woolsey, Theodore D., 23, 25
words: in arrangement of whole composition, 165, 166; positioning of, 115; selection of, 115, 189, 190, 191; as tools of composition, 71

The Working Principles of Rhetoric
(Genung), 103, 128, 148,
196
Wozniak, John Michael, viii
*Writing Instruction in Nineteenth-
Century American Colleges*
(Berlin), viii
Wundt, Wilhelm, 4–5. Work:
*Principles of Physiological
Psychology,* 4

Yale College: emergence of science
at, 12; graduate program of,
13, 16; leadership of, 17;
literary society of, 32; as
model of conservative
education, 20–26, 40; study of
philology at, 37–38; textbooks
in use at, 50. *See also* College
of New Jersey
Youmans, E. L., 10

About the Author

ALBERT R. KITZHABER, born in Cedar Rapids, Iowa, graduated from Coe College in 1939, received his master's degree from Washington State College in 1941, then taught at Iowa State College before serving in the U.S. Army in Europe until discharged in 1945. He studied rhetoric under Porter G. Perrin at the University of Washington and wrote under Perrin's direction the dissertation published here. From 1952 to 1958 he directed freshman and sophomore English at the University of Kansas, then resigned to direct an intensive study of the college-preparatory curriculum in the Portland, Oregon, high schools (1958–1960) for the Ford Foundation. The study's report, written in collaboration with Paul Roberts and Robert Gorrell, was published as *Education for College: Improving the High School Curriculum*. From 1960 to 1962 he was research professor of English at Dartmouth College, where he directed the Dartmouth Study of Student Writing, published in the Carnegie Series in American Education as *Themes, Theories, and Therapy: The Teaching of Writing in College*.

During his tenure at the University of Oregon, 1962–1980, Kitzhaber directed two five-year projects under the U.S. Office of Education's "Project English," producing and testing experimental curricula in the "New English" for grades 7–12, and later for grades 1–6.

Kitzhaber has served on various committees and commissions of the College Entrance Examination Board, was a panelist at the White House Conference on Education (1965), and a consultant to the U.S. Office of Education (1962–1970). He was a member of the English Program Advisory Committee of the Modern Language Association (1966–1970); an organizer of and participant in the Dartmouth International Seminar on the Teaching of English (1966); a member of the advisory committee for the Study of the Ph.D. in English and American Literature, Modern Language Association (1967–1968); a member of the Commission on the Humanities in the Schools, Carnegie Corporation; and Associate Dean of the Graduate School, University of Oregon (1967–1972).

Besides being general editor of two textbook series growing out of the "Project English" work, he is the author of numerous articles on composition, freshman English, and educational policy and problems.

Photo by Kennell-Ellis